高等学校试用教材

建筑类专业英语
暖通与燃气

第一册

赵三元　阎岫峰　主编
王　鸣　马立山
王建华　张素宁　编
杨印芳　　　　　主审

中国建筑工业出版社

《建筑类专业英语》编审委员会

总 主 编　徐铁城
总 主 审　杨匡汉
副总主编　（以姓氏笔划为序）
　　　　　王庆昌　乔梦铎　陆铁镛
　　　　　周保强　蔡英俊
编　　委　（以姓氏笔划为序）
　　　　　王久愉　王学玲　王翰邦　卢世伟
　　　　　孙　玮　李明章　朱满才　向小林
　　　　　向　阳　刘文瑛　余曼筠　孟祥杰
　　　　　张少凡　张文洁　张新建　赵三元
　　　　　阎岫峰　傅兴海　褚羞花　蔡慧俭
　　　　　濮宏魁
责任编辑　程素荣

前　　言

　　经过几十年的探索，外语教学界许多人认为，工科院校外语教学的主要目的应该是："使学生能够利用外语这个工具，通过阅读去获取国外的与本专业有关的科技信息。"这既是我们建设有中国特色的社会主义的客观需要，也是在当前条件下工科院校外语教学可能完成的最高目标。事实上，教学大纲规定要使学生具有"较强"的阅读能力，而对其他方面的能力只有"一般"要求，就是这个意思。

　　大学本科的一、二年级，为外语教学的基础阶段。就英语来说，这个阶段要求掌握的词汇量为2400个（去掉遗忘，平均每个课时10个单词）。加上中学阶段已经学会的1600个单词，基础阶段结束时应掌握的词汇量为4000个。仅仅掌握4000个单词，能否看懂专业英文书刊呢？还不能。据统计，掌握4000个单词，阅读一般的英文科技文献，生词量仍将有6%左右，即平均每百词有六个生词，还不能自由阅读。国外的外语教学专家认为，生词量在3%以下，才能不借助词典，自由阅读。此时可以通过上下文的联系，把不认识的生词猜出来，那么，怎么样才能把6%的生词量降低到3%以下呢？自然，需要让学生增加一部分词汇积累。问题是，要增加多少单词？要增加哪一些单词？统计资料表明，在每一个专业的科技文献中，本专业最常用的科技术语大约只有几百个，而且它们在文献中重复出现的频率很高。因此，在已经掌握4000个单词的基础上，在专业阅读阶段中，有针对性地通过大量阅读，扩充大约1000个与本专业密切有关的科技词汇，便可以逐步达到自由阅读本专业科技文献的目的。

　　早在八十年代中期，建设部系统院校外语教学研究会就组织编写了一套《土木建筑系列英语》，分八个专业，共12册。每个专业可选读其中的3、4册。那套教材在有关院校相应的专业使用多年，学生和任课教师反映良好。但是，根据当时的情况，那套教材定的起点较低（1000词起点），已不适合今天学生的情况。为此，在得到建设部人事教育劳动司的大力支持，并征得五个相关专业教学指导委员会同意之后，由建设部系统十几所院校一百余名外语教师和专业课教师按照统一的编写规划和要求，编写了这一套《建筑类专业英语》教材。

　　《建筑类专业英语》是根据国家教委颁发的《大学英语专业阅读阶段教学基本要求》编写的专业阅读教材，按照建筑类院校共同设置的五个较大的专业类别对口编写。五个专业类别为：建筑学与城市规划；建筑工程（即工业与民用建筑）；给水排水与环境保护；暖通、空调与燃气；建筑管理与财务会计。每个专业类别分别编写三册专业英语阅读教材，供该专业类别的学生在修完基础阶段英语后，在第五至第七学期专业阅读阶段使用，每学期一册。

　　上述五种专业英语教材语言规范，题材广泛，覆盖相关专业各自的主要内容：包括专业基础课、专业主干课及主要专业选修课，语言材料的难易度切合学生的实际水平；词汇以大学英语"通用词汇表"的4000个单词为起点，每个专业类别的三册书将增加1000～1200个阅读本专业必需掌握的词汇。本教材重视语言技能训练，突出对阅读、翻译和写作能力的培养，以求达到《大学英语专业阅读阶段教学基本要求》所提出的教学目标："通过指导学生阅读有关专业的英语书刊和文献，使他们进一步提高阅读和翻译科技资料的能力，并能以英语为工具获取专业所需的信息。"

《建筑类专业英语》每册16个单元，每个单元一篇正课文（TEXT），两篇副课文（Reading Material A & B），每个单元平均2000个词，三册48个单元，总共约有十万个词，相当于原版书三百多页。要培养较强的阅读能力，读十万个词的文献，是起码的要求。如果专业课教师在第六和第七学期，在学生通过学习本教材已经掌握了数百个专业科技词汇的基础上，配合专业课程的学习，再指定学生看一部分相应的专业英语科技文献，那将会既促进专业课的学习，又提高英语阅读能力，实为两得之举。

本教材不仅适用于在校学生，对于有志提高专业英语阅读能力的建筑行业广大在职工程技术人员，也是一套适用的自学教材。

建设部人事教育劳动司高教处和中国建设教育协会对这套教材的编写自始至终给予关注和支持；中国建筑工业出版社第五编辑室密切配合，参与从制定编写方案到审稿各个阶段的重要会议，给了我们很多帮助。在编写过程中，各参编学校相关专业的许多专家、教授对材料的选取、译文的审定都提出了许多宝贵意见，谨此致谢。

《建筑类专业英语》是我们编写对口专业阅读教材的又一次尝试，由于编写者水平及经验有限，教材中不妥之处在所难免，敬请广大读者批评指正。

《建筑类专业英语》
编审委员会

Contents

UNIT ONE
    Text   Basic Concepts and Definitions 1
    Reading Material A   Thermodynamic Systems 6
    Reading Material B   Pressure 8

UNIT TWO
    Text   Application of the Principles of Thermodynamics to Steady-Flow
            Components of Engineering Systems 10
    Reading Material A   Power and Enthalpy 14
    Reading Material B   The First Law of Thermodynamics 16

UNIT THREE
    Text   Equations of State 18
    Reading Material A   Van Der Waals Equation of State 23
    Reading Material B   Equilibrium 25

UNIT FOUR
    Text   The Ideal Basic Vapor Compression Refrigeration Cycle 27
    Reading Material A   Probability and Entropy 33
    Reading Material B   Entropy and the Third Law 35

UNIT FIVE
    Text   Variation of Pressure in A Static Fluid 37
    Reading Material A   Viscosity 42
    Reading Material B   Compressible and Incompressible Fluids 46

UNIT SIX
    Text   Hydraulic Grade Line and Energy Line 48
    Reading Material A   Eulerian and Lagrangian Flow Descriptions 53
    Reading Material B   Static, Stagnation (total), and Dynamic Pressure 54

UNIT SEVEN
    Text   Incompressible, Steady and Uniform Turbulent Flow in Circular
            Cross-section Pipes 57
    Reading Material A   Laminar and Turbulent Flow 62
    Reading Material B   Pipe Networks 64

UNIT EIGHT
    Text   Conduction 66
    Reading Material A   General Characteristics 71
    Reading Material B   Transient Heat Flow 73

UNIT NINE

Text　　　Definition of Similitude ··· 75
　　　Reading Material A　Comments about Dimensional Analysis ······················· 80
　　　Reading Material B　Reynolds Number and Similarity ······································ 81
UNIT TEN
　　　Text　　　Natural Convection ··· 84
　　　Reading Material A　Forced Convection ··· 89
　　　Reading Material B　Convection ·· 90
UNIT ELEVEN
　　　Text　　　Drag of Three-Dimensional Bodies (Incompressible Flow) ············· 92
　　　Reading Material A　Lift and Drag Concepts ·· 97
　　　Reading Material B　Boundary-layer Separation and Pressure Drag ············· 99
UNIT TWELVE
　　　Text　　　Actual Radiation ··· 102
　　　Reading Material A　Radiation in Gases ··· 107
　　　Reading Material B　Radiation ··· 109
UNIT THIRTEEN
　　　Text　　　Categories of Compressible Flow ··· 112
　　　Reading Material A　Effect of Flow Cross Section Area Variations ············· 118
　　　Reading Material B　Converging-diverging Duct Flow ··································· 120
UNIT FOURTEEN
　　　Text　　　Eddy Diffusivity and Application to Turbulent Flow ················ 123
　　　Reading Material A　Mean Temperature Differences for Parallel Flow and
　　　　　　　　　　　　　Counterflow Heat Exchangers ·· 128
　　　Reading Material B　Finned-Tube Heat Transfer ··· 131
UNIT FIFTEEN
　　　Text　　　Centrifugal Pumps and Fans ·· 133
　　　Reading Material A　Pump and the Pipe System ··· 139
　　　Reading Material B　Cavitation ··· 142
UNIT SIXTEEN
　　　Text　　　Manufactured Gases ··· 145
　　　Reading Material A　Gaseous Fuels ··· 151
　　　Reading Material B　The Future of Plastic Pipe at Higher Pressures ········· 153
Appendix I　　　　Vocabulary ·· 155
Appendix II　　　 Translation for Reference ··· 161
Appendix III　　　Key to Exercises ··· 182

UNIT ONE

Text   Basic Concepts and Definitions

[1]   Most applications of thermodynamics require that the system and its surroundings be defined. A thermodynamic system is defined as a region in space or a quantity of matter bounded by a closed surface. The surroundings include everything external to the system, and the system is separated from the surroundings by the system boundaries. These boundaries can be either movable or fixed; either real or imaginary.

[2]   Two master concepts operate in any thermodynamic system, energy and entropy. Entropy (s) measures the molecular disorder of a given system. The more shuffled a system is, the greater its entropy; conversely, an orderly or unmixed configuration is one of low entropy. [1]

[3]   Energy is the capacity for producing an effect, and can be categorized into either stored or transient forms. Stored forms of energy include:

   thermal (internal) energy, u—the energy possessed by a system caused by the motion of the molecules and/or intermolecular forces [2]

   potential energy, P. E. —the energy possessed by a system caused by the attractive forces existing between molecules, or the elevation of the system:

$$P.E. = mgz \quad (1.1)$$

where

   m = mass

   g = local acceleration of gravity

   z = elevation above a horizontal reference plane

   kinetic energy, K. E. —the energy possessed by a system caused by the velocity of the molecules:

$$K.E. = mv^2/2 \quad (1.2)$$

where

   m = mass

   v = velocity of the fluid streams crossing system boundaries

   chemical energy, Ec—energy possessed by the system caused by the arrangement of atoms composing the molecules.

nuclear (atomic) energy, Ea—energy possessed by the system from the cohesive forces holding protons and neutrons together as the atom's nucleus. [3]

[4]   Transient energy forms include:

   heat, Q —the mechanism that transfers energy across the boundary of systems with differing temperatures, always in the direction of the lower temperature. [4]

   work—the mechanism that transfers energy across the boundary of systems with differing pressures (or force of any kind), always in the direction of the lower pressure; if the total effect produced in the system can be reduced to the raising of a weight, then nothing but work has crossed the boundary. ⑤ Mechanical or shaft work, W, is the energy delivered or absorbed by a mechanism, such as a turbine, air compressor or internal combustion engine.

Flow work is energy carried into or transmitted across the system boundary because a pumping process occurs somewhere outside the system, causing fluid to enter the system. ⑥ It can be more easily understood as the work done by the fluid just outside the system on the adjacent fluid entering the system to force or push it into the system. ⑦ Flow work also occurs as fluid leaves the system.

$$\text{Flow Work (per unit mass)} = Pv \qquad (1.3)$$

where P is the pressure and v is the specific volume, or the volume displaced per unit mass.

[5]　A property of a system is any observable characteristic of the system. The state of a system is defined by listing its properties. The most common thermodynamic properties are: temperature (T), pressure (P) and specific volume (v) or density (ρ). Additional thermodynamic properties include entropy, stored forms of energy and enthalpy.

Frequently, thermodynamic properties combine to form new properties. Enthalpy (h), a result of combining properties, is defined as:

$$h = u + Pv \qquad (1.4)$$

where
　　u = internal energy
　　p = pressure
　　v = specific volume

Each property in a given state has only one definite value, and any property always has the same value for a given state, regardless of how the substance arrived at that state.

[6]　A process is a change in state that can be defined as any change in the properties of a system. A process is described by specifying the initial and final equilibrium states, the path (if identifiable) and the interactions that take place across system boundaries during the process. A cycle is a process, or more frequently, a series of processes wherein the initial and final states of the system are identical. Therefore, at the conclusion of a cycle all the properties have the same value they had at the beginning.

[7]　A pure substance has a homogeneous and invariable chemical composition. It can exist in more than one phase, but the chemical composition is the same in all phases.

[8]　If a substance exists as vapor at the saturation temperature, it is called saturated vapor. (Sometimes the term dry saturated vapor is used to emphasize that the quality is 100%). ⑧ When the vapor is at a temperature greater than the saturation temperature, it is superheated vapor. The pressure and temperature of superheated vapor are independent properties, since the temperature can increase while the pressure remains constant. Gases are highly superheated vapors.

New Words and Expressions

thermodynamics [ˌθəməudaiˈnæmiks]	n.	热力学
entropy [ˈentrəpi]	n.	熵（热力学函数）
shuffle [ˈʃʌfl]	vt.	搅乱，弄混
configuration * [kənˌfigjuˈreiʃən]	n.	构造，结构
categorize * [ˌkætigənaiz]	v.	把…分类
transient [ˈtrænziənt]	a.	（物）瞬变的
thermal * [ˈθəːməl]	a.	热的
elevation * [ˌeliˈveiʃən]	n.	高度
acceleration * [ækˌseləˈreiʃən]	n.	（物）加速，加速度
kinetic [kaiˈnetik]	a.	动力（学）的，动力的
cohesive [kəuˈhiːsiv]	a.	内聚的
cohesive forces		内聚力
proton [ˈprəutɔn]	n.	质子
neutron [ˈnjuːtrɔn]	n.	中子
mechanism * [ˈmekənizəm]	n.	机械装置，机械结构
shaft * [ʃɑːft]	n.	轴
compressor [kəmˈpresə]	n.	压缩机，压气机
combustion [kəmˈbʌstʃən]	n.	燃烧
adjacent * [əˈdʒeisənt]	a.	邻近的，因此相连的
specific volume		比容
displace [disˈpleis]	vt	排（水）
enthalpy [enˈθælpi]	n.	焓
equilibrium * [ˌiːkwiˈlibriəm]	n.	平衡，均衡
homogeneous * [ˌhɔməˈdʒiːnəs]	a.	均匀的
saturation [ˌsætʃəˈreiʃən]	n.	饱和（状态）
saturated [ˈsætʃəreitid]	a.	饱和

Notes

①The more shuffled... the greater...：这是"越……越……"句型。

②... the motion of the molecules and/or intermolecular forces：应理解为... the motion of the molecules and intermolecular forces 以及 the motion of the molecules or intermolecular forces.

③... energy possessed by... forces holding... together as the atom's nucleus.：possessed by... forces 过去分词短语作定语修饰 energy; holding ... as... 现在分词短语

作定语修饰 cohesive forces。

④... the mechanism that transfers... with..., always in the direction of the lower temperature：

句中 that 引起的定语从句修饰 mechanism；with 短语修饰 systems；always in the direction of... 短语修饰 transfers。

⑤... nothing but：只有。

⑥... a pumping process occurs somewhere outside the system, causing fluid to enter the system：

causing... 现在分词短语作 a pumping process ... the system 的结果状语。

⑦... the work... on...：对……做的功。

⑧quality：本文译为干度。

Exercises

Reading Comprehension

I. Match Column A with Column B according to the text.

A	B
1. A thermodynamic system	a. Energy possessed by the system from the cohesive forces holding protons and neutrons together as the atom's nucleus.
2. Entropy	b. Energy possessed by the system caused by the arrangement of atoms composing the molecules.
3. Energy	c. The energy possessed by a system caused by the velocity of the molecules.
4. Thermal (internal) energy	d. The energy possessed by a system caused by the attractive forces existing between molecules, or the elevation of the system
5. Potential energy	e. The energy possessed by a system caused by the motion of the molecules and/or intermolecular forces.
6. Kinetic Energy	f. The capacity for producing an effect.
7. Chemical energy	g. Measures the molecular disorder of a given system.
8. Nuclear (atomic) energy	h. a region in space or a quantity of matter bounded by a closed surface.

II. Separate the two types of properties according to the text.

> temperature, entropy, pressure, specific volume
> stored forms of energy and enthalpy,

1. The most common thermodynamic properties are:
2. Additional thermodynamic properties include:

Ⅲ. Do the following exercises according to the text.

1. Skim through the text and complete the following table.

```
           Energy
          /      \
   Stored forms   Transient forms
```

1) _____   1) _____
2) _____   2) _____
3) _____   3) _____
4) _____
5) _____

2. Give the definitions to the following terms:
   1) Heat _____
   2) Work _____
   3) Mechanical or shaft work _____
   4) Flow work _____

3. Fill in the blanks with the information given in the last three paragraphs:
   1) What is a process?
      (a) A process is a change in state _____
      _____
      _____
      (b) A process is described by _____
      _____
      _____

   2) What are the saturated vapor and superheated vapor?
      (a) If a substance _____ it is called _____.
      (b) When the vapor is _____ it is _____.

Vocabulary

Ⅰ. Find words in the text which mean almost the same as the following.
  1. Para. 2: being mixed in a mass confusion (_____)
  2. Para. 2: not lasting or staying long (_____)
  3. Para. 3: of or relating to the motion of material bodies and the forces and energy associated therewith (_____)

4. Para. 4: the process of burning (＿＿＿＿＿＿＿＿)
5. Para. 7: the state of being saturated (＿＿＿＿＿＿＿＿)

Now use the words you have found to complete the following sentences. Change the forms if necessary.

6. The more ＿＿＿＿＿ a system is, the greater difficulty it will have in its operation.
7. We have several kinds of engines and internal ＿＿＿＿＿ engine is one of them.
8. A substance can exist as vapor at the ＿＿＿＿＿ temperature.
9. ＿＿＿＿＿ energy is one kind of stored forms of energy.
10. Heat, work, mechanical or shaft work and flow work are included in the ＿＿＿＿＿ energy forms.

II. Fill in the blanks with the words given below. Change the forms if necessary

| elevation, categorize, acceleration, adjacent, homogeneous |

1. The house is at an ＿＿＿＿＿ of 2000 meters.
2. The ＿＿＿＿＿ of decay is caused by enzymes.
3. They live in the ＿＿＿＿＿ rooms in the same building.
4. The students are helping the librarians to ＿＿＿＿＿ all the books into several kinds.
5. A ＿＿＿＿＿ and invariable chemical composition is indispensable in a pure substance.

Reading Material A

Thermodynamic Systems

In the engineering world, objects normally are not isolated from one another. In most engineering problems many objects enter into a given problem. Some of these objects, all of these objects, or even additional ones may enter into a second problem. The nature of a problem and its solution are dependent on which objects are under consideration. Thus, it is necessary to specify which objects are under consideration in a particular situation. In thermodynamics this is done either by placing an imaginary envelope around the objects under consideration or by using an actual envelope if such exists. ① The term system refers to everything lying inside the envelope. The envelope, real or imaginary, is referred to as the boundaries of the system. It is essential that the boundaries of the system be specified very carefully. For example, when one is dealing with a gas in a cylinder where the boundaries are located on the outside of the cylinder, the system includes both the cylinder and its contained gas. ② On the other hand, when the boundaries are placed at the inner face of the cylinder, the system consists solely of the gas itself.

When the boundaries of a system are such that it cannot exchange matter with the surroundings, the system is said to be a closed system (see Fig. 1-1a). ③ The system, however, may exchange energy in the form of heat or work with the surroundings. The boundaries of a closed system may be rigid or may expand or contract, but the mass of a closed system cannot change. Hence, the term control mass sometimes is used for this type of system. When the energy crossing the boundaries of a closed system is zero or substantially so, the system may be treated as an isolated system④ (Fig. 1-1b).

In most engineering problems, matter, generally a fluid, crosses the boundaries of a system in one or more places. Such a system is known as an open system (see Fig. 1-1c). The boundaries of an open system are so placed that their location does not change with time. Thus, the boundaries enclose a fixed volume, commonly known as the control volume.

Sometimes a system may be a closed system at one moment and an open one the next. For example, consider the cylinder of an internal combustion engine with the boundaries at the inner walls. With the valves closed, the system is a closed one. However, with either or both of the valves open, the system becomes an open system.⑤

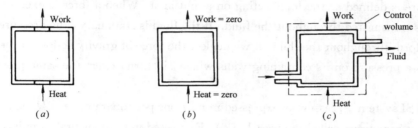

Fig. 1-1 Types of systems
(a) Closed system   (b) Isolated system   (c) Open system

Frequently the total system to be considered may be large and complicated. The system may be broken down into component parts and an analysis of the component parts made. Then the performance of the entire system can be determined by the summation of the performance of the individual component systems. For example, consider the liquid-vapor part of a steam power plant as an entire system.⑥ This system, which is closed, contains the steam generator, the steam turbine, the steam condenser, the feed-water pumps, and the feed-water heaters. Any or all of these units may be considered separately by throwing a boundary around them.⑦ Since a fluid enters and leaves each of these smaller systems, each one is an open system and must be analyzed as such.

Notes

①在热力学中,这点是通过下列两种方法中的任何一种来实现的,即在研究的物体周围设置假想的封闭面或者使用实际封闭面,如果这样的实际封闭面存在的话。
②例如:当我们研究气缸内的气体时,如果边界位于气缸之外,则该系统包括气缸和气缸内的气体。
③当系统的边界使得系统不能与其环境交换物质时,则该系统称为闭口系统。
  such that:(是)这样(以致)。

④当越过闭口系统边界的能量是零或者实质是这样的时候，这种系统就可以按孤立（隔离）系统对待。

⑤如果阀门关闭，系统就是闭口系统。但是，如果两个阀门都关闭或者其中一个关闭，该系统就变成开口系统。

⑥例如：把蒸汽动力厂的液—汽部分作为一个完整系统来考虑。

⑦任何一个或所有这些装置都可以通过在它们周围加一个边界而分别予以考虑。

Reading Material B

Pressure

Pressure is defined as the force acting on a unit area. When a force is exerted on a fluid, this force is transmitted throughout the fluid. If the fluid is stationary, the pressure within the fluid is uniform throughout the fluid, if we neglect the force of gravity action on the fluid. The fluid exerts a pressure on its containing walls which, in turn, exert the same pressure on the fluid.①

In the SI system, pressure is expressed in newtons per square meter (N/m^2).② This unit of pressure is sometimes called the pascal (Pa). Expressed in fundamental SI units, the dimensions of the pascal $kg/m \cdot s^2$.③ In the English system, pressures are expressed generally in pounds per square inch (psi).

Thermodynamically speaking, there is only one kind of pressure and that is absolute pressure. Although there are devices available to measure absolute pressures, most pressure measuring devices measure pressure differences.

A very common pressure measuring device is the Bourdon-tube type of pressure gage.④ Fundamentally, this gage consists of a coiled elliptical tube that is fixed at one end and free to move at the other end. The pressure to be measured is transmitted to the inside of the tube. There will be movement of the free end of the tube when the pressure within the tube differs from that outside the tube. The movement of the tube is transmitted to the needle of the gage. Because the pressure on the outside of the tube is atmospheric, the reading on the gage is the pressure above or below that of the atmosphere. In general, then, gage pressure is defined as the pressure above or below that of the atmosphere.

Another type of pressure device is the manometer. The U-tube type of manometer is illustrated in Fig. 1-2. Here the fluid pressure to be measured is balanced against the weight of a column of a liquid. Liquids commonly used for this purpose are water, mercury, and special manometer oil. A knowledge of the specific weight, or the weight per unit volume, of the fluid and the height of the column that balances the pressure permits the determination of the pressure. Thus, the product of the specific weight in pounds per cubic inch and the column height in inches equals the pressure in pounds per square inch.⑤ In general terms, since the force exerted by liquid, $F=W=wV=wAz$, then

$$p = \frac{force}{area} = wz \tag{1.5}$$

where p=pressure
  w=specific weight
  z=column height

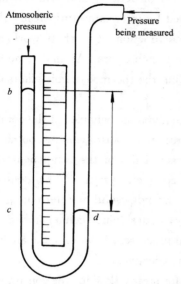

Fig. 1-2 U-tube type of manometer

In Eq. 1.5, the units of pressure will be fixed by the selection of the units of specific weight and the column height.

The atmospheric pressure must be added to the gage pressure to obtain the true or absolute pressure. Barometers generally are used to determine the atmospheric pressure. Hence, atmospheric pressure frequently is referred to as the barometric pressure. Standard atmospheric pressure (i.e., pressure of the standard atmosphere) is defined as being equivalent to a mercury column 760 mm high, where the mercury has a temperature of 0℃.⑥ This is equivalent to a pressure of 14.6960 psi.

When the pressure is less than atmospheric, a vacuum is said to exist. The magnitude of the vacuum denotes how much the pressure is below that of the atmosphere. Vacuum generally is expressed as the height of a mercury column.

Notes

①流体对容器壁施加压力，而容器壁则又对流体施加等压。
②SI：国际单位制。
③该压力单位有时称为帕斯卡（帕），用基本的国际单位表示，帕斯卡的因次为千克/米·秒²。
④the Bourdon-tube type of pressure gage：弹簧管压力计，布尔登（管式）压力计。
⑤这样，比重（磅/英寸³）和柱高（英寸）的乘积就等于压力（磅/英寸²）。
⑥标准大气压（即标准大气的压力）就是760毫米水银柱高，这儿水银是0℃。

UNIT TWO

Text Application of the Principles of Thermodynamics to Steady-Flow Components of Engineering Systems

[1]　　Many complex engineering systems operate with steady or periodic flow which simplifies the thermodynamic analysis. The systems are constructed by interconnecting steady-flow components which are grouped into four classes according to function: (1) shaft work machines, (2) nozzles and diffusers, (3) throttles, and (4) heat exchangers. An understanding of the behavior of these components is the key to understanding the thermodynamic plants discussed in the next chapter.[①]

[2]　　Our objective in this chapter is to determine the thermodynamic behavior of the components of each class by applying the principles of thermodynamics to a control volume containing the component. This approach yields the "black box" characteristics of the component that must be known in order to evaluate the performance of the complete system.[②] This does not mean that the principles of thermodynamics do not apply or are not useful in determining the detailed internal processes of the component. On the contrary, in designing such a component, thorough consideration must be given to the complex internal processes; however, the analysis of these internal processes is outside the scope of our present objective.

[3]　　The analysis of this chapter is based on the equations for steady flow for the control volume with one inlet port and one exit port. In addition it will be useful to consider a control volume of infinitesimal extent in the direction of flow.[③] The fluid experiences an infinitesimal change of state between inlet and outlet in response to infinitesimal rates of heat transfer and shear work transfer. Thus we can get differential relations:

$$\frac{\delta \dot{Q}}{\dot{m}} - \frac{\delta \dot{Q}_{shear}}{\dot{m}} = dh + vdv - gdz$$

[4]　　The analysis will be illustrated by application to the flow of an incompressible fluid, the flow of an ideal gas, and to the flow of a pure substance in two phase states. These cases illustrate the basic behavior of each of four classes of steady-flow components.

[5]　　The first class of components is comprised of machines which change the state of a stream by positive or negative shaft work transfer. Machines with positive shaft work transfer are commonly called turbines, reciprocating engines, expanders, or fluid motors, depending upon the application and the method of developing the pressure forces that produce the shaft work transfer. Machines with negative shaft work transfer are commonly called compressors, pumps, or fans depending upon the application.

[6]　　The operation of a shaft work machine does not depend upon the attainment of thermal equilibrium between the flowing fluid and the walls of the apparatus; consequently, the rate of work transfer is not limited by the relatively slow thermal conduction process. Rather, the

work transfer depends upon the pressure forces on the moving surfaces internal to the apparatus (turbine or compressor blades or piston faces). ④ Thus, the limit on the rate of work transfer is related to the velocity of propagation of pressure waves (sound) in the fluid. This rate is often fast enough that the rate of work transfer for the machine is actually limited by the forces which result from the accelerations of the solid parts of the machine (inertia stress limit).

[7]　Since the work transfer rate is rapid, the shaft work machine is small enough that the fluid remains within the machine for a time period that is small compared to the time period required to attain thermal equilibrium. ⑤ Thus, the apparatus is essentially adiabatic. Note that some heat transfer does occur in virtually every case; however, the magnitude is negligible compared to the shaft work transfer. This situation is especially true for turbo machines in which the high work transfer rate is the result of internal pressure differences (across the blades) produced by accelerating (deflecting) the moving stream of fluid. ⑥ In reciprocating or positive displacement machines, the internal forces are the result of equilibrium pressure (spatially uniform) acting on a moving piston face or the equivalent moving surface.

[8]　A second result of the relatively rapid work transfer rate and the resulting small size of the machine is that the change in gravitational potential energy is usually negligible. This is usually true even for the large water turbines used in hydroelectric power stations provided the control volume does not include the penstock.

[9]　The preceding discussion indicates that shaft work machines can be reasonably modeled as adiabatic devices with negligible changes in gravitational potential energy. Further, in many practical cases the change in kinetic energy of the bulk flow is also negligible. Thus the first law of thermodynamics, applied to a control volume representing a machine of this type reduces to

$$-\dot{W}_{shaft} = \dot{m}(h_{out} - h_{in})$$

New Words and Expressions

nozzle ['nɔzl]	n.	喷管（嘴）
diffuser * [di'fjuːzə]	n.	扩散器，喷雾器，扩压管
throttle ['θrɔtl]	n.	节流阀
inlet * ['inlet]	n.	进（入）口
infinitesimal [infini'tesiməl]	a.	无穷小的，无限小的
differential [,difə'renʃəl]	a.	微分（的）
incompressible [inkəm'presəbl]	a.	不可压缩的
reciprocating [ri'siprəkeitiŋ]	a.	往复的，来回的
expander [ikspændə]	n.	膨胀器，扩张器
piston ['pistən]	n.	活塞
propagation * [prɔpə'geiʃən]	n.	传播
inertia * [i'nəːʃjə]	n.	惯性，惰性，惯量

adiabatic	[ˌædiəˈbætik]	a.	绝热的
magnitude *	[ˈmægnitjuːd]	n.	量（级），数值
negligible *	[ˈneglidʒəbl]	a.	可以忽略的
turbo	[ˈtəːbəu]	n.	涡轮，透平
deflect	[diˈflekt]	vt. & vi.	使偏离（斜），使转向
spatially *	[ˈspeiʃəli]	ad.	在空间上
gravitational	[ˌgræviˈteiʃnl]	a.	重力的
hydroelectric	[ˈhaidrəuiˈlektrik]	a.	水力发电的
penstock	[ˈpenstək]	n.	进水管，压力水管，闸门
model	[mɔdl]	v.	模拟（造）

Notes

①behavior：这里译为"变化特性"。
②"black box"："黑箱原则"一种预算预测方法。用"投入"和"产出"的概念来说明预测目标。
③infinitesimal extent：这里译为"微元长度"。
④... the moving surfaces internal to the apparatus...：internal to the apparatus 形容词短语作后置定语修饰 the moving surfaces。
⑤Since the work... small enough that... a time period that... required... equilibrium.：that the fluid remains... 是由于 small enough 引出的结果状语从句；that is... 引出的定语从句修饰 a time period；required to attain thermal equilibrium 过去分词短语修饰 the time period。
⑥This situation is especially... in which... produced by... of fluid.：in which... 引出的是定语从句，which 的先行词是 turbo machines；produced by accelerating... the moving stream of fluid 过去分词短语作 internal pressure differences 的定语。

Exercises

Reading Comprehension

I. Fill in the blanks with the information given in the text

1. Our objective of this chapter is to _____
   _____
   _____.

2. The analysis of this chapter is based on _____
   _____
   _____.

3. The analysis will be illustrated by application to
   1) _____
   2) _____
   3) _____

II. Separate the following according to the text.

| turbines | compressors | pumps | reciprocating engines |
| expanders | fans | fluid motors | |

1. Machines with positive shaft work transfer are commonly called:
_____

2. Machines with negative shaft work transfer are commonly called:
_____

III. Make a good match according to the information given in the last four paragraphs.

1.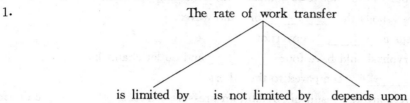

(1)	(2)	(3)
the relatively slow thermal conduction process.	the pressure forces on the moving surfaces internal to the apparatus.	the forces which result from the accelerations of the solid parts of the machine.

2.

Items	Match	Information
1) The magnitude of some heat transfer is 2) The high work transfer rate is 3) The internal forces (in reciprocating or positive displacement machines) are 4) The change is usually 5) The change in kinetic energy of the bulk flow is	negligible the result of	a) in many practical cases. b) equilibrium pressure acting on a moving piston face or the equivalent moving surface. c) internal pressure differences produced by accelerating the moving stream of fluid. d) compared to the shaft work transfer. e) in gravitational potential energy.

Vocabulary

I. Find words in the text which mean almost the same as the following.
1. Para. 3: a way in (for water, liquid, etc.) (_____)
2. Para. 6: the act of propagating or being propagated. (_____)
3. Para. 6: the force which prevents a thing from being moved when it is standing still, and keeps it moving (or prevents it from being stopped) when it is moving. (_____)
4. Para. 7: too slight or unimportant to make any difference or to be worth any attention. (_____)
5. Para. 7: of, concerning, or being in space. (_____)

Now use the words from (1—5) above to complete the following sentences:
6. The sun sometimes spoils the _____ of radio waves.
7. This machine needs a _____ governor.
8. This kind of reservoir should have four _____ and outlet channels.
9. The quantity is _____ compared to the others.
10. The internal forces are the result of equilibrium pressure which is _____ uniform.

II. Fill in the blanks with some of the words given below. Change the forms if necessary.

| adiabatic | deflect | hydroelectric |
| reciprocating | differential | |

1. This is an _____ curve.
2. There is a _____ power station outside the city.
3. The bullet struck a wall and was _____ from its course.
4. A _____ engine should be used here.
5. Because they are the middle school students they cannot understand _____ calculus.

Reading Material A

Power and Enthalpy

The size of work-producing devices is dependent not on the total work to be delivered, but on the rate at which it is delivered, that is, on the power required[①] Power is defined as the time rate of doing work. In the SI system, the fundamental unit of power is the watt (W). The watt is defined as the work done at the rate of a joule per second. Since the watt is a small unit of power, the kilowatt (KW), which is a thousand watts, is used extensively. For still larger amounts of power, the megawatt (MW), which is a million watts, may be used.

Although rates of heat addition to a system may be expressed in terms of watts, care must be taken not to think of this amount of heat as being equal to the electrical energy deliverable.[2] For example, a nuclear reactor, rated at 1000 MW, may produce steam for a steam turbogenerator unit. The electrical output of the generator may be only 320 MW and not 1000 MW. To avoid this difficulty when dealing with rates of heat transfers expressed in watts, it is customary to express them as watts thermal. Thus, the rating of the reactor could be expressed as 1000 MWt.

The terms U and pV represent the energy of a given mass, m, of fluid entering the system. But $U=mu$ and $V=mv$. Then $U+pV=m(u+pv)$, where u is the internal energy per unit mass and v is the specific volume. As will be discussed in some detail later one, when the state of the fluid is fixed, the summation of $u+pv$ is also fixed, and hence, has a specific value. This eliminates the necessity of evaluating each term individually. Credit for using this combination is given to Professor Williard Gibbs of Yale University who, in 1879, designated it as his χ function. Unfortunately, at the turn of the century, other terms such as total heat and heat content, were applied to this function. These terms are entirely erroneous in their implications and hence led to considerable confusion.[3] Some years later, the term enthalpy was selected for this function and was given the symbol H. The defining equation for enthalpy is

$$H = U + pV \tag{2.1}$$

and

$$h = u + pv \tag{2.1.a}$$

Since U, p, and V all are properties, H must also be a property.[4] Because it is composed of several properties, it is known as a compound property. As a property, it can be tabulated in tables of properties of various substances. Methods will be developed later on to evaluate enthalpy changes for both ideal and actual gases.

Although the concept of enthalpy is a very valuable one when dealing with flow, care must be taken in its use in nonflow conditions. The term pV was shown to be the energy necessary to force a given mass of a fluid across a given boundary of a system; hence, pV represents energy transmitted by the fluid as it crosses the boundary of the system.[5] Thus, for a fluid in motion, its enthalpy is truly energy. On the other hand, for a substance at rest, the pV term cannot represent energy being transmitted since no energy is being transmitted. Thus, for a substance at rest, the PV term is not energy. Hence, enthalpy cannot be energy and must not be used as such.

Although enthalpy can be used as energy only in the case of flow, it may be useful for other purposes. In certain cases, such as for closed systems, it may be necessary to determine changes in internal energies. However, some tables of properties list values of enthalpies but not internal energies. Internal energies may be calculated readily by using the defining equation of enthalpy, $H = U + pV$, or $U = H - pV$.

Notes

① 作功装置的大小取决于要输出的总功量,但是也取决于输出的功率,也就是需要的功率。
② 尽管对一个系统的加热量可以用瓦特来表示,但要注意不要把这部分热量看作等于传递的电能。
③ 这些术语在内涵上是完全错误的,这样就引起了相当大的混乱。
④ property:参数。
⑤ 术语 pV 是使一定质量的流体穿过指定系统边界所需的能量。

Reading Material B

The First Law of Thermodynamics

The first law of thermodynamics plays a significant role in the analysis of thermodynamic systems, and for this reason we shall devote considerable attention to its development. However, it is useful for us to outline briefly the essential features of the first law of thermodynamics as it applies to closed systems.① With this information, we will be better prepared to organize and interpret the details of the succeeding development.

In essence, the first law of thermodynamics is a generalization of the observed facts about the energy interactions between a system and its environment. Specifically, it relates the various energy interactions between a system and its environment to changes of state experienced by that system during these interactions.② All physical experience has confirmed that the generalizations embodied in the first law of thermodynamics must be satisfied to describe realistically a physical situation.

There are many ways in which the first law of thermodynamics can be stated, and some rather complex arguments are required to prove the equivalence of these statements. However, the simplest of these statements can be formulated by considering a system which executes a cycle.③ By definition, the system experiences no net change of state. Therefore, there can be no net energy interaction between the system and its environment. For our purposes it will be sufficient to consider only two forms of energy interaction between a system and its environment: work transfers W, and heat transfers Q. Thus, we may state the first law of thermodynamics in a formal way as:

The net energy interaction between a system and its environment is zero for a cycle executed by the system.

The mathematical equivalent of this statement is

$$\oint \delta Q - \oint \delta W = 0 \qquad (2.2)$$

The integral sign indicates the algebraic summation of each infinitesimal heat transfer δQ or work transfer δW over the complete cycle. The negative sign is introduced because historically in thermodynamics, work transfer from a system is taken as positive which is the inverse of the sign convention used in mechanics.④

The major difficulty in applying the first law to physical situations lies in the determination and formulation of the heat transfers and work transfers. This will soon become apparent as we take the basic concepts of work transfer directly from mechanics and electromechanics, and reformulate them from a thermodynamics point of view. However, as we deal with progressively more complex systems, it may be necessary to extend these definitions of work transfer to avoid any ambiguity. Since heat transfer is unique to thermodynamics, it is not possible to rely on other disciplines for its formulation. In fact, one of the most difficult aspects of the formalism of thermodynamics is a rigorous definition of heat transfer. Therefore, we shall delay its discussion until later in our development. Presently, it is sufficient to regard heat transfer simply as one method of energy interaction, distinct from work transfer, between a system and its environment.⑤

As we shall see later, it will become increasingly important for us to distinguish between the energy transfer interactions Q and W and the property which changes by virtue of these interactions. This latter quantity is defined as the energy, E, of the system at a given state. It is simply the stored energy of the system. The change in the stored energy of a system due to a change of state of the system from state 1 to state 2 is defined by

$$\int_1^2 \delta Q - \int_1^2 \delta W = E_2 - E_1 \tag{2.3}$$

Notes

①因此简要概述热力学第一定律在闭口系统中应用时的主要特点对我们是有用的。
②具体地讲，它把一个系统和环境之间的各种能量的相互作用与该系统在相互作用过程中所经历的状态变化联系起来。
③然而，在这些论述中最简单的就是通过考虑一个实现循环的系统来阐述。
④这里引入了负号，因为从历史角度讲，在热力学中，从系统传出的功被认为是正的，而这是与机械中通常使用的符号相反的。
⑤这里，把热量传递作为系统和环境之间能量相互作用的方法（不同于功传递）来看待就行了。

UNIT THREE

Text   Equations of State

[1]   An equation of state of a pure substance is a mathematical relation between pressure, specific volume and temperature, when the system is in thermodynamic equilibrium:

$$f(P,v,T) = 0 \tag{3.1}$$

[2]   Theoreticians use principles of statistical mechanics to (1) explore the fundamental properties of matter, (2) predict an equation of state based on the statistical nature of a particulate system or (3) propose a functional form for an equation of state with unknown parameters that are determined by measuring thermodynamic properties of a substance.[①] A fundamental equation with this basis is the virial equation.

[3]   The virial equation is expressed as an expansion in pressure P or in reciprocal values of volume per unit mass, y:

$$\frac{Pv}{RT} = 1 + B'P + C'P^2 + D'P^3 + \cdots \tag{3.2}$$

$$\frac{Pv}{RT} = 1 + (B/v) + (C/v^2) + (D/v^3) + \cdots \tag{3.3}$$

where coefficients B', C', D', etc., and B, C, D and so forth are called virial coefficients. B' and B are second virial coefficients; C' and C are third virial coefficients, etc. The virial coefficients are functions of temperature only, and values of the respective coefficients in Eq. (20) and (21) are related. For example, $B' = B/RT$ and $C' = (C - B^2)/(RT)^2$

[4]   The quantity R is the ideal gas constant defined as:

$$R = \lim_{p \to 0} (Pv)_T / T_{tp} \tag{3.4}$$

where $(Pv)_T$ is the product of pressure and volume along an isotherm, and T_{tp} is the defined temperature of the triple point of water $T_{tp} = 273.16$K. The current best value of R is 8.31434 J/g mol·K.

[5]   The quantity Pv/RT is also referred to as the compressibility factor, $Z = Pv/RT$, or:

$$Z = 1 + (B/v) + (C/v^2) + (D/v^3) + \cdots \tag{3.5}$$

[6]   An advantage of the virial form is that statistical mechanics can be used to predict the lower order coefficients, and provide physical significance to the virial coefficients. For example, in Eq. (3.5), the term B/v is a function of interactions between two molecules, C/v^2 between three molecules and so forth.[②] Since the lower order interactions are common, the contributions of the higher order terms are successively less. Thermodynamicists use the partition or distribution function to determine virial coefficients. In general, however, experimental values of the second and third coefficients are preferred. For dense fluid, many higher order terms are necessary that can neither be satisfactorily predicted from theory nor determined

from experimental measurements.[3] In general, a truncated virial expansion of four terms is valid for densities of less than one-half the value at the critical point.[4] For higher densities, additional terms can be used and determined empirically.

[7]   Digital computers allow use of far more complex equations of state in calculating P-v-T values, even to high densities. The Benedict-Webb-Rubin (B-W-R) equation of state and the Martin-Hou equation have had considerable use, but should generally be limited to densities less than the critical value. Strobridge has suggested a modified Benedict-Webb-Rubin relation that gives excellent results at higher densities and can be used for a P-v-T surface that extends into the liquid phase.

[8]   Strobridge suggested an equation of state that was developed for nitrogen properties, and used for most cryogenic fluids. This equation combines the B-W-R equation of state with an equation for high density nitrogen suggested by Benedict. These equations have been used successfully for liquid and vapor phases, extending in the liquid to the triple point temperature and the freezing line, and in the vapor phase from 10 to 1000K, with pressures to 1000 mPa. The equation suggested by Strobridge is accurate within the uncertainty of the measured P-v-T data. This equation, as originally reported by Strobridge, is:

$$P = RT\rho + \left[Rn_1 T + n_2 + \frac{n_3}{T} + \frac{n_4}{T^2} + \frac{n_5}{T^4} \right] \rho^2$$
$$+ (Rn_6 T + n_7)\rho^3 + n_8 T \rho^4$$
$$+ \rho^3 \left[\frac{n_9}{T^2} + \frac{n_{10}}{T^3} + \frac{n_{11}}{T^4} \right] e^{(-n_{16}\rho^2)}$$
$$+ \rho^5 \left[\frac{n_{12}}{T^2} + \frac{n_{13}}{T^3} + \frac{n_{14}}{T^4} \right] e^{(-n_{16}\rho^2)} + n_{15}\rho^6 \quad (3.6)$$

[9]   The 15 coefficients of this equation's linear terms are determined by a least-square fit to experimental data. For further information on methods and techniques for determining equations of state, see reference books.

[10]   In the absence of experimental data, Van der Waals' principle of corresponding states can predict fluid properties.[5] Modifications of Van der Waals' principle, as suggested by Kamerlingh Onnes, have been used to improve correspondence at low pressures. The principle of corresponding states provides useful approximations, and numerous modifications have been reported in the literature. More complex treatments for predicting property values, which recognize similarity of fluid properties, are by generalized equations of state.[6] These equations ordinarily allow for adjustment of the P-v-T surface by introduction of parameters. One example allows for departures from the principle of corresponding states by adding two correlating parameters.

New Words and Expressions

theoretician	[ˌθiəre'tiʃən]	n.	理论家
particulate	[pə'tikjulit]	n.	微粒
parameter *	[pə'ræmitə]	n.	参数
virial equation			维里方程
reciprocal	[ri'siprəkəl]	a.	倒数的
coefficient	[ˌkəui'fiʃənts]	n.	系数
isotherm	['aisəuθə:m]	n.	等温线，恒温线
triple (point) *	['tripl]	a.	三相的（三相点）
compressibility	[kəmˌpresi'biliti]	n.	压缩（性）
contribution	[ˌkɔntri'bju:ʃən]	n.	分配，分布
partition *	[pɑ:'tiʃən]	n.	分开，划分
partition function			分配函数
truncated	['trʌŋkeitid]	a.	截短（断）的
empirically *	[em'pirikəli]	ad.	经验地，实验地
critical value			临界值
cryogenic	[ˌkraiə'dʒenik]	a.	低温（学）的
linear	['liniə]	a.	线性的
a least-square fit			最小二乘拟合
modification	[ˌmɔdifi'keiʃən]	n.	修改，改进
scale	[skeil]	vt.	换算
correspondence *	[ˌkɔris'pɔndəns]	n.	对应
approximation	[əˌprɔksi'meiʃən]	n.	近似，近似值
generalize *	['dʒenərəlaiz]	vt.	归纳出
correlating *	['kɔrileitiŋ]	a.	相关的

Notes

①Theoreticians use... a substance：
  句中（1）、（2）、（3）三个并列的动词不定式短语作目的状语；with unknown parameters 短语作 an equation of state 的定语；that are determined... 引出定语从句修饰 unknown parameters。

②For example... and so forth：
  句中 C/v^2 between three molecules 省掉了与前句中相同的部分，也就是 C/v^2 is a function of interactions between three molecules。

③For dense fluid... experimental measurements：

句中 that 引出的定语从句先行词是 many higher order terms 中间被 are necessary 分隔。

④... less than one-half the value at the critical point：

介词短语 at the critical point 的定语 less than one-half 后面省略了介词 of。

⑤in the absence of：无……时，缺少……时；Van der Waals 为 J. D. van der Waals（1837—1923），荷兰物理学家，研究分子吸引力，1910 年获诺贝尔奖。

⑥More complex treatments... equations of state：

句中 which 引出的非限制性定语从句修饰 more complex treatments。

Exercises

Reading Comprehension

Ⅰ. What do the theoreticians use principles of statistical mechanics to do according to the text? Put a tick before the correct ones.
1. To explore the fundamental properties of matter.
2. To express an expansion in pressure.
3. To predict an equation of state based on the statistical nature of a particulate system.
4. To predict the lower order coefficients.
5. To propose a functional form for an equation of state with unknown parameters that are determined by measuring thermodynamic properties of a substance.
6. To provide physical significance to the virial coefficients.

Ⅱ. Say whether the following statements are True (T) or False (F) according to the text.
( ) 1. The virial equation is a fundamental equation which is expressed as an expansion in pressure P or in reciprocal values of volume per unit mass, V.
( ) 2. In this equation only $B. C. D.$ are called virial coefficients.
( ) 3. The virial coefficients are functions of temperature only.
( ) 4. The quantity R is also referred to as the compressibility factor.
( ) 5. Since the higher order interactions are common, the contributions of the lower order terms are successively less.

Ⅲ. Choose the best answer.
1. An advantage of the virial form is that _____.
   A. the partition or distribution function can be used to determine virial coefficients.
   B. experimental values of the second and third coefficients are preferred.
   C. the lower order coefficients can be predicted by statistical mechanics and physical significance can be provided to the virial coefficients.
   D. many higher order terms can neither be satisfactorily predicted from theory nor determined from experimental measurements.
2. Which relation or equation can give excellent results at higher densities and can be used for a P-v-T surface that extends into the liquid phase.

A. The Benedict-Webb-Rubin equation
B. The Martin-Hou equation
C. Strobridge equation
D. A modified Benedict-Webb-Rubin relation

3. The following statements are true except _____.
   A. An equation of state suggested by Strobridge was developed for nitrogen properties and used for most cryogenic fluids.
   B. This equation combines the B-W-R equation of state with an equation for high density nitrogen suggested by Benedict.
   C. These equations have been used successfully for liquid and vapor phases.
   D. The 15 coefficients of this equation's linear terms are determined by further information on methods and techniques.

4. What can Van der Waals' principle of corresponding states do in the absence of experimental data?
   A. It can relate suitable reducing factors.
   B. It can define reducing parameters.
   C. It can predict fluid properties.
   D. It can improve correspondence.

5. The equations discussed in the text are following except _____.
   A. the virial equation
   B. P-v-T equation
   C. B-W-R equation
   D. the Martin-Hou equation

Vocabulary

I. Complete each of the following statements with one of the four choices given below.

1. This is an equation of state with unknown _____ that are determined by measuring thermodynamic properties of a substance.
   A. paramatta   B. parameters
   C. paramnesia   D. paramecin

2. In this equation T_{tp} is the defined temperature of the _____ point of water.
   A. triple   B. triplet
   C. tripod   D. tripper

3. It is also customary for the teacher to provide grammar notes to help the student _____ what he has learned.
   A. generalize   B. produce
   C. sum into   D. conclude

4. Modifications of this principle have been used to improve _____ at low pressures.

A. adaptation B. coherence
C. correspondence D. affection

5. The 15 coefficients of this equation's _____ terms are determined by a least-square fit to experimental data.
    A. liny B. linear
    C. slim D. stripy

II. Match the words in Column A with their corresponding definitions in Column B:

A	B
1. coefficient	a. curve for changes in physical system at constant temperature.
2. particulate	b. (physics) multiplier that measures some property
3. truncated	c. (matter) in the form of separate particles
4. isotherm	d. shortened by cutting the tip, top, or end from something.
5. approximation	e. almost correct amount or estimate.

Use the words from (1—5) above to complete the following sentences. Change the forms if necessary.

6. The _____ of displacement in this system is very important.
7. The students are asked to calculate the area of the _____ cone.
8. The _____ inheritance belongs to the study of biology.
9. In this equation, $(Pv)_T$ is the product pressure and volume along an _____.
10. They only want the _____ of the square root.

Reading Material A

Van Der Waals Equation of State

Over the years, some 50 to 60 equations of state have been developed to give more accurate results than the ideal gas equation. Some of these equations are based on analytical considerations; others are empirical or semiempirical. Some equations are relatively simple; others are very complex. All of these equations of state have some merit in that they produce acceptable results for some conditions.① No equation, regardless of its complexity, is wholly satisfactory for all conditions of temperature and pressure.②

One of the earliest equations of state was that proposed by J. D. van der Waals, a Dutch physicist in 1873. The van der Waals equation is a simple one. It is therefore valuable for illustrating the use of an equation of state to obtain various properties of gases without becoming involved in the excessive mathematical calculations required by use of the more complicated equations of state.[3] Moreover, the van der Waals equation gives fairly satisfactory results for low to moderate pressures and moderate to high temperatures. The van der Waals equation will be examined in some detail and then other equations of state will be considered.

It was stated that intermolecular attractions cause deviations from the ideal equation of state. As an illustration, consider a particular gas molecule that is ready to strike its containing wall. According to the ideal-gas equation of state, it will exert a certain pressure on the containing wall. However, other molecules that are close enough to exert an attractive force will prevent the particular molecule from exerting its full pressure on the containing wall (see Fig. 3-1). This reduction in pressure caused by intermolecular attractive forces is known as the internal pressure. Because of intermolecular forces, the reduction in pressure exerted on a certain area of the wall by each molecule is proportional to the number of molecules in the sphere of action around that area. Furthermore, the combined reduction in pressure exerted by all the molecules in that partial sphere of action is proportional to the number of molecules in the partial sphere. Hence, the internal pressure exerted by all molecules in a sphere of action may be considered proportional to the square of the number of molecules in a given volume or proportional to the square of the density of the gas.[4] The sum of the external or observable pressure and the internal pressure represents the total pressure that would be exerted by an ideal gas.

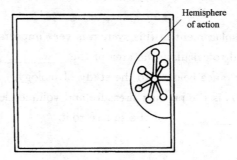

Fig. 3-1 Pressure reduction by adjacent molecules

The ideal-gas equation of state is based on the assumption that the volume of the molecules is negligible. Hence, the free volume (volume free of molecules) equals the entire volume, which, per unit mass, is v.[5] In addition, it assumes that the pressure exerted by the molecules with no intermolecular attractions equals the observable pressure, p. To deal with actual gases, van der Waals introduced a term b which is subtracted from the total volume to obtain the free volume. He also introduced the term a/v^2 which, when added to the observed pressure, indicates the total molecular pressure. Thus, the van der Waals equation of state becomes

$$\left(p + \frac{a}{v^2}\right)(v - b) = R_0 T \tag{3.7}$$

Values of the constants a and b depend on the kind of gas and the units used in Eq. 3.7. When the pressures are expressed in bars, the volume in cubic meters per kilogram mole, and the temperature in degrees Kelvin, R_0 has a value of 0.08314 bar-m³/kg mole-K.[6]

Notes

① 所有这些状态方程都有有利之处，在某些条件下，它们可以产生可接受的结果。
② 状态方程不管多么复杂，没有一个能在各种温度和压力下完全令人满意的。
③ 用一个状态方程可以在没有（因为使用较为复杂的状态方程所需的）过多的数学计算情况下获得气体的参数。这点可以用 Van der Waals 方程来证明，因此 Van der Waals 方程是有价值的。
④ 因此，由于运转中的球体内的所有分子的作用而产生的内压可以认为与一定空间内的分子数量的平方成正比或者与气体密度的平方成正比。
⑤ the free volume 这里译为：自由空间。
⑥ bar 巴（压力单位）。

Reading Material B

Equilibrium

Consider now two thermodynamic systems which are free to interact in any possible manner. If the state of one system is changed by some external agent, the two systems will interact with one another. Eventually, they will reach a particular state, known as the equilibrium state, determined by the physical situation. In this state, the interaction between systems ceases. Once this state has been established, the two systems cannot be made to interact any further unless the imposed circumstances are altered. In this sense, the two systems are in a state of mutual equilibrium. On the other hand, the two interacting systems may actually be part of a larger system. When all subsystems of this larger system reach a state of mutual equilibrum, the composite system is said to be in a state of internal equilibrium. That is, any one part of the composite system is in equilibrium with any other part.

It is worth noting that the underlying principle of thermodynamics is this tendency for all systems to seek the equilibrium state as defined by the particular physical circumstances. On the basis of this principle, it is possible to derive the relations of thermodynamics.

Although it is not specifically mentioned, the variable time does play an important role in the definition of equilibrium. Perhaps this point can be clarified by rephrasing the definition: "When a system is in an equilibrium state, it is impossible for the system to experience a change of state without also experiencing an interaction of some sort". ① In a manner of speaking, an equilibrium state is a state of "rest"; nothing is happening. ② We note, however, that this static nature of the equilibrium state exists only on a macroscopic scale. If we observe any system on a microscopic scale, we see that the system is in a state of constant fluctuation and is far from being at "rest". The magnitudes of these microscopic fluctuations are so minute that in most cases they are undetectable on a macroscopic scale. However, the possibility does exist for a large number of these minute fluctuations to "happen" simultaneously so that a spontaneous macroscopic fluctuation is observed. If this possibility exists for every system, then how can we talk about equilibrium states in such absolute terms? This question can be answered by noting that the probability of this occurring in most systems is so small that the event would probably happen only once during a time period comparable with the age of the universe. Therefore, a system not experiencing any interactions when allowed to do so can be regarded as being in equilibrium.③

The point is that this equilibrium is relative rather than absolute. We have just stated (although not explicitly) that if the probability of a system executing a spontaneous change of state is small during the time scale of a typical observation, then the system is assumed to be in equilibrium. Simply, if a system is undergoing a change of state which is "slow" relative to the time scale of the physical phenomenon which dominates the overall physical picture, such a system can be treated as though it were in equilibrium.④

In the present treatment there are four types of equilibrium which will concern us. These types are characterized by the nature of the interaction which is necessary for the system to reach equilibrium. Accordingly they are called mechanical equilibrium, thermal equilibrium, chemical equilibrium, and diffusion equilibrium. Detailed definitions of these various types of equilibrium will be presented at the appropriate points in our development.

Notes

①如果系统处于平衡状态,那末系统不经历某种相互作用而发生状态变化是不可能的。
②in a manner of speaking：不妨说；说起来。
③因此,一个可以相互作用而没有经历相互作用的系统可被看作是处于平衡状态。
④简单地说,如果一个系统正在进行"慢速"的状态变化,这样的系统可以按似乎处于平衡状态来对待。所谓"慢速"是相对于物理现象的时间标尺而言的。这种时间标尺控制着总的物理状态。

UNIT FOUR

Text   The Ideal Basic Vapor Compression Refrigeration Cycle

[1]   The equipment diagram for the basic vapor compression cycle is illustrated in Fig. 4-1. Minimum components of this cycle include compressor, condenser, expansion valve and evaporator. The ideal cycle considers heat transfer in the condenser and evaporator without pressure losses, a reversible adiabatic (isentropic) compressor, and an adiabatic expansion valve, connected by piping that has neither pressure loss nor heat transfer with the surroundings.① The refrigerant leaves the evaporator at point 1 as a low pressure, low temperature, saturated vapor and enters the compressor, where it is compressed reversibly and adiabatically (isentropic). At point 2, it leaves the compressor as a high temperature, high pressure, superheated vapor and enters the condenser, where it is first desuperheated and then condensed at constant pressure. At point 3, the refrigerant leaves the condenser as a high pressure, medium temperature, saturated liquid and enters the expansion valve where it expands irreversibly and adiabatically (constant enthalpy). At point 4, it leaves the expansion valve as a low pressure, low temperature, low quality vapor and enters the evaporator, where it is evaporated reversibly at constant pressure to the saturated state at point 1. Heat transfer to the evaporator and from the condenser occurs without a finite temperature difference between the fluid emitting the heat and the fluid that absorbs the heat, except during the desuperheating process in the condenser.②

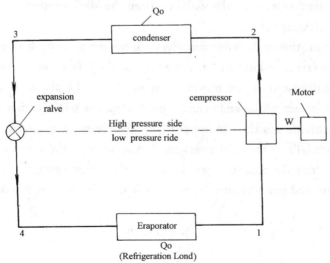

Fig. 4-1 Equipment Diagram for Basic Vapor Compression Cycle

[2]   An energy balance and certain performance parameters can be derived from the first law of thermodynamics. Applying the steady flow equation for the first law to each of the components of the basic vapor compression cycle, the following relationships are derived:

1-2	Compression	$_1\dot{W}_2 = -(h_2 - h_1)\dot{m}$	(4.1)
2-3	Condensing	$_2\dot{Q}_3 = -(h_2 - h_3)\dot{m}$	(4.2)
3-4	Expansion Valve	$h_3 = h_4$	
4-1	Evaporator	$_4\dot{Q}_1 = (h_1 - h_4)\dot{m}$	(4.3)

[3]　In applying the steady flow equation, kinetic energy and potential energy terms were omitted; because flow velocities are low to avoid fluid friction and undesirable pressure losses, and height variation within a given refrigeration system is usually small, these terms are numerically insignificant. Since the system is cyclic, the heat rejected in the condenser must be equal to the sum of the heat absorbed in the evaporator and the work of compression.

[4]　Coefficient of Performance (COP) is used to evaluate the performance of a refrigeration system. COP = refrigeration effect/net work input.

[5]　For the basic vapor compression cycle, from Eq. (4.1) and (4.3), the COP is:
$$COP = (h_1 - h_4)/(h_2 - h_1)$$

[6]　Performance characteristics and applications of compressors to the refrigeration cycle are reviewed in Chapter 12 of the 1983 Equipment Volume. Types considered include positive displacement compressors (e.g., reciprocating piston, rotary and helical rotary) and centrifugal compressors.

[7]　In evaluating contributions of the compressor to thermodynamic systems, it is necessary to consider properties of the refrigerants at the inlet and outlet of the compressor, with the change in state between these points being (1) reversible and adiabatic (isentropic) for the ideal compressor; or (2) adiabatic and irreversible (with an increase in entropy in the fluid passing through the compressor) with the variation from the ideal compressor described by the adiabatic compressor efficiency.[3]

[8]　An important thermodynamic consideration for the positive displacement compressor is the effect of the clearance volume, i.e., the volume the refrigerant occupies within the compressor that is not displaced by the moving member.[4] For the piston compressor consider the clearance volume between piston and cylinder head when the piston is in a top, center position. After the cylinder discharges the compressed gas, the clearance gas reexpands to a larger volume as the pressure falls to the inlet pressure. Consequently, the compressor discharges a refrigerant mass less than the mass that would occupy the volume swept by the piston, measured at the inlet pressure and temperature. This effect is quantitatively expressed by the volumetric efficiency, η_v:
$$\eta_v = m_a/m_t \tag{4.4}$$
where
　　m_a = actual mass of new gas entering the compressor per stroke
　　m_t = theoretical mass of gas represented by the displacement volume and determined at the pressure and temperature at the compressor inlet

[9]　Volumetric efficiency measures the effectiveness of the compressor's piston displacement

(size) in moving the refrigerant vapor through the cycle. Since refrigerants differ greatly in their specific volumes v_1, choice of refrigerant can affect the mass flow delivered by compressor displacement.

[10]　One of the design parameters of a multistage compressor is selection of the interstage pressure at which the refrigerant temperature is reduced by an intercooler. At optimum interstage pressure, total work is minimum. For two-stage compression of an ideal gas ($Pv = RT$), this occurs at the geometric mean of the suction and discharge pressures and results in equal work for the stages. The application of multistage compressors to refrigeration systems, however, differs from gas compressors since cooling at the interstage pressure is usually accomplished by refrigerant diverted from some other part of the cycle.

New Words and Expressions

compression [kəm'preʃən]	n.	压缩
refrigeration [ri͵fridʒə'reiʃən]	n.	制冷
condenser [kən'densə]	n.	冷凝器
valve [vælv]	n.	阀门
evaporator [i'væpəreitə]	n.	蒸发器
reversible [ri'və:səbl]	a.	可逆的
reversibly [ri'və:səbli]	ad.	可逆（倒）地
irreversibly [͵iri'və:səbli]	ad.	不可逆（转）地
isentropic [aisen'trɔp:k]	a.	等（定）熵的
refrigerant [ri'fridʒərənt]	n.	致冷剂，冷冻剂，冷媒
adiabatically [͵ædiəbətikli]	ad.	绝热地
superheated [sju:pəhi:tid]	a.	过热的
desuperheated [di:'sju:pə'hi:tid]	a.	降温，降低蒸气过热度
undesirable ['ʌndi'zaiərəbl]	a.	令人不快的，讨厌的
numerically * [nju(:)'merikəli]	ad.	在数字上
insignificant [insig'nifikənt]	a.	小的，微不足道的
cyclic ['saiklik]	a.	循环的
helical [helikəl]	a.	螺旋的，螺旋形的
centrifugal [sen'trifjugəl]	a.	离心的，
clearance volume		余隙，容积
cylinder * ['silində]	n.	气缸，圆筒
reexpand ['ri:iks'pænd]	v.	再膨胀
quantitatively * ['kwɔntitətivli]	ad.	定量地
volumetric [͵vɔlju'metrik]	a.	容积的
interstage [intə(:) 'steidʒ]	a.	级间的，中间的

Notes

①The ideal cycle... connected by... surroundings:

句中 connected by piping 过去分词结构修饰 the condenser and evaporator without pressure losses, a reversible adiabatic (isentropic) compressor, and an adiabatic expansion valve; that 引出定语从句修饰 piping。

②Heat transfer... in the condenser:

句中 to the evaporator and from the condenser 两个介词短语并列修饰 heat transfer; between 后面是 the fluid... and the fluid...; that 引出定语从句修饰第二个 fluid; except during... 介词短语修饰全句。

③In evaluating contributions... compressor efficiency:

句中 with the change in state... being (1), or (2)... 是 with + 名词 + 分词 being 独立结构作状语。

④... the volume... moving member:

the refrigerant occupies within the compressor 和 that is not displaced by moving member 两个定语从句修饰 the volume。

Exercises

Reading Comprehension

Ⅰ. Match Column A with Column B according to the text and fill in the missing words where necessary.

1. The Table for Basic Vapor Compression Cycle

A

The refrigerant
- leaves
- ①first enters and ②then leaves
- enters

B

1) the evaporator as _____.

2) the compressor, ①where it is _____.
   ②as _____.

3) the condenser, ①where it is _____.
   ②_____.

4) the expansion valve ①where _____.
   ②as _____.

5) the evaporator, where it is _____.

2.

A	B
1. The ideal cycle considers	a. the first law of thermodynamics
2. Heat transfer to the evaporator and from the condernser occurs	b. the effectiveness of the compres-sor's piston displacement in moving the refrigerant vapor through the cycle
3. An energy balance and certain performance parameters can be derived from	c. selection of the interstage pressure at which the refrigerant temperature is reduced by an intercooler
4. Volumetric efficiency measures	d. without a finite temperature difference between the fluid emitting the heat and the fluid that absorbs the heat, except during the desuperheating process in the condenser.
5. One of the design parameters of a multistage compressor is	e. heat transfer in the condenser and evaporator without pressure losses

Ⅱ. Separate the two different groups of words according to the text.

> compressor, positive displacement compressors, reciprocating piston, condenser, rotary, expansion valve, helical rotary, evaporator centrifugal compressors

1. Minimum components of this cycle include:

2. Types of compressors considered include:

Ⅲ. Answer the questions by completing the following.
 1. Tell the kinds of compressors mentioned in the text:

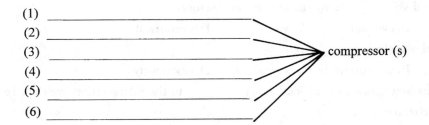

(1) _____
(2) _____
(3) _____
(4) _____
(5) _____
(6) _____
→ compressor (s)

2. Try to find the words in the text which are used to modify the following words:

(1) _____
(2) _____
(3) _____ → pressure (s)
(4) _____   (a)
(5) _____
(6) _____

(1) _____
(2) _____ → temperature (s)
(3) _____   (b)
(4) _____

(1) _____
(2) _____ → vapor (s)
(3) _____   (c)
(4) _____

Vocabulary

I. Complete each of the following statements with one of the four choices given below.
1. This kind of machines needs a rotary and a safety _____
   A. value   B. valse   C. valve   D. valise
2. The enemy were _____ superior.
   A. numerically   B. fruitlessly   C. blindly   D. hardly
3. There are several six-_____ motor-cars in this factory.
   A. cyclical   B. cylinder   C. cylindric   D. cylindrical
4. We can make the analysis _____.
   A. splendidly   B. quantitatively   C. heartlessly   D. laboriously
5. Performance characteristics and applications of _____ to the refrigeration cycle are reviewed in this chapter.
   A. compressor   B. engine   C. heater   D. breaker

II. Fill in the blanks with the words given below. Change the forms if necessary.

> cylinder, valve, compression, refrigeration, cyclic, refrigerants, volumetric, centrifugal, quantitatively, numerically

1. There are many kinds of _____ which are used in different pipes, machines and places. Butterfly _____ and control _____ are two examples.

32

2. They will apply the steady flow equation for the first law to each of the components of the basic vapor _____ cycle.
3. Since the system is _____, the heat rejected in the condenser must be equal to the sum of the heat absorbed in the evaporator and the work of compression.
4. In evaluating contributions of the compressor to thermodynamic systems, it is necessary to consider properties of _____ at the inlet and outlet of the compressor.
5. This effect is _____ expressed by the volumetric efficiency.
6. Types considered include positive displacement compressors and _____ compressors.
7. _____ efficiency measures the effectiveness of the compressor's piston displacement in moving the refrigerant vapor through the cycle.
8. Here these terms are _____ insignificant.
9. After the _____ discharges the compressed gas, the clearance gas reexpands to a larger volume as the pressure falls to the inlet pressure.
10. The application of multistage compressors to _____ systems differs from gas compressors.

Reading Material A

Probability and Entropy

It was stated that all irreversible processes produce increases in entropy. A common irreversible process is a free-expansion one (see Fig. 4-2). Cylinder A contains a gas under high pressure. Cylinder B is completely evacuated. When the valve between the two cylinders is open, gas rushes into cylinder B until the pressure between the two cylinders becomes equalized. If the system is isolated, its internal energy cannot change. Assuming that the gas is an ideal one, then there can be no net change in its temperature.

Since there is no net change in temperature, the change in entropy for the free expansion of an ideal gas,

$$S_2 - S_1 = mR \frac{V_2}{V_1}$$

During the free-expansion process, the molecules moved from a highly improbable state to the most probable state.[①] The equation given before may be used to evaluate the probabilities of each state. This equation involves the quantity N, which is the number of cells under consideration. Since these cells must be of equal volumes, the above-mentioned equation may be rewritten as:

$$\Psi = V^n \tag{4.5}$$

where V is the total number of units of volumes under consideration.

After the valve in Figure 4-2 has been opened, the possible number of microscopic states equals $(V_T/V_A)^n$ where V_T is the total volume and V_A is the volume of cylinder A. The probability of finding all the molecules in cylinder A is one chance out of $(V_T/V_A)^n$ or the probability of this occurrence equals $(V_T/V_A)^n$. [2] The probability of finding all the molecules in the total volume is unity. [3] The ratio of the probability Ψ_2 of the final state to that of the initial state, Ψ_1, is

$$\frac{\Psi_2}{\Psi_1} = \frac{1}{(V_1/V_2)^n} \tag{4.6}$$

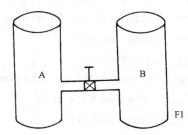

Fig. 4-2 Free-expansion system

the change in entropy, k, the gas constant per molecule

$$S_2 - S_1 = k(\ln\Psi_2 - \ln\Psi_1) \tag{4.7}$$

Equation 4.7 states that when an isolated system moves from a less probable state to a more probable state, the increase in entropy is directly proportional to the increase in the natural logarithm of the probability of the state of the system. [4]

Return to the free-expansion process. Before the valve was opened, each and every molecule was in cylinder A. Their positions could be specified. After the free-expansion process, it is not possible to specify whether any given molecule is in cylinder A or in cylinder B at any specified instant. Thus, we say that the final state of the system is a random one or a disorderly one. The system passed from a more orderly state to a less orderly state. Furthermore, the system passed from a less probable state to a more probable state. In so doing, there was an increase in entropy of the system.

The concepts developed here for a free-expansion process may be adapted to all irreversible processes. In all such processes, the system proceeds from an orderly state to a less orderly state and from a state of low probability to its most probable state. This change of state is accompanied by an increase in entropy, the change in entropy being a function of the probabilities of existence of the initial and final states.

When an isolated system is not in its most probable state, it tends to move to this state. In so doing, its entropy must increase. When the system attains its most probable state, its entropy cannot increase. Thus, if an isolated system cannot experience a change in entropy, it must be in its most probable state. But if the entropy of the system can increase, the system cannot be in its most probable state, and hence, the system is not in equilibrium. These facts may be used in determining whether or not a system is in equilibrium. If calculations show that the entropy of an isolated system can increase, then the system cannot be in equilibrium

Notes

① from a highly improbable state to the most probable：从一种不太可能的状态到最有可能的状态。
② 在气缸A中找到所有分子的可能性是$(V_T/V_A)^n$的可能性之一。或者说这种情况的可能性是$(V_T/V_A)^n$。
③ unity：这里译为"不变的"。
④ from a less probable state to a more probable state：从不大可能的状态到较为可能的状态。

Reading Material B

Entropy and the Third Law

Some authors hesitate to call that which is known as the Third Law of Thermodynamics a law.① The first law deals with energy relationships during energy exchanges and transformations. The second law places certain limitations on energy transformations and establishes a new property, entropy, which is needed to deal with energy transformations. The third law presents no concepts about new areas of thermodynamics. However, since it formulates a conclusion relative to an important area of thermodynamics that is in agreement with our experiences, it will be treated as a law in this text.②

The concepts of the third law were put forth first by Nernst in 1906 as his heat theorem. This work was augmented by Planck in 1911. Perhaps the all-inclusive statement of what is now recognized as the third law was made by Lewis and Randall in 1923. Their statement is: "If the entropy of each element in some crystalline state be taken as zero at the absolute zero of temperature, every substance has a finite positive entropy; but at the absolute zero of temperature the entropy may become zero and does so become in the case of perfect crystalline substances."

It is difficult to prove the third law. However, there are two ways of arriving at the reasonableness of this law. Two or more elements that exist as pure crystalline substances at absolute zero of temperature may be heated, changed into liquids, further heated, vaporized, and then combined chemically. The resultant products may be cooled down, liquefied, solidified, and finally cooled down to absolute zero of temperature. If the product becomes a pure crystalline substance, the result will be zero when the entropy changes for all these processes are evaluated and summed up. This means that the entropies of all pure crystalline substances are equal at zero degrees absolute. Either this value of entropy is zero, or it may be treated as such in all problems.

The second approach to determining the value of the entropy of a pure crystalline substance at an absolute zero of temperature is to make use of a postulate formulated by L. Boltzmann in 1890 and M. Planck in 1912. This postulate is

$$S = k\ln\Psi \tag{4.8}$$

There is no rigid proof of this postulate but experience has shown its validity. A pure crystalline substance is perfectly ordered at a temperature of zero degrees absolute, that is, there is one probable state. Since Ψ is then unity and $\ln\Psi = 0$, the entropy must be zero at zero degrees absolute temperature.

When changes in entropy are desired for systems in which chemical reactions are not involved, these changes can be determined by the methods presented before.[③] However, when chemical reactions are involved, absolute values of entropy of both the reacting substances and the products of reactions are required. Absolute values of entropy of a gas may be obtained by recognizing that the absolute value of entropy of a pure crystalline substance is zero at zero degrees absolute and by finding the summation of (1) the change in entropy as the substance is heated to its fusion temperature, (2) the entropy change during melting, (3) the change in entropy as the liquid is heated to the vaporization temperature, (4) the entropy change during vaporization, and (5) the entropy change as the gas is heated to the temperature at which its entropy is desired.[④] This method of determining the absolute entropy of a gas is a laborious one and, furthermore, requires an accurate knowledge of the specific heats of the solid, the liquid, and the gas, the fusion and vaporization temperatures, and also the latent heats of both fusion and vaporization.

Notes

①有些作者在把热力学第三定律称为定律时犹豫不决。
②但是既然第三定律在热力学的一个重要方面得出了结论，而且这个结论与我们的经验是一致的，因此在本课文中就按定律来对待。
③对没有涉及到化学反应的系统，要求出其熵的变化时，可由以前给的方法得出。
④气体熵的绝对值可以通过认为纯晶体物质在绝对零度时，熵的绝对值为零，并找出下列总和来得到：
（1）将物质加热到它的熔点温度时，熵的变化。
（4）熔化期间熵的变化。
（3）液体加热到气化温度时熵的变化。
（4）气化期间熵的变化。
（5）将气体加热到可以得到所需要的熵的温度时，熵的变化。

UNIT FIVE

Text   Variation of Pressure in A Static Fluid

[1]   Consider the differential element of static fluid shown in Fig. 5-1. Since the element is very small, we can assume that the density of the fluid within the element is constant. Assume the pressure at the center of the element is p. And assume the dimensions of the element are δx, δy and δz. The forces acting on the fluid element in the vertical direction are the body force. That is action of gravity on the mass within the elements. And the surface forces transmitted from the surrounding fluid and acting at right angles against the top, bottom, and sides of the element. Since the fluid is at rest, the element is in equilibrium and the summation of forces acting on the element in any direction must be zero.① If forces are summed up in the horizontal direction, that is, x or y, the only forces acting are the pressure forces on the vertical faces of the element. To satisfy $\Sigma F_x = 0$ and $\Sigma F_y = 0$, the pressure on the opposite vertical faces must be equal. Thus $\partial p/\partial x = \partial p/\partial y = 0$ for the case of the fluid at rest.

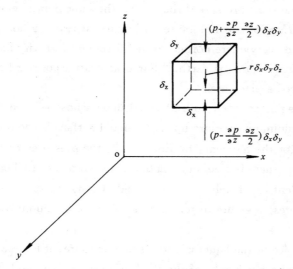

Fig. 5-1

[2]   Summing up forces in the vertical direction and setting equal to zero, the results can be written as

$$\frac{dp}{dz} = -\gamma \tag{5.1}$$

[3]   This is the general expression that relates variation of pressure in a static fluid to vertical position. The minus sign indicates that as z gets larger (increasing elevation), the pressure gets smaller.

[4]   To evaluate pressure variation in a fluid at rest one must integrate Eq. (5.1) between appropriately chosen limits. For incompressible fluids (γ=constant), Eq. (5.1) can be inte-

grated directly. It was shown that

$$p - p_1 = -\gamma(z - z_1) \tag{5.2}$$

p is the pressure at an elevation z. This expression is generally applicable to liquids since they are only slightly compressible. Only where there are large changes in elevation, as in the ocean, need the compressibility of the liquid be considered, to arrive at an accurate determination of pressure variation.[②] For small changes in elevation, Eq. (5.2) will give accurate results when applied to gases.[③]

[5]　For the case of a liquid at rest, it is convenient to measure distances vertically downward from the free liquid surface. If h is the distance below the free liquid surface and if the pressure of air and vapor on the surface is arbitrarily taken to be zero, Eq. (5.2) can be written as

$$p = \gamma h \tag{5.3}$$

[6]　As there must always be some pressure on the surface of any liquid, the total pressure at any depth h is given by Eq. (5.3) plus the pressure on the surface. In many situations this surface pressure may be disregarded.

[7]　From Eq. (5.3) it may be seen that all points in a connected body of constant density fluid at rest are under the same pressure if they are at the same depth below the liquid surface. This indicates that a surface of equal pressure for a liquid at rest is a horizontal plane. Strictly speaking, it is a surface everywhere normal to the direction of gravity and is approximately a spherical surface concentric with the earth.[④] For practical purposes a limited portion of this surface may be considered a plane area.

[8]　In Fig. 5-2 imagine an open tank of liquid upon whose surface there is no pressure. Though in reality the minimum pressure upon any liquid surface is the pressure of its own vapor. Disregarding this for the moment, by Eq. (5.3) the pressure at any depth h is $p = \gamma h$. If γ is assumed constant, there is a definite relation between p and h. That is, pressure (force per unit area) is equivalent to a height h of some fluid of constant specific weight γ. It is often more convenient to express pressure in terms of a height of a column of fluid rather than in pressure per unit area.

[9]　Even if the surface of the liquid is under some pressure, it is necessary only to convert this pressure into an equivalent height of the fluid in question, and add this to the value of h shown in Fig. 5-2, to obtain the total pressure.

[10]　The preceding discussion has been applied to a liquid. And it is equally possible to use it for a gas or vapor by specifying some constant specific weight γ for the gas or vapor in question. Thus pressure p may be expressed in the height of a column of any fluid by the relation.

$$h = \frac{p}{\gamma} \tag{5.4}$$

Equation (5.2) may be expressed as follows:

$$z + \frac{p}{\gamma} = z_1 + \frac{p_1}{\gamma} = const \tag{5.5}$$

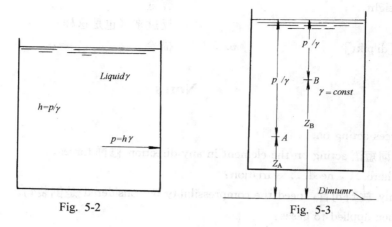

Fig. 5-2   Fig. 5-3

[11] This shows that for incompressible fluid at rest the summation of the elevation z at any point in a fluid plus the pressure head p/γ at that point is equal to the sum of these two quantities at any other point. The significance of this statement is that, in a fluid at rest with an increase in elevation, there is a decrease in pressure head and vice versa.⑤ This concept is depicted in Fig. 5-3.

New Words and Expressions

body force		质量力
surface force		表面力
summation [sʌˈmeiʃən]	n.	和，总数
at rest		静止
integrate * [ˈintigreit]	v.	积分
appropriately [əˈproupritli]	ad.	适可地
expression [iksˈpreʃən]	n.	式，符号
compressible [kʌmˈpresəbl]	a.	可压缩
arrive at		得出
determination [diˌtə:miˈneiʃən]	n.	测定
vertically [ˈvə:tikəli]	ad.	纵向地
arbitrarily [ˈɑ:bitrərili]	ad.	随意地，任意地
disregard [ˈdisriˈgɑ:d]	vt.	忽视，不考虑
approximately [əˈprɔksimitli]	ad.	大体上
spherical [ˈsferikəl]	a.	球形的
concentric [kənˈsentrik]	a.	同轴心的
in terms of		用…来表示
in question		正被谈论的

specific weight 容重
vice versa 反过来（也是这样）
depict * ［di'pikt］   v. 描绘

Notes

① ... forces acting on...：
现在分词短语 acting on the element in any direction 修饰 forces。

② Only where..., need... variation：
由于 only 放到句首，need the compressibility be considered 是倒装句。

③ ... when applied to gases：
是省略句，全句是 when Eq.（5.2）is applied to gases。

④ Strictly speaking..., with the earth：
形容词短语 normal to the directon of gravity 修饰 a surface everywhere；形容词短语 concentric with the earth 修饰 a spherical surface。

⑤ The significance of this statement is that, in a fluid at rest ...and vice versa：此句为 SVC 句型，that 引起的是表语从句。

Exercises

Reading Comprehension

Ⅰ. Choose the best answer.

1. The body force can be regarded as the forces _____.
    A. acting on the fluid element in the horizontal direction
    B. acting on the fluid element in the vertical direction
    C. acting on the fluid element in no direction

2. The surface forces are the forces transmitted from _____.
    A. the above surface
    B. the surrounding surface
    C. the surrounding fluid and acting at right angles against the top, bottom, and sides of the element

3. For a sealed vessel, whose specific weight is $9800N/m^3$ and the pressure 2-meters below the surface is $49000N/m^2$. Then the pressure 5-meters below the surface must be _____.
    A. $49000N/m^2$
    B. $78400N/m^2$
    C. $19600N/m^2$

4. As there must always be some pressure on the surface of any liquid, the total pressure at any depth h is given by Eq. 5.3 plus the pressure _____.
   A. at the bottom
   B. in the middle
   C. on the surface
5. It may be seen that all points in a connected body of constant density fluid at rest are under the same pressure if they are at the same depth _____.
   A. below the liquid surface
   B. on the liquid surface
   C. above the liquid surface

II. Complete the following statements with the information given in the text.
1. The forces _____ in the vertical direction are _____.
2. Since the fluid is _____, the element is in equilibrium and the summation of forces acting on the element in any direction _____.
3. To satisfy $\Sigma F_x=0$ and $\Sigma F_y=0$, the pressure on the opposite vertical faces _____.
4. The minus sign indicates that as Z gets _____, the pressure gets _____.
5. Only where there are _____ in elevation, need _____ be considered, to _____ an accurate determination of pressure variation.
6. For the case of a liquid at rest, it is convenient to measure distances vertically _____ from _____.
7. All points in a connected body of constant density fluid at rest are under _____ if they are at _____ below the liquid surface.
8. If γ is assumed constant, there is _____ between p and h.
9. It is often more convenient to express pressure _____ rather than in _____.
10. Even if the surface of the liquid is _____, it is necessary only to _____ an equivalent height of the fluid in question.

Vocabulary

I. Find words in the text which mean almost the same as the following.
1. Para. 1: sum total obtained by adding together numbers or amounts (_____)
2. Para. 4: combine parts into a whole (_____)
3. Para. 7: having or sharing a common centre (with another circle, etc.) (_____)
4. Para. 8: pay no attention to; show no respect for (_____)
5. Para. 11: show in the form of a picture; describe in words (_____)

II. Fill in the blanks with the words given below. Change the forms if necessary.

summation	integrate	arbitrarily	disregard	spherical
concentric	depict	compressibility	body force	specific weight

1. The forces acting on the fluid element in the vertical direction are called the _____.
2. He is a man of great humour and he can often _____ dull things vividly and interestingly.
3. A _____ valve is something like a ball and actually it is not a ball at all.
4. In order to evaluate pressure variation in a fluid at rest you should _____ $dp/dz=-\gamma$ between appropriately chosen limits.
5. Pressure (force per unit area) is equivalent to a height h of some fluid of constant _____.
6. The drag _____ on a body is the sum of the friction drag and the pressure drag.
7. We should do things according to the rules of nature and cannot do anything _____ to violate the objective law.
8. _____ all difficulties, we are determined to fight it out to the end.
9. Strictly speaking, it is a surface everywhere normal to the direction of gravity and is approximately a spherical surface _____ with the earth.
10. Only where there are large changes in elevation, as in the ocean, need the _____ of the liquid be considered, to arrive at an accurate determination of pressure variation.

Reading Material A

Viscosity

The viscosity of a fluid is a measure of its resistance to shear or angular deformation. The friction forces in fluid flow result from the cohesion and momentum interchange between molecules in the fluid. The viscosities of typical fluids are shown in Figs. 5-4 and 5-5. As the temperature increases, the viscosities of all liquids decrease. The viscosities of all gases increase. This is because the force of cohesion, which diminishes with temperature, predominates with liquids, while with gases the predominating factor is the interchange of molecules between the layers of different velocities.[①] Thus a rapidly moving molecule shifting into a slower-moving layer tends to speed up the latter. And a slow-moving molecule entering a faster-moving layer tends to slow it down. This molecule interchange sets up a shear, or produces a friction force between adjacent layers. Increased molecular activity at higher temperatures causes the viscosity of gases to increase with temperature.

Consider two parallel plates (Fig. 5-6), sufficiently large so that edge conditions may be neglected, placed a small distance Y apart, the space between being filled with the fluid.[②] The lower surface is assumed to be stationary, while the upper one is moved parallel to it with a velocity U by the application of a force F corresponding to some area A of the moving plate. Such a condition is approximated, for instance, in the clearance space of a flooded journal bearing (any radial load being neglected).

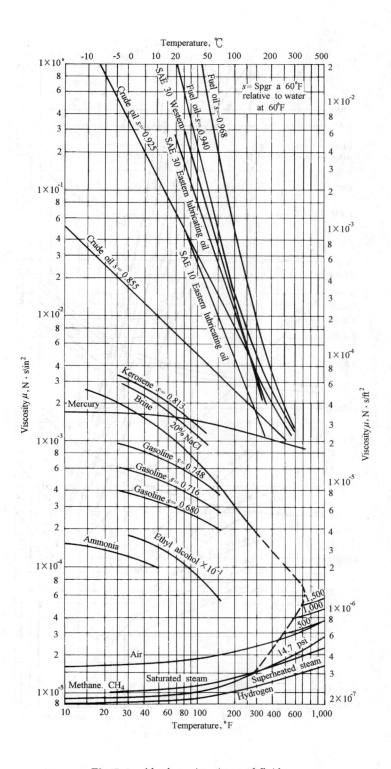

Fig. 5-4　Absolute viscosity μ of fluids

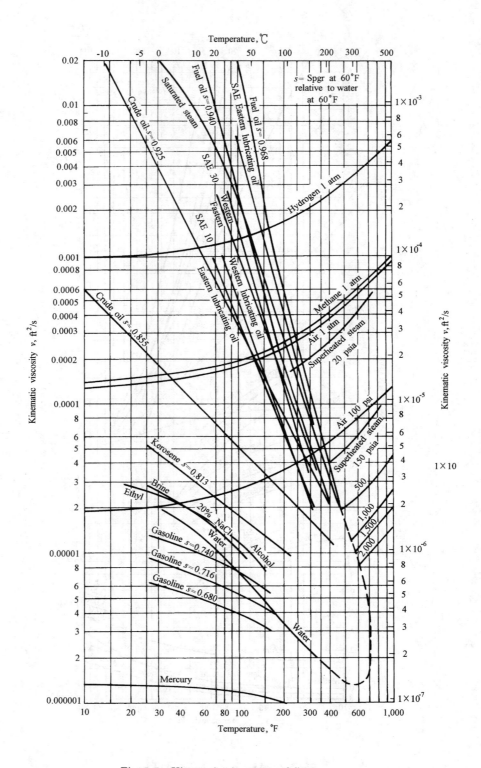

Fig. 5-5 Kinematic viscosity ν of fluids

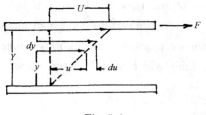

Fig. 5-6

Particles of the fluid in contact with each plate will adhere to it. And if the distance Y is not too great or the velocity U too high, the velocity gradient will be a straight line.③ The action is much as if the fluid were made up of a series of thin sheets, each of which would slip a little relative to the next. Experiment has shown that for a large class of fluids

$$F \sim \frac{AU}{Y}$$

It may be seen from similar triangles in Fig. 5-6 that U/Y can be replaced by the velocity gradient du/dy. If a constant of proportionality μ is now introduced, the shearing stress τ between any two thin sheets of fluid may be expressed by

$$\tau = \frac{F}{A} = \mu \frac{U}{Y} = \mu \frac{du}{dy} \tag{5.6}$$

Equation (5.6) is called Newton's equation of viscosity, and in transposed form it serves to define the proportionality constant

$$\mu = \frac{\tau}{du/dy} \tag{5.7}$$

It is called the coefficient of viscosity, the absolute viscosity, dynamic viscosity (since it involves force), or simply the viscosity of the fluid.

It has been explained that the distinction between a solid and a fluid lies in the manner in which each can resist shearing stresses. A further distinction among various kinds of fluids and solids will be clarified by reference to Fig. 5-7, In the case of a solid, shear stress is proportional to the magnitude of the deformation. Yet Eq. (5.6) shows that in many fluids the shear stress is proportional to the time rate of (angular) deformation.

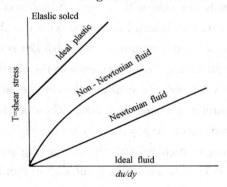

Fig. 5-7

A fluid for which the constant of proportionality does not change with rate of deformation is said to be a Newtonian fluid. It can be represented by a straight line in Fig. 5.7. The slope of this line is determined by the viscosity. The ideal fluid, with no viscosity, is represented by the horizontal axis. And the true elastic solid is represented by the vertical axis. A plastic which sustains a certain amount of stress before suffering a plastic flow can be shown by a straight line intersecting the vertical axis at the yield stress.④ There are certain non-Newtonian fluids in which μ varies with the rate of deformation. These are relatively uncommon, hence the remainder of this text will be restricted to the common fluids which obey Newton's law.

Notes

①这是由于粘滞力支配着流体,粘滞力随温度增加而降低。而支配气体的因素则是不同速度层的分子互变。
②现在来考虑一下这种情况,假设有两个平行板块（图5-6）,面积很大以致边界条件可以略去不计,两块之间距离（Y）很小,之间充满流体。
③各面相接触的流体粒子将依附在面上,如果距离 Y 不是太大,或者速度 U 不是太高,速度梯度将是一条直线。
④能在发生塑性流动前承受一定应力的塑料可以用与纵坐标轴在屈服应力处相交的直线来表示。

Reading Material B

Compressible and Incompressible Fluids

Fluid mechanics deals with both incompressible and compressible fluids, that is, with fluids of either constant or variable density. Although there is no such thing in reality as an incompressible fluid, this term is applied where the change in density with pressure is so small as to be negligible. This is usually the case with liquids. Gases, too, may be considered incompressible when the pressure variation is small compared with the absolute pressure.①

Liquids are ordinarily considered incompressible fluids. But sound waves, which are really pressure waves, travel through them. This is evidence of the elasticity of liquids. In problems involving water hammer, it is necessary to consider the compressibility of the liquid.

The flow of air in a ventilating system is a case. There a gas may be treated as incompressible, for the pressure variation is so small that the change in density is of no importance. But for a gas or steam flowing at high velocity through a long pipeline, the drop in pressure may be so great that change in density cannot be ignored.② For an airplane flying at speeds below 100 m/s, the air may be considered to be of constant density. But as an object moving through the air approaches the velocity of sound, which is of the order of 300 m/s, the pressure and density of the air adjacent to the body become materially different from those of the air at some distance away. And the air must then be treated as a compressible fluid.

The compressibility of a liquid is inversely proportional to its volume modulus of elasticity, also known as the bulk modulus.③ This modulus is defined as, $Ev=-vdp/dv=-(v/dv)dp$, where v = specific volume and p = unit pressure. As v/dv is a dimensionless ratio, the units of Ev and p are the same. The bulk modulus is analogous to the modulus of elasticity for solids. However, for fluids it is defined on a volume basis rather than in terms of the familiar one-dimensional stress-strain relation for solid bodies.

In most engineering problems the bulk modulus at or near atmospheric pressure is the one of interest. The bulk modulus is a property of the fluid. And it is a function of temperature and pressure. In Table 5.1 are shown a few value of the bulk modulus for water. At any temperature it can be noted that the value of Ev increases continuously with pressure, but at any one pressure the value of Ev is a maximum at about 50℃. Thus water has a minimum compressibility at about 50℃.

Table 5.1　　　　　　　　　　Bulk modulus of water, psi

Pressure, psia	Temperature F				
	32°	68°	120°	200°	300°
15	292,000	320,000	332,000	308,000	
1,500	300,000	330,000	342,000	319,000	248,000
4,500	317,000	348,000	362,000	338,000	271,000
15,000	380,000	410,000	426,000	405,000	350,000

The volume modulus of mild steel is about 170,000 MN/m². Taking a typical value for the volume modulus of cold water to be 2,200 MN/m², it is seen that water is about 80 times as compressible as steel. The compressibility of liquids covers a wide range. Mercury, for example, is approximately 8 percent as compressible as water, while the compressibility of nitric acid is nearly six times greater than that of water.④

Table 5.1 shows that at any one temperature the bulk modulus does not vary a great deal for a moderate range in pressure, and thus as an approximation one may use

$$\frac{\Delta v}{v_1} = -\frac{\Delta p}{Ev} \qquad (5.8)$$

where Ev is the mean value of the modulus for the pressure range.

Assuming Ev to have a value of 2,200 MN/m², it may be seen that increasing the pressure of water by 6.875 MN/m² will compress it only 1/320 or 0.3 percent, of its original volume. Therefore it is seen that the usual assumption regarding water as incompressible is justified.

Notes

①当压力变化和绝对压力相比较显得特别微小时，气体也可被认为是不可压缩的。
②但是，对以高速度在长距离管道里流动的气体或气流来说，压降可能很大以致密度变化不可忽视。
③... is inversely proportional to...：与……成反比。
④各种流体的可压缩性差异很大。例如，水银约是水压缩性的8%，而硝酸却几乎是水的6倍。

UNIT SIX

Text   Hydraulic Grade Line and Energy Line

[1]   The term $z+p/\gamma$ is referred to as the piezometric head, because it represents the level to which liquid will rise in a piezometer tube. The hydraulic grade line (HGL) is a line drawn through the tops of the piezometer columns. A pitot tube, a small open tube with its open end pointing upstream, will intercept the kinetic energy of the flow and hence indicate the total energy head, $z+p/\gamma+u^2/2g$.

[2]   Familiarity with the concept of the energy line and hydraulic grade line is useful in the solution of flow problems involving incompressible fluids.

[3]   If a series of piezometrers were erected along the pipe, the liquid would rise in them to various levels. The line drawn through the summits of such an imaginary series of liquid columns is called the hydraulic grade line. It may be observed that the hydraulic grade line represents what would be the free surface if one could exist and maintain the same conditions of flow.

[4]   The hydraulic grade line indicates the pressure along the pipe, as at any point the vertical distance from the pipe to the hydraulic grade line is the pressure head at that point, assuming the profile to be drawn to scale. See Fig. 6-1. At C this distance is zero, thus indicating that the absolute pressure within the pipe at that point is atmospheric. At D the pipe is above the hydraulic grade line, indicating that there the pressure head is $-DN$.

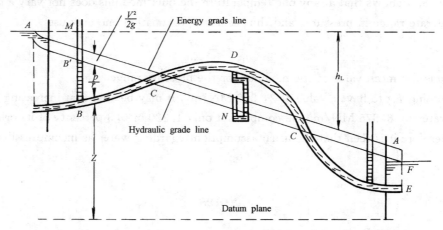

Fig. 6-1   Hydraulic and energy grade lines

[5]   If the profile of a pipeline is drawn to scale, then not only does the hydraulic grade line enable the pressure head to be determined at any point by measurement on the diagram, but it shows by mere inspection the variation of the pressure in the entire length of the pipe.[①] The hydraulic grade line is a straight line only if the pipe is straight and of uniform diameter. But for the gradual curvatures that are often found in long pipelines, the deviation from a straight

line will be small. Of course, if there are local losses of head, aside from those due to normal pipe friction, there may be abrupt drops in the hydraulic grade line.② Changes in diameter with resultant changes in velocity will also cause abrupt changes in the hydraulic grade line.③

[6] If the velocity head is constant, as in Fig. 6-1, the drop in the hydraulic grade line between any two points is the value of the loss of head between those two points. Thus in Fig. 6-2 the rate of loss in the larger pipe is much less than in the smaller pipe. If the velocity changes, the hydraulic grade line might actually rise in the direction of flow, as shown in Figs. 6-2 and 6-3.

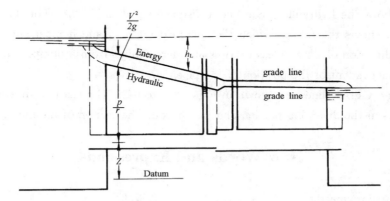

Fig. 6-2 Plotted to scale from measurements

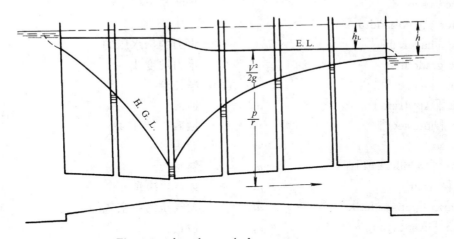

Fig. 6-3 plotted to scale from measurements

[7] The vertical distance from the level of the surface at A in Fig 6-1 down to the hydraulic grade line represents $V^2/2g + h_L$ from A to any point in question. Hence the position of the grade line is independent of the position of the pipe. Thus it is not necessary to compute pressure heads at various points in the pipe to plot the hydraulic grade line. Instead, values of $V^2/2g + h_L$ from A to various points can be laid off below the horizontal line through A, and this procedure is often more convenient. If the pipe is of uniform diameter, it is necessary to locate only a few points, and often only two are required.

[8]   If Fig. 6-1 represents to scale the profile of a pipe of uniform diameter, the hydraulic grade line can be drawn as follows. At the intake to the pipe there will be a drop below the surface at A, which should be laid off equal to $V^2/2g$ plus a local entrance loss. At E the pressure is EF, and hence the grade line must end at F. If the pipe discharged freely into the air at E, the line would pass through E. The location of other points, such as B' and N, may be computed if desired.

[9]   If values of h_L are laid off below the horizontal line through A, the resulting line represents values of the total energy head H measured above any arbitrary datum plane inasmuch as this line is above the hydraulic grade line a distance equal to $V^2/2g$. This line is the energy grade line. It shows the rate at which the energy decreases, and it must always drop downward in the direction of flow unless there is an energy input from a pump. The energy grade line is also independent of the position of the pipeline.

[10]   Energy grade lines are shown in Figs. 6-1 to 6-3. The last one shows that the chief loss of head is in the diverging portion and just beyond the section of minimum diameter.

New Words and Expressions

piezometric [ˌpaiəzə'metrik]	a.	测压的
piezometric head		测压管水头
be referred to as…		指的是…
piezometer [ˌpaiə'zɔmitə]	n.	测压计
hydraulic [hai'drɔːlik]	a.	水力的,水压的
hydraulic grade line		水力坡度线
pitot tube		毕托管
upstream ['ʌp'striːm]	ad.	逆流
intercept ['intə'sept]	vt.	拦截
energy head		能头
familiarity [fəˌmili'æriti]	n.	熟悉
summit ['sʌmit]	n.	顶点,决顶
atmospheric [ˌætməs'ferik]	a.	大气压的,空气的
inspection [in'spekʃən]	n.	检查
curvature ['kəːvətʃə]	n.	弯曲
deviation [ˌdiːvi'eiʃən]	n.	偏离,偏向
resultant * [ri'zʌltənt]	a.	作为结果而发生的
intake ['in-teik]	n.	吸入,入口
resulting [ri'zʌltiŋ]	a.	由此产生的
datum ['deitəm]	n.	基准(点,面)
inasmuch (as) [ˌinəz'mʌtʃ]	ad.	因为,由于
energy grade line		能量坡度线

pipeline ['paiplain]	n.	管线，管道
plot [plɔt]	vt.	划分，标出
diverge [dai'və:dʒ]	vi.	岔开

Notes

①... then not only... but it shows...：
句中 not only 放到句首引起部分倒装；but 后省略了 also。

②of course, if there are local losses of head, aside from those due to normal pipe friction, there may be abrupt drops in the hydraulic grade line. aside from：除……之外（除了由于正常的管道摩擦力以外）；those 代前面的 losses of head：能源损耗。

③Changes in diameter with resultant changes in velocity…resultant：作为结果而产生的。直径的变化及随之而产生的速度变化……。

Exercises

Reading Comprehension

Ⅰ. Match Column A with Column B according to the text：

A	B
1. piezometric head	a. the line above the hydraulic grade line and showing the rate at which the energy decreasing
2. piezometer tube	b. the tube used for measuring pressure
3. pitot tube	c. the head representing the level to which liquid will rise in a piezometer tube
4. total energy head	d. the tube used for measuring the speed of the flow
5. kinetic energy	e. the total energy or force existing in the tube or pipe coming from the flow
6. hydraulic grade line	f. the energy coming from the motion of something
7. pressure head	g. the line drawn through the summits of the piezometer columns
8. pipe friction	h. the head showing how much the pressure is
9. velocity head	i. the friction coming from the liquid flowing through a pipe
10. energy grade line	j. the head showing the speed of the flow

Ⅱ. Complete the following sentences with the information given in the text.

1. The term $z + p/\gamma$ is referred to as the _____ and because it represents

_____.

2. A pitot tube is a small open tube _____ and it will intercept the kinetic energy of the flow and hence indicate _____.
3. At C this distance is _____, thus indicating that the absolute pressure within the pipe at that point is _____.
4. The hydraulic grade line is a straight line only if _____.
5. Changes in diameter with resultant changes in velocity will also cause abrupt changes in _____.

Vocabulary

I. Fill in the blanks with the words given below. Change the forms if necessary.

plot	upstream	intercept	familiarity
summit	inspection	curvature	deviation
resultant	inasmuch as		

1. We should adhere to our set line and guard against "Left" and "Right" _____.
2. During the World War II, the British fighter-planes _____ the German bombers over the English Channel.
3. On the _____ of the mountain there was a cottage in which my grandfather lived thirty years ago.
4. _____ with standard pronunciation he often helps others with their pronunciation and their spoken English.
5. Since the time is quite limited and we ought to _____ out our time carefully and finish our work in time.
6. The _____ in this long pipeline will cause some troubles to our work.
7. There will be a house-to-house _____ for the lost pistol which had been used to kill the mayor.
8. A boat sailing _____ must forge ahead or it will be driven back.
9. Changes in diameter with _____ changes in velocity will also cause abrupt changes in the hydraulic grade line.
10. _____ we serve the people, we are not afraid to have our shortcomings being pointed out and actually we are eager to correct them.

II. Match the words in Column A with their corresponding definitions in Column B.

        A   B

1. inasmuch as   a. stop, catch (sb. or sth.) between starting-point and destination

2. resultant
3. deviation
4. curvature
5. intercept

b. (with from) (of lines, paths, opinions, etc.) get farther apart from a point or from each other as they progress; turn or branch away from
c. since; as; because
d. coming as a result; product or outcome (of sth.)
e. curving; the state of being curved

Reading Material A

Eulerian and Lagrangian Flow Descriptions

There are two general approaches in analyzing fluid mechanics problems. The first method, called the Eulerian method, uses the field concept. In this case, the fluid motion is given by completely prescribing the necessary properties as functions of space and time. From this method we obtain information about the flow in terms of what happens at fixed points in space as the fluid flows past those points.

The second method, called the Lagrangian method, involves following individual fluid particles. That is, the fluid particles are "tagged" or identified, and their properties determined as they move.

The difference between the two methods of analyzing fluid flow problems can be seen in the example of smoke discharging from a chimney, as is shown in Fig. 6-4.[①] In the Eulerian method one may attach a temperature-measuring device to the top of the chimney (point 0) and record the temperature at that point as a function of time. At different times there are different fluid particles passing by the stationary device. Thus, one would obtain the temperature, T, for that locations ($x=x_0$, $y=y_0$, and $z=z_0$) as a function of time, that is, $T=T(x_0, y_0, z_0, t)$. The use of numerous temperature measuring devices fixed at various locations would provide the temperature field, $T=T(x, y, z, t)$. The temperature of a particle as a function of time would not be known unless the location of the particle were known as a function of time.

In the Lagrangian method, one would attach the temperature-measuring device to a particular fluid particle (particle A) and record that particle's temperature as it moves about. Thus, one would obtain that particle's temperature as a function of time $T_A=T_A(t)$. The use of many such measuring devices moving with various fluid particles would provide the temperature of these fluid particles as a function of time. The temperature would not be known as a function of position unless the location of each particle were known as a function of time. If enough information in Eulerian form is available, Lagrangian information can be derived from the Eulerian data—and vice versa.[②]

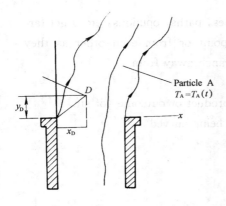

Fig. 6-4 Eulerian and Lagrangian description of temperature of a flowing fluid

In fluid mechanics it is usually easier to use the Eulerian method to describe a flow. There are, however, certain instances in which the Lagrangian method is more convenient. For example, some numerical fluid mechanics calculations are based on determining the motion of individual fluid particles, thereby describing the motion in Lagrangian terms. Similarly, in some experiments individual fluid particles are "tagged" and are followed throughout their motion, providing a Lagrangian description. A Lagrangian description may also be useful in describing fluid machinery in which fluid particles gain or lose energy as they move along their flow paths.

Another illustration of the difference between the Eulerian and Lagrangian descriptions can be seen in the following biological example. Each year thousands of birds migrate between their summer and winter habitats. Ornithologists study these migrations to obtain various types of important information. One set of data obtained is the rate at which birds pass a certain location on their migration route. This corresponds to an Eulerian description—"flowrate" at a given location as a function of time.③ Individual birds need not be followed to obtain this information. Another type of information is obtained by "tagging" certain birds with radio transmitters and following their motion along the migration route. This corresponds to a Lagrangian description — "position" of a given particle as a function of time.④

Notes

①这两种分析流体流动问题方法的不同之处可以从烟筒排烟的例子中看到。
②如果 Eulerian 方法有足够的数据可供使用的话，那么，我们可以从此数据中导出 Lagrangian 数据，反过来也一样，即：如果 Lagrangian 方法有足够的数据可供使用的话，我们也可从这些数据中导出 Eulerian 数据。
③这与 Eulerian 的描述一致——给定地点的"流量"为时间的函数。
④这与 Lagrangian 的描述一致——某一粒子的"位置"为时间的函数。

Reading Material B

Static, Stagnation (total), and Dynamic Pressure

A useful concept associated with the Bernoulli equation deals with the stagnation and dynamic pressures. These pressures arise from the conversion of kinetic energy in a flowing fluid into a "pressure rise" as the fluid is brought to rest. In this section we explore various results of this process. Each term of the Bernoulli equation has the dimensions of force per unit area - psi, lb/ft², N/m². The first term, p, is the actual thermodynamic pressure of the fluid as it flows. To measure its value, one could move along with the fluid, thus being "static" relative to the moving fluid. Hence, it is normally termed the static pressure. Another way to measure the static pressure would be to drill a hole in a flat surface and fasten a piezometer tube as indicated by the location of point (3) in Fig. 6-5. ① The pressure in the flowing fluid at (1) is $p_1 = \gamma h_{3-1} + p_3$, the same as if the fluid were static. We know that $p_3 = \gamma h_{4-3}$. Thus, since $h_{3-1} + h_{4-3} = h$ it follows that $p_1 = \gamma h$.

The third term, γz, is termed the hydrostatic pressure, in obvious regard to the hydrostatic pressure variation discussed. It is not actually a pressure, but does represent the change in pressure possible due to potential energy variations of the fluid as a result of elevation changes.

The second term in the Bernoulli equation, $\rho V^2/2$, is termed the dynamic pressure. Its interpretation can be seen in Fig. 6-5 by considering the pressure at the end of a small tube inserted into the flow and pointing upstream. ② After the initial transient motion has died out, the liquid will fill the tube to a height of H as shown. The fluid in the tube, including that at its tip, (2), will be stationary. That is, $V_2 = 0$, or point (2) is a stagnation point.

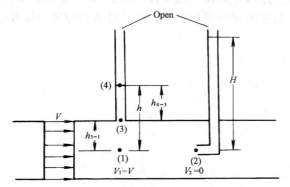

Fig. 6-5   Measurement of static and stagnation pressures

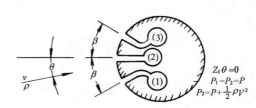

Fig. 6-6   Cross section of a direction finding Pitot-static tube

If we apply the Bernoulli equation between points (1) and (2), (see Fig. 6-5) using $V_2 = 0$ and assuming that $z_1 = z_2$, we find that

$$p_2 = p_1 + \frac{1}{2}\rho V_1^2$$

Hence the pressure at the stagnation point is greater than the static pressure, p_1, by an amount $\rho V_1^2/2$, the dynamic pressure.

If elevation effects are neglected, the stagnation pressure, $p + \rho V^2/2$, is the largest pressure obtainable along a given streamline. It represents the conversion of all of the kinetic energy into a pressure rise. ③ The sum of the static pressure, hydrostatic pressure, and dynamic pressure is termed the total pressure p_T. The Bernoulli equation is a statement that the total pressure remains constant along a streamline.

Again, we must be careful that the assumptions used in the derivation of this equation are appropriate for the flow being considered.

One method of determining the flow direction and its speed (Thus the veloity) is to use a directional finding Pitot tube as is illustrated in Fig. 6-6. Three pressure taps are drilled into a small circular cylinder, fitter with small tubes, and connected to three pressure transducers. The cylinder is rotated until the pressures in the two side holes are equal, thus indicating that the center hole points directly upstream. The center tap then measures the stagnation pressure. The two side holes are located at a specific angle ($\beta = 29.5°$) so that they measure the static pressure. The speed is then obtained from $V = [2(p_2 - p_1)/\rho]^{1/2}$

The above discussion is valid for incompressigle flows. At high speeds compressibility becomes important (the density is not constant) and other phenomena occur.

The concepts of static, dynamic, stagnation, and total pressure are useful in a variety of flow problems.

Notes

① 另外一种测量静压的方法就是在一平面上打孔并安装一测压管，如图6-5点3位置所示。

② 伯努利方程的第二项，$\rho V^2/2$ 叫做动压。对它的解释可在图6-5中通过考察插进流体并指向上游的小管的端压看出。

③ 这就是说所有的重力能都转化成为压升。

UNIT SEVEN

Text   Incompressible, Steady and Uniform Turbulent Flow In Circular Cross-section Pipes

[1]   The head loss in turbulent flow in a closed section pipe is given by the Darcy equation:
$$h_f = \frac{4fL}{d} \cdot \frac{\bar{v}^2}{2g}$$

[2]   It will be seen from the above expression that all the parameters, with the exception of the friction factor f, are measurable.[①] Results of extensive experimentation in this area led to the establishment of the following proportional relationships:

(1) $h_f \propto l$;

(2) $h_f \propto \bar{v}^2$;

(3) $h_f \propto l/d$;

(4) h_f depends on the surface roughness of the pipe walls;

(5) h_f depends on fluid density and viscosity;

(6) h_f is independent of pressure.

[3]   The value of f must be selected so that the correct value of h_f will always be given by the Darcy equation and so cannot be a single-value constant. The value of f must depend on all the parameters listed above. Expressed in a form suitable for dimensional analysis this implies that
$$f = \phi(\bar{v}, d, \rho, \mu, k, k', \alpha) \tag{7.1}$$
where k is a measure of the size of the wall roughness, k' is a measure of the spacing of the roughness particles, both having dimensions of length, and α is a form factor, a dimensionless parameter whose value depends on the shape of the roughness particles. In the general rough pipe case, dimensional analysis yields an expression:
$$f = \phi_2(\text{Re}, k/d, k'/d, \alpha) \tag{7.2}$$

[4]   Dimensional analysis can only indicate the best combination of parameters for an empirical solution; the actual algebraic format of the relation for friction factor in terms of the variables listed must be determined by experimentation.[②].

[5]   Blasius, in 1913, was the first to propose an accurate empirical relation for friction factor in turbulent flow in smooth pipes, namely
$$f = 0.079/\text{Re}^{1/4} \tag{7.3}$$
This expression yields results for head loss to ±5 per cent for smooth pipes at Reynolds numbers up to 100,000.

[6]   For rough pipes, Nikuradse, in 1933, proved the validity of the f dependence on the relative roughness ratio k/d by investigating the head loss in a number of pipes which had been treated internally with a coating of sand particles whose size could be varied. These tests in no

way investigated the effect of particle spacing k'/d, or of particle shape factor α, on the friction factor, but did show that, for one type of roughness,

$$f = \phi_3(\text{Re}, k/d) \tag{7.4}$$

It may well be argued that experimental problems would make it virtually impossible to hold k'/d and α constant so that the effect of roughness size k/d might be investigated in isolation.[3] However, the accuracy of the results obtained by basing the value of f simply on Reynolds number and k/d does suggest that the effects of particle spacing and shape are negligible compared to that of the relative roughness based solely on k/d.[4]

[7]   Thus, the calculation of losses in turbulent pipe flow is dependent on the use of empirical results and the most common reference source is the Moody chart, which is a logarithmic plot of f vs. Re for a range of k/d values. This type of data presentation is commonly referred to as a Staton diagram. A typical Moody chart is presented as Fig. 7-1 and a number of distinct regions may be identified and commented on.

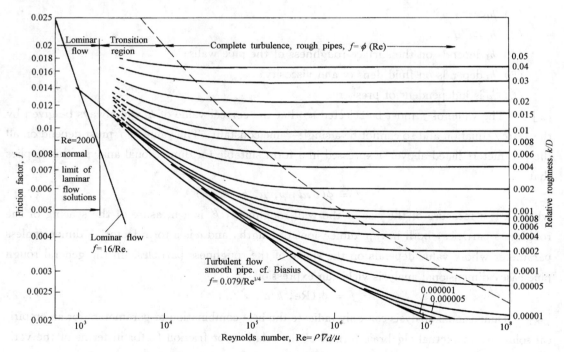

Fig. 7-1   Variation of friction factor f with Reynolds number and pipe wall roughness for ducts of circular cross-section

[8]   (i) The straight line labelled 'laminar flow', representing $f = 16/\text{Re}$, is a graphical representation of the Poiseuille equation. $f = 16/\text{Re}$ plots as a straight line of slope-1 on a log-log plot and is independent of pipe surface roughness. This relation also shows that the Darcy equation may be applied to the laminar flow regime provided that the correct f value is employed.

[9]   (ii) For values of $k/d < 0.001$ the rough pipe curves of Fig 7-1 approach the Blasius smooth pipe curve due to the presence of the laminar sub-layer, which develops in turbulent

flow close to the pipe wall and whose thickness decreases with increasing Reynolds number. Thus, for certain combinations of surface roughness and Reynolds number, the thickness of the laminar sub-layer is sufficient to cover the wall roughness and the flow behaves as if the pipe wall were smooth. ⑤ For higher Reynolds numbers the roughness particles project above the now decreased thickness laminar sub-layer and contribute to an increased head loss.

[10]　(iii) At high Reynolds numbers, or for pipes having a high k/d value, all the roughness particles are exposed to the flow above the laminar sub-layer. In this condition, the head loss is totally due to the generation of a wake of eddies by each particle making up the pipe roughness. This form of head loss is known as 'form drag' and is directly proportional to the square of the mean flow velocity, thus $h_f \propto \bar{v}^2$ and, hence, from Darcy's equation, f is a constant, depending only on the roughness particle size. This condition is represented on the Moody chart by portions of the f vs. Re curves which are parallel to the Re axis and which occur at high values of Re and k/d.

New Words and Expressions

turbulent ['tə:bjulənt]	a.	紊流，湍流
cross-section	n.	横断面，截面
measurable ['meʒərəbl]	a.	可测量的
experimentation [eks‚perimen'teiʃən]	n.	试验，试验
roughness ['rʌfnis]	n.	粗糙度
viscosity [vis'kɔsiti]	n.	粘度
single-value	n.	单值
spacing ['speisiŋ]	n.	空隙
dimensionless [di'menʃənlis]	a.	无量纲的
algebraic [‚ældʒi'breiik]	a.	代数的
format * ['fɔ:mæt]	n.	形式
empirical * [em'pirikəl]	a.	以经验为根据的
validity * [və'liditi]	n.	有效，效力
coating ['kəutiŋ]	n.	涂层
isolation [‚aisə'leiʃən]	n.	隔绝，隔离
Reynolds number		雷诺数
logarithmic [lɔgə'riθmik]	a.	对数的
laminar ['læminə]	a.	流层的
graphical ['græfikəl]	a.	图的
log-log plot		双对数图
regime * [rei'ʒi:m]	n.	格率，制度
sub-layer		底层
eddy ['edi]	n.	涡流

Moody chart	莫迪图
Re curves	Re 曲线
Re axis	Re 轴

Notes

①It will be…are measurable:

句中 that 引出主语从句；the above expression：上式。

②Dimensional analysis…by experimentation:

分号前后是两个分句。第一分句的结构是 analysis（主语）indicate（谓语）combination（宾语）；第二分句的结构是 the actual algebraic format of the relation for friction factor in terms of the variables（主语结构），must be determined（谓语）。

③It may well…in isolation:

句中 that…in isolation 是主语从句；…make it virtually…中 it 是形式宾语，动词不定式 to hold k'/d and α constant 是宾语，impossible 是宾语补足语；so that 是主语从句中的结果状语从句。

④However, the accuracy…on k/d:

句中 obtained by…是 results 的定语；basing…on…and k/d 动名词短语作 by 的宾语；does 强调谓语动词 suggest；compared to that of…中 that 代 effect。

⑤…as if the pipe wall were smooth:

由于 as if，本句是虚拟语气。

Exercises

Reading Comprehension

I. Match Column A with Column B according to the text.

A	B
1. turbulent flow	a. a flow which is violent, in disorder and uncontrolled
2. head loss	b. a flow which is laminar and in good order
3. Blasius	c. a man who, in 1913, was the first to propose an accurate empirical relation for friction factor in turbulent flow in smooth pipes
4. Nikuradse	d. a man who, in 1933, proved the validity of the f dependence on the relative roughness ratio k/d by investigating the head loss in a number of pipes
5. laminar flow	e. energy loss

6. laminar sub-layer   f. the lowest layer of the laminar flow
7. laminar flow regime   g. the area in which the flow is laminar flow
8. k is   h. a measure of the size of the wall roughness
9. k′ is   i. a form factor
10. α is   j. a measure of the spacing of the roughness particles

II. Complete the following sentences with the information given in the text.
1. From the expression $h_f = \dfrac{4fL}{d} \cdot \dfrac{V^2}{2g}$ we know that all the parameters are measurable except the _____.
2. The head loss h_f depends on the surface _____, and fluid _____, and it is independent of _____.
3. _____ is a form factor, a dimensionless _____ and whose value depends on the _____ the roughness particles.
4. The expression $f = 0.079 \text{Re}^{1/4}$ yields results for head loss to ±5 _____ for smooth pipes at Reynolds numbers up to 100,000.
5. At high Reynolds numbers, or for pipes having a high k/d value, all the roughness particles are _____ to the flow above the laminar sub-layer.

Vocabulary

I. Fill in the blanks with the words given below Change the forms if necessary.

turbulent	empirical	measurable	experimentation
format	validity	coating	isolation
laminar	eddies		

1. The criminal will be sentenced for his case is still in the term of _____, though it happened a long time ago.
2. The _____ of paint is fresh and don't touch it.
3. In straight pipes of constant diameter, flow can be assumed to be _____ if the Reynolds number exceeds 40000.
4. Whether you will amount to anything or not depends on how hard you study and we might see the result within the _____ future.
5. The actual algebraic _____ of the relation for friction factor in terms of the variables listed must be determined by experimentation.
6. The _____ will determine the actual algebraic format of the relation for friction factor in terms of the variables listed.
7. In chemistry there are many _____ formulas.
8. The old man lives in _____ but he knows quite well everything happening around the world.

9. Anyone who wants to swim across the river must be careful for the _____ in the river.
10. In pipes, at values of the Reynolds number > 2000, flow will not necessarily be turbulent, and _____ flow has been maintained up to Re = 50000.

Ⅱ. Match the words in Column A with their corresponding definitions in Column B.

A	B
1. format	a. shape and size (of a book, including the type, paper, and binding); form
2. empirical	b. relying solely on observation and experiment, not on theory
3. coating	c. like those in a fluid in which several layers exist
4. laminar	d. thin layer or covering
5. eddy	e. (of wind, smoke, fog, mist, dust, water) circular or spiral

Reading Material A

Laminar and Turbulent Flow

Observation shows that two entirely different types of fluid flow exist This was demonstrated by Osborne Reynolds in 1883 through an experiment in which water was discharged from a tank through a glass tube.① The rate of flow could be controlled by a valve at the outlet, and a fine filament of dye injected at the entrance to the tube.② At low velocities, it was found that the dye filament remained intact throughout the length of the tube, showing that the particles of water moved in parallel linesThis type of flow is known as laminar, viscous or streamline, the particles of fluid moving in an orderly manner and retaining the same relative positions in successive cross-sections.

As the velocity in the tube was increased by opening the outlet valve, a point was eventually reached at which the dye filament at first began to oscillate and then broke up so that the colour was diffused over the whole cross-section, showing that the particles of fluid no longer moved in an orderly manner but occupied different relative positions in successive cross-sections.③ This type of flow is known as turbulent and is characterized by continuous small fluctuations in the magnitude and direction of the velocity of the fluid particles, which are accompanied by corresponding small fluctuations of pressure.

When the motion of a fluid particle in a stream is disturbed, its inertia will tend to carry it on in the new direction, but the viscous forces due to the surrounding fluid will tend to make it conform to the motion of the rest of the stream In viscous flow, the viscous shear stresses are sufficient to eliminate the effects of any deviation, but in turbulent flow they are inadequate The criterion which determines whether flow will be viscous or turbulent is therefore the ratio of the inertial force to the viscous force acting on the particle.④

The ratio
$$\frac{Inertial\ force}{Viscous\ force} = const \times \frac{\rho v l}{\mu}$$

Thus, the criterion which determines whether flow is viscous or turbulent is the quantity $\rho v l / \mu$, known as the Reynolds number. It is a ratio of forces and, therefore, a pure number and may also be written as ul/v where is the kinematic viscosity ($v = \mu/\rho$).

Experiments carried out with a number of different fluids in straight pipes of different diameters have established that if the Reynolds number is calculated by making l equal to the pipe diameter and using the mean velocity $\bar{v}$, then, below a critical value of $\rho \bar{v} d/\mu = 2000$, flow will normally be laminar (viscous), any tendency to turbulence being damped out by viscous friction.⑤ This value of the Reynolds number applies only to flow in pipes, but critical values of the Reynolds number can be established for other types of flow, choosing a suitable characteristic length such as the chord of an aerofoil in place of the pipe diameter. For a given fluid flowing in a pipe of a given diameter, there will be a critical velocity of flow $\bar{v}_c$ corresponding to the critical value of the Reynolds number, below which flow will be viscous.

In pipes, at values of the Reynolds number >2000, flow will not necessarily be turbulent Laminar flow has been maintained up to $Re = 50,000$, but conditions are unstable and any disturbance will cause reversion to normal turbulent flow. In straight pipes of constant diameter, flow can be assumed to be turbulent if the Reynolds number exceeds 4000.

Notes

①（有两种完全不同的流体流动）这一点在 1883 年就由 Osberne Reynolds 用试验演示证明。在试验里，水通过玻璃管从水箱里放出。

②流量由出口处的阀门来控制，一股很细的染色流束由入口注入玻璃管内。

③打开出口阀门，管子里的速度就提高．随着速度提高，最后会达到这样的程度，即染色流束起初开始摆动然后破碎，这样颜色就扩散在整个截面上这表明流体粒子已不再有次序流动却在连续的截面上占有相对不同的位置。

④因此，确定流动是粘滞性的还是紊流性的标准就是作用在粒子上的惯性力和粘滞力之比。

⑤在不同管径的直管里用许多不同流体所进行的试验已经证实，如雷诺数是通过使 L 等于管径并且使用平均速度 $\bar{v}$ 来计算，那末在低于临界值 $\rho \bar{v} d/\mu = 2000$ 的条件下流动一般是层流（粘滞流动），任何紊流的倾向都会由于粘滞摩擦而受到抑制。

Reading Material B

Pipe Networks

An extension of compound pipes in parallel is a case frequently encountered in municipal distribution systems, in which the pipes are interconnected so that the flow to a given outlet may come by several different paths. Indeed, it is frequently impossible to tell by inspection which way the flow travels.[①] Nevertheless, the flow in any network, however complicated, must satisfy the basic relations of continuity and energy as follows:
1. The flow into any junction must equal the flow out of it
2. The flow in each pipe must satisfy the pipe-friction laws for flow in a single pipe.
3. The algebraic sum of the head losses around any closed circuit must be zero.

Pipe networks are generally too complicated to solve analytically, as was possible in the simpler cases of parallel pipes. A practical procedure is the method of successive approximations, introduced by Cross. It consists of the following elements, in order:
1. By careful inspection assume the most reasonable distribution of flows that satisfies condition 1.
2. Write condition 2 for each pipe in the form

$$h_L = KQ^n \tag{7.5}$$

where K is a constant for each pipe. For example, the standard pipe-friction equation would yield $K=1/C^2$ and $n=2$ for constant f. Minor losses within any circuit may be included, but minor losses at the junction points are neglected.

3. To investigate condition 3, compute the algebraic sum of the head losses around each elementary circuit. $\Sigma h_L = \Sigma KQ^n$. Consider losses from clockwise flows as positive, counterclockwise negative. Only by good luck will these add to zero on the first trial.

4. Adjust the flow in each circuit by a correction, ΔQ, to balance the head in that circuit and give $\Sigma KQ^n = 0$ The heart of this method lies in the determination of ΔQ For any pipe we may write

$$Q = Q_0 + \Delta Q$$

where Q is the correct discharge and Q_0 is the assumed discharge Then, for a circuit

$$\Delta Q = \frac{-\Sigma K Q_0^n}{\Sigma |KnQ_0^{n-1}|} = \frac{-\Sigma h_L}{n\Sigma |h_L/Q_0|} \tag{7.6}$$

It must be emphasized again that the numerator of Eq. (7.6) is to be summed algebraically, with due account of sign, while the denominator is summed arithmetically. The negative sign in Eq. (7.6) indicates that when there is an excess of head loss around a loop in the clock-wise direction, the ΔQ must be subtracted from clockwise Q_0's and added to counterclockwise ones. The reverse is true if there is a deficiency of head loss around a loop in the clockwise direction.

5. After each circuit is given a first correction, the losses will still not balance because of the interaction of one circuit upon another (pipes which are common to two circuits receive two independent corrections, one for each circuit) The procedure is repeated, arriving at a second correction, and so on, until the corrections become negligible.

Either form of Eq. (7.6) may be used to find ΔQ. As values of K appear in both numerator and denominator of the first form, values proportional to the actual K may be used to find the distribution. The second form will be found most convenient for use with pipe-friction diagrams for water pipes.

An attractive feature of the approximation method is that errors in computation have the same effect as errors in judgment and will eventually be corrected by the process.

The pipe-network problem lends itself well to solution by use of a digital computer. Programming takes time and care, but once set up, there is great flexibility and many man-hours of labor can be saved.[2]

Notes

[1]的确，通过观察往往很难说清楚流体将流经哪一个管路。
[2]编制程序需花费大量的时间和精力，但是一旦完成，就有很大的机动灵活性，许多耗人费时的劳动就可省去。

UNIT EIGHT

Text   Conduction

[1] Heat transfer by conduction may be thought of as the heat transferred through a substance (or combination of substances) from a region of high temperature to a region of low temperature by the progressive exchange of energy between the molecules of the substance.[①] In the process of transferring heat by conduction, no bodily displacement of the molecules occurs. In the case of metals, however, electron movement greatly assists in heat transfer by conduction.

[2] The fundamental law of conduction is credited to Fourier. This law may be illustrated as follows. Consider steady-state, unidirectional heat flow through a solid, as is indicated in Fig. 8-1.[②] Take a slab of the solid having a cross-sectional area A normal to the path of heat flow. Let the thickness of the slab be dx, and let the temperature difference across the slab be dt. From his experimental work Fourier developed the following relationship:

$$\dot{Q} = -kA\frac{dT}{dx} \tag{8.1}$$

where $\dot{Q}$ = heat flow per unit of time

k = proportionality factor, called the thermal conductivity

dT/dx = rate of change in temperature with distance in the direction of heat flow

In the SI system of units, thermal conductivity may be expressed as

$$W/m^2 \div K/m = W/mK$$

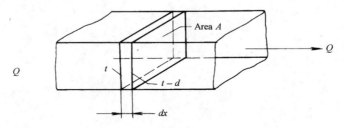

Fig. 8-1 Fourier's law of heat conduction

[3] Extensive experimental investigations have established the values of thermal conductivities of many substances and the effect of temperature on these conductivities. Note that the thermal conductivity of any metal is very high in comparison with that of any gas. The reported values of thermal conductivities of metals are valid only for metals of a given degree of purity. Particularly for those metals with the highest values of thermal conductivity, the introduction of a slight amount of another metal will cause a significant change in the thermal conductivity.

[4] The best heat-insulating solids owe their insulating properties to the air or to other gas-

es contained in cells within the material. These cells cause the heat to flow through the solid material through a long tortuous passage. In addition, the available cross-sectional area of the solid material is much less than the projected area. Experimental evidence shows that many small unicellular pockets of gas are much more effective than a series of connected cells having the same total volume in giving insulating value to a substance. There may be considerable variation in the thermal conductivity of any given insulating material because the conductivity depends on its density, the size and number of its air cells, and its absorbed moisture.

[5]　　There are several accepted methods of experimentally determining the thermal conductivity of solids. When proper care is used, fairly accurate values can be obtained for the thermal conductivity of a given solid of specified composition. It is much more difficult, however, to determine the thermal conductivity of a gas, a vapor, or a liquid, since it is almost impossible to eliminate the heat transferred by convection, which occurs simultaneously with that transferred by conduction, without introducing difficulties in the accurate measurement of other factors.[3] For these reasons there are differences of perhaps 10 to 25 percent in reported values of the thermal conductivities of fluids.

[6]　　Fig. 8-2 shows the heat conduction in a simple wall. It is assumed that the width and height of the wall are so large in comparison with the thickness of the wall that the heat flow may be considered to be unidirectional.[4] One face of the wall is maintained at a uniform temperature t_1, and the other face is kept at temperature t_2. The heat flow through the wall may be obtained by integration of Eq. 8.1.

[7]　　An examination of the thermal conductivities of the various materials shows that, for many materials, the thermal conductivity may be taken as constant over an appreciable range in temperature. Furthermore, for most materials, the thermal conductivity is a straight-line function of temperature within the range of temperature for which[5] information is available. Thus, the arithmetic mean thermal conductivity k_m may be used as the true thermal conductivity. For the simple wall, Eq. 8.1 may be integrated as follows:

$$Q = \frac{k_m A}{X}(T_1 - T_2) \tag{8.2}$$

[8]　　According to Eq. 8.2, the rate of heat flow is proportional to the heat-flow area, the temperature difference causing heat flow, and the term k_m/x. This term is known as the thermal conductance.

[9]　　When the thermal conductivity does not vary linearly with temperature, the mean thermal conductivity k_m cannot be determined readily. In such a case it becomes desirable to express the thermal conductivity as a function of temperature in Eq. 8.1 and then to perform the integration.

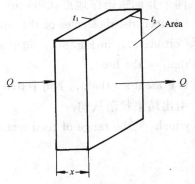

Fig. 8-2　Conduction throught a single wall

New Words and Expressions

progressive	[prə'gresiv]	a.	进行的
bodily	['bɔdili]	a.	具体的，有形的
credit (to)		v.	把……归于，认为……
Fourier's Law			付立叶定律
unidirectional	['juːnidi'rekʃənl]	a.	单向的
slab	[slæb]	n.	厚片
cross-sectional area			横截面积
proportionality *	[prə'pɔːʃə'næliti]	n.	比例
conductivity	[ˌkɔndʌk'tiviti]	n.	导热系数
purity	['pjuəriti]	n.	纯度
insulating *	['insjuleitiŋ]	a.	绝热的
tortuous	['tɔːtjuəs]	a.	弯曲的
projected area			投影面积
unicellular	['juːni'seljulə]	a.	单细胞的，单孔的
convection	[kən'vekʃən]	n.	对流
integration	[ˌinti'greiʃən]	n.	积分
appreciable *	[ə'priːʃiəbl]	a.	相当大的
conductance	[kən'dʌktəns]	n.	导热率
linearly *	['liniəli]	ad.	线性地

Notes

①Heat transfer... the substance：
  句中 through a substance (or combination of substances) from a region... to a region... 两个介词短语作地点状语；by the progressive exchange of energy 介词短语作方式状语；between the molecules of the substance 修饰 the progressive exchange。

②Consider... in Fig. 8-1：句中 as 引出非限制性定语从句，as 修饰全句。

③that = the heat。

④It is assumed that...：句中 that 引出主语从句；so large... that the heat flow... 中的 that 引出结果状语从句。

⑤which = the range of temperature。

Exercises

Reading Comprehension

Ⅰ. Match Column A with Column B according to the first four paragraphs.

A	B
1. Heat transfer by conduction	a. owe their insulating properties to the air or to other gases contained in cells within the material.
2. Electron movement	b. is very high in comparison with that of any gas.
3. Extensive experimental	c. greatly assists in heat transfer by investigations conduction.
4. Thermal conductivity of any metal	d. have established the values of thermal conductivities of many substances.
5. The best heat-insulating solids	e. may be thought of as the heat transferred through a substance or combination of substances.

Ⅱ. Separate the following according to the paragraph 2 and 6.
   A. Consider steady-state, unidirectional heat flow through a solid
   B. The width and height of the wall are so large in comparison with the thickness of the wall that the heat flow may be considered to be unidirectional.
   C. Take a slab of the solid having a cross-sectional area A normal to the path of heat flow.
   D. One face of the wall is maintained at a uniform temperature t_1.
   E. Let the thickness of the slab be d_x.
   F. The other face is kept at temperature t_2.
   G. Let the temperature difference across the slab be d_t.
   H. The heat flow through the wall may be obtained by integration of Eq8. 1.
   I. From his experimental work Fouries developed the relationship:

   1. The fundamental law of conduction may be illustrated as follows

   1) _____A_____
   2) _____
   3) _____
   4) _____
   5) _____

   2. The heat conduction in a simple wall

may be described as follows:
1) _____B_____
2) _____
3) _____
4) _____

III. Say whether the following statements are True (T) or False (F) according to the text, making use of the given paragraph reference number.
1. No bodily displacement of the molecules occurs in the process of heat transfer by conduction (Para. 1)
2. Fourier owes the fundamental law of conduction to someone (Para. 2)
3. The thermal conductivity of any gas is low in comparison with that of any metal (Para. 3)
4. The reported values of thermal conductivities of metals are sound only for metals of any degree of purity (Para. 3)
5. A significant change in the thermal conductivity will be caused if a slight amount of another metal is introduced. (Para. 3)
6. A series of connected cells having the same total volume will be much less effective than many small unicellular pockets of gas in giving insulating value to a substance. (Para. 4)
7. Since it is much more difficult to eliminate the heat transferred by convection it is almost impossible to determine the thermal conductivity of solids. (Para. 5)
8. An examination of the thermal conductivities of the various materials shows two important factors. (Para. 7)
9. The term k_m/x is known as the thermal conductiving. (Para. 8)
10. When the thermal conductivity varies linearly with temperature, the mean thermal conductivity Km can be determined readily. (Para. 9)

Vocabulary

I. Find words in the text which mean almost the same as the following.
   1. para. (1): having a material form, physical; (_____)
   2. para. (2): the state of being in proportion (_____)
   3. para. (4): covering or separating (sth.) with non-conducting materials to prevent loss of heat. (_____)
   4. para. (7): large enough to be recognized and measured (_____)
   5. para. (9): in linear manner (_____)
Now use the words you have found to complete the following sentences.
   6. In the equation, the "k" stands for the _____ factor.
   7. We have many _____ ways and one of them is insulating a cooking-stove with asbestos.

8. Does any _____ displacement of the molecules occur-in the process of transferring heat by conduction?
9. The city has an _____ change in the temperature all the year round.
10. When the thermal conductivity does not vary _____ with temperature, the mean thermal conductivity km cannot be determined readily.

II. Fill in the blanks with the words given below. Change the forms if necessary.

| tortuous | cross-sectional | area |
| conductivities | unicellular | convection |

1. These cells cause the heat to flow through the solid material through a long _____ passage.
2. The available _____ of the solid material is much less than the projected area.
3. The reported values of thermal _____ of metals are valid only for metals of a given degree of purity.
4. Experimental evidence shows that many small _____ pockets of gas are much more effective than a series of connected cells having the same total volume in giving insulating value to a substance.
5. The conveying of heat from one part of a liquid or gas to another by the movement of heated substances is called _____.

Reading Material A

General Characteristics

Heat or thermal energy is transferred from one region to another by three modes: conduction, convection and radiation. Each is important in the design or application of heating, air-conditioning or refrigeration equipment. Heat transfer is among the transport phenomena that include mass transfer, momentum transfer or fluid friction and electrical conduction. Transport phenomena have similar rate equations and flux is proportional to a potential difference. In heat transfer by conduction and convection, the potential difference is the temperature difference. Heat, mass and momentum transfer, because of their similarities and interrelationship in many common physical processes, receive unified treatment in some textbooks.[1]

Thermal conduction is the mechanism of heat transfer whereby energy is transported between parts of a continuum from the transfer of kinetic energy between particles or groups of particles at the atomic level.[2] In gases. conduction is a result of elastic collision of molecules; in liquids and electrically nonconducting solids, it is believed to be caused by longitudinal oscillations of the lattice structure. Thermal conduction in metals occurs like electrical conduction, through motions of free electrons. The second Law of Thermodynamics states that thermal transfer occurs in the direction of decreasing temperature. In solid opaque bodies, the significant heat transfer mechanism is thermal conduction, since there is no net material flow in the process. With flowing fluids, thermal conduction dominates in the region very close to a solid boundary where the flow is laminar and parallel to the surface, and there is no eddy motion.③

Thermal convection may involve energy transfer by eddy mixing and diffusion in addition to conduction. Consider heat transfer to a fluid flowing inside a pipe. If the Reynolds number is sufficiently great, three different flow regions will exist. Immediately adjacent to the wall is a laminar sublayer where heat transfer occurs by thermal conduction; outside the laminar sublayer is a transition region called the buffer layer, where both eddy mixing and conduction effects are significant; beyond the buffer layer and extending to the center of the pipe is the turbulent region, where the dominant mechanism of transfer is eddy mixing④.

In most equipment, the main body of fluid is in turbulent flow, and the laminar layer exists at the solid walls only. In cases of low velocity flow in small tubes, or with viscous liquids such as oil (i. e. , at low Reynolds numbers), the entire flow may be laminar with no transition or eddy region.

When fluid currents are produced by sources external to the heat transfer region, for example, a blower or pump, the solid-to-fluid heat transfer is termed forced convection. If the fluid flow is generated internally by nonhomogeneous densities caused by temperature variation, the heat transfer is termed free or natural convection.

In conduction and convection, heat transfer takes place through matter. For radiant heat transfer, there is a change in energy form; from internal energy at the source to electromagnetic energy for transmission, then back to internal energy at the receiver.⑤ Whereas conduction and convection are affected primarily by temperature difference and somewhat by temperature level, the heat transferred by radiation increases rapidly as the temperature increases.

Although some generalized heat transfer equations have been mathematically derived from fundamentals, usually they are obtained from correlations of experimental data. Normally, the correlations employ certain dimensionless numbers from analyses such as dimensional analysis or analogy.

Notes

①热量、质量和动量传递由于在许多常见的物理过程中的相似性和相互关系，因此在一些教科书中作了一致的处理。
②热传导是指连续体各部分之间依靠原子级的微粒或微粒群之间的动能传递来传递能量的传热机理。
③对流动流体，在紧靠固体边界的区域，流动是平行于表面的层流，且没有涡旋运动，导热占主导地位。
④紧靠管壁的是层流层，在这里通过热传导进行热交换；层流层外面是过渡层叫缓冲层，在

这里涡旋混合和传导效应很明显；缓冲层向外延伸到管中心是紊流区，在这里占统治地位的传递手段是涡旋混合。

⑤就辐射热传递而言，存在能量形式的变化；传递在热源处从内能变成电磁能，然后又在受热体处转回内能。

Reading Material B

Transient Heat Flow

Often, it is necessary to know the heat transfer and temperature distribution under unsteady state (varying with time) conditions. Examples are: cold storage temperature variations on starting or stopping a refrigeration unit; daily periodic variation of external air temperature and sun-load affecting the heat load of a clod storage room or wall temperatures; the time required to freeze a given material under certain conditions in a storage room; quick freezing of objects by direct immersion in brines; or the time required for heating or cooling fluids to certain temperatures.

The fundamental equation for unsteady state conduction in solids or fluids in which there is no substantial motion is:

$$\frac{\partial t}{\partial \tau} = \alpha \left(\frac{\partial^2 t}{\partial x^2} + \frac{\partial^2 t}{\partial y^2} + \frac{\partial^2 t}{\partial z^2} \right) \tag{8.3}$$

where the thermal diffusivity, α, is the ratio, $k/\rho c_p$; k is the thermal conductivity; ρ the density; and c_p the specific heat. If α is large (high conductivity; low density and specific heat or both), heat will diffuse faster.

To predict the rate of temperature change of a body with uniform temperature, such as a well-stirred reservoir of fluid, whose temperature is changing because of a net rate of heat gain or loss, the applicable equation can be written.①

$$q_{net} = Mc_v dt/d\tau \tag{8.4}$$

where M is the mass of the body and c_v is its specific heat at constant volume. For liquids and solids, c_v and c_p are nearly equal, and c_p can be used with negligible error. The term q_{net} may include heat transfer by conduction, convection or radiation, and is the difference between the rate of heat transfer to and away from the body, Equation (8.4) is simply an extension of the definition of the specific heat.

Problems of transient convective heating often can be solved with reasonable accuracy by using steady state relationships. Most relationships for convection are based on assumption of steady temperature and flow, and may not be valid for rapid transients. From Eq. (8.3), it is possible to derive expressions for temperature and heat flow variations at different instants and different locations. Most common cases have been solved and presented in graphical forms. In other cases, it is simpler to use numerical methods.

Cooling times for materials can be estimated by employing Gurnie-Lurie charts, which are graphical solutions for the heating or cooling of infinite cylinders, infinite slabs and spheres. These charts assume an initial uniform temperature distribution and no change of phase. The charts cannot be used to calculate freezing times, because of the change of phase that occurs in freezing.

By using Gurnie-Lurie charts, it is possible to estimate the temperature at any point and the average temperature in a homogeneous mass of material as a function of time in a cooling process. In cooling, it is assumed that no freezing occurs. It is possible to estimate the cooling times for rectangular-shaped solids. cubes, cylinders and spheres.

From a heat transfer point of view, a cylinder insulated on its ends behaves as a cylinder of infinite length, and a rectangular solid insulated so that only two parallel faces allow heat transfer behaves as an infinite slab.[②] Also, a thin slab or a long, thin cylinder may be considered infenite objects.

Notes

①为了预测物体对均匀温度的温度变化率，如搅拌充分的液体储罐，其温度由于净得热或失热而在变化，适用的方程可写成：

②从热传递的观点出发，两端绝热的圆柱体性能象无限长圆柱体一样，而只有两个平行面允许热传递的绝热长方体类似于一个无限大的平板。

UNIT NINE

Text   Definition of Similitude

[1]   It is usually impossible to determine all the essential facts for a given fluid flow by pure theory, and hence dependence must often be placed upon experimental investigations. The number of tests to be made can be greatly reduced by a systematic program based on dimensional analysis and specifically on the laws of similitude or similarity, which permit the application of certain relations by which test data can be applied to other cases. ①

[2]   Thus the similarity laws enable us to make experiments with a convenient fluid such as water or air. Also, in both hydraulics and aeronautics, valuable results can be obtained at a minimum cost by tests made with small-scale models of the full-size apparatus. ② The laws of similitude make it possible to determine the performance of the prototype, which means the full-size device, from tests made with the model. It is not necessary that the same fluid be used for the model and its prototype. Neither is the model necessarily smaller than its prototype. Thus the flow in a carburetor might be studied in a very large model. And the flow of water at the entrance to a small centrifugal-pump runner might be investigated by the flow of air at the entrance to a large model of the runner.

[3]   It should be emphasized that the model need not necessarily be different in size from its prototype. In fact, it may be the same device, the variables in the case being the velocity and the physical properties of the fluid. ③

[4]   One of the desirable features in model studies is that there be geometric similarity. The important consideration is that the flow patterns be geometrically similar. If the scale ratio is denoted by L_r, which means the ratio of the linear dimensions of the prototype to corresponding dimensions in the model it follows that areas vary as L_r^2 and volumes as L_r^3. Complete geometric similarity is not always easy to attain. ④ Thus the surface roughness of a small model may not be reduced in proportion unless it is possible to make its surface very much smoother than that of the prototype. In the study of sediment transportation, it may not be possible to scale down the bed materials without having material so fine as to be impractical. Thus fine powder does not simulate the behavior of sand. Again in the case of a river, the horizontal scale is usually limited by the available floor space, and this same scale used for the vertical dimensions may produce a stream so shallow that capillarity has an appreciable effect and also the slope may be such that the flow is laminar. ⑤ In such cases it is necessary to use a distorted model, which means that the vertical scale is larger than the horizontal scale. If the horizontal scale ratio is denoted by L_r and the vertical scale ratio by L_r', the cross section area ratio is $L_r L_r'$.

[5]   Kinematic similarity implies geometric similarity and in addition it implies that the ratio of the velocities at all corresponding points in the flow is the same. If subscripts p and m de-

note prototype and model, respectively, the velocity ratio V_r is

$$V_r = \frac{V_p}{V_m} \tag{9.1}$$

and its value in terms of L_r will be determined by dynamic considerations as explained in the following section.

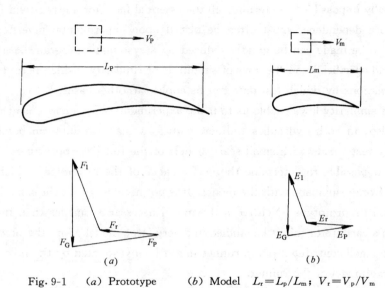

Fig. 9-1 (a) Prototype (b) Model $L_r = L_p/L_m$; $V_r = V_p/V_m$

[6]　As time T is dimensionally L/V, the time scale is

$$T_r = \frac{L_r}{V_r} \tag{9.2}$$

and in a similar manner the acceleration scale is

$$a_r = \frac{L_r}{T_r^2} = \frac{V_r^2}{L_r} \tag{9.3}$$

If two systems are dynamically similar, corresponding forces must be in the same ratio in the two. Forces that may act on a fluid element include those due to gravity F_G, pressure F_P, viscosity F_V, and elasticity F_E. Also, if the element of fluid is at a liquid-gas interface, there are forces due to surface tension F_T. If the summation of forces on a fluid element does not add up to zero, the element will accelerate in accordance with Newton's law. Such an unbalanced force system can be transformed into a balanced system by adding an inertia force F_I that is equal and opposite to the resultant R of the acting forces.⑧ Thus, generally, $F_G + F_P + F_V + F_E + F_T + F_I = 0$.

[7]　In many flow problems some of these forces are either not present or insignificant. In Fig. 9-1 are depicted two geometrically similar flow systems. Let it be assumed that they also possess kinematic similarity and that the forces acting are F_G, F_P, F_V, and F_I. Then dynamic similarity will be achieved if

$$\frac{F_{G_p}}{F_{G_m}} = \frac{F_{P_p}}{F_{P_m}} = \frac{F_{V_p}}{F_{V_m}} = \frac{F_{I_p}}{F_{I_m}}$$

where subscripts p and m refer to prototype and model as before. These relations can be expressed as

$$\left(\frac{F_I}{F_G}\right)_P = \left(\frac{F_I}{F_G}\right)_m \quad \left(\frac{F_I}{F_P}\right)_P = \left(\frac{F_I}{F_P}\right)_m \quad \left(\frac{F_I}{F_V}\right)_P = \left(\frac{F_I}{F_V}\right)_m$$

Each of the quantities is dimensionless. With four forces acting, there are three independent expressions that must be satisfied; for three forces there are two independent expressions.

New Words and Expressions

investigation [in,vesti'geiʃən]	n.	调查
similitude [si'militju:d]	n.	相同点，相似物
specifically [spi'sifikəli]	ad.	尤其
similarity [simi'læriti]	n.	类似，相似
hydraulics [hai'drɔ:liks]	n.	水力学
aeronautics [,ɛərə'nɔ:tiks]	n.	航空学
small-scale	n.	成比例缩小
apparatus [,æpə:reitəs]	n.	装置
prototype * ['prəutətaip]	n.	原形，足尺装置
full-size		原尺寸
carburetor ['kɑ:bjuretə]	n.	汽化器
geometric [dʒiə'metrik]	n.	几何图形
denote * [di'nəut]	vt.	指示，表示
sediment ['sedimənt]	n.	沉淀，沉淀物
scale down		按比例缩减，降低
impractical [im'præktikəl]	a.	不切合实际
capillarity [,kæpi'læriti]	n.	毛细作用现象
distorted [dis'tɔ:tid]	a.	失真了的
kinematic [,kaini'mætik]	a.	运动学的
subscript ['sʌbskript]	n.	下符，下标
dynamically [dai'næmikəli]	ad.	在动力学方面
elasticity [,elæs'tisiti]	n.	弹力，弹性
interface ['intəfeis]	n.	结合面，分界面
insignificant [,insig'nifikənt]	a.	不重要的，轻微的

Notes

①The number of tests... to other cases:
　句中 to be made 动词不定式被动式作定语修饰 the number of tests；based on... and on... 过去分词作定语修饰 a sustematic program；which permit... 是非限定性定语从句，which

的先行词是 the laws of similitude or similarity；... by which 引出定语从句。

②Also, in both... full-size apparatus：at a minimum cost：以最低的代价；tests made with small-scale models：用按比例缩小的模型做的试验。

③..., the variables... being the velocity and physical properties of the fluid 是名词＋分词（being...）独立结构起补充说明作用。

④... without having material...：
句中 so fine as to be impractical 形容词短语作后置定语修饰 material。

⑤... may produce a stream... such that...：
句中 so shallow that capillarity has an appreciable effect 形容词短语作后置定语修饰 a stream；such that：如此以致于……。

⑥... force system can be transformed... by... that...：
此句结构为：主语＋被动式＋方式状语＋定语从句。

Exercises

Reading Comprehension

Ⅰ. Match Column A with Column B According to the text.

A	B
1. small-scale models	a. science of using water to produce power
2. aeronautics	b. set of instruments or other mechanical appliances put together for a purpose with the same size as the prototype
3. hydraulics	c. science of aviation
4. full-size apparatus	d. models which are made in small proportion
5. carburetor	e. the part of an internal-combustion engine in which petrol and air are mixed to make an explosive mixture
6. scale ratio	f. if an object is in motion, it continues in the same direction and in a straight line unless it is acted upon by an external force, property of matter being such
7. geometric similarity	g. the scale which is made horizontally
8. vertical scale	h. the scale which is made vertically
9. horizontal scale	i. geometrically similar
10. inertia force	j. proportion between the size of something.

Ⅱ. Give the definitions to the following terms.

1. A systematic program is _____
_____
_____.

2. The similarity laws are _____
   _____
   _____
   _____.
3. Geometric similarity is _____
   _____.
4. Kinematic similarity is _____
   _____.
5. Dynamic similarity is _____
   _____
   _____.

Vocabulary

Ⅰ. Fill in the blanks with the words given below. Change the forms if necessary.

investigation	similitude	denote	sediment
distort	similarity	prototype	impractical
interface	resultant	elasticity	subscript

1. We have turned out much more products comparing with the _____ period of the preceding year.
2. No _____, no right to speak. The matter is under _____ and we had better not say anything about it.
3. Can you tell me which one is the _____ and which one is the imitation?
4. The head nodding sign _____ "yes" and the head shaking sign "no".
5. First, we ought to pump the water out and then we have to remove the _____ on the floor and at this time we can repair the pond.
6. I'm sorry to say that I did not mean that and you've _____ what I said.
7. The plan you put forward was _____ and we can not put it into practice.
8. You can lend me some wood and I will return you with the _____ products produced with the borrowed wood.
9. What about the _____ of your new spring mattress?
10. In the formula $V_r = V_P/V_m$ what do the _____ p and m stand for?

Ⅱ. Find words in the text which mean almost the same as the following.
1. Para. 2: resemblance; appearance (_____)
2. Para. 2: first or original example (e. g. of an aircraft) from which others have been or will be copied or developed (_____)
3. Para. 4: matter (e. g. sand, dirt, gravel) that settles to the bottom of a liquid (e. g. mud left on fields after a river has been in flood over them (_____)

4. Para. 4: pull, twist, out of the usual shape (＿＿＿＿)
5. Para. 6: the part that two things contact or that which has something to do with two things (＿＿＿＿)

Reading Material A

Comments about Dimensional Analysis

One of the most important, and difficult, steps in applying dimensional analysis to any given problem is the selection of the variables that are involved.① As noted previously, for convenience we will use the term variable to indicate any quantity involved, including dimensional and nondimensional constants. There is no simple procedure whereby the variables can be easily identified. Generally one must rely on a good understanding of the phenomenon involved and the governing physical laws. If extraneous variables are included, then too many pi terms appear in the final solution, and it may be difficult, time consuming, and expensive to eliminate these experimentally. If important variables are omitted, then an incorrect result will be obtained; and again, this may prove to be costly and difficult to ascertain. It is, therefore, imperative that sufficient time and attention be given to this first step in which the variables are determined.

Most engineering problems involve certain simplifying assumptions that have an influence on the variables to be considered. Usually we wish to keep the problem as simple as possible, perhaps even if some accuracy is sacrificed. A suitable balance between simplicity and accuracy is a desirable goal. How "accurate" the solution must be depends on the objective of the study;② that is, we may be only concerned with general trends and, therefore, some variables that are thought to have only a minor influence in the problem may be neglected for simplicity.

For most engineering problems pertinent variables can be classified into three general groups-geometry, material properties and external effects.

Geometry: The geometric characteristics can usually be prescribed by a series of lengths and angles.

Material Properties: Since the response of a system to applied external effects such as forces, pressures, and changes in temperature is dependent on the nature of the materials involved in the system, the material properties that relate the external effects and the responses must be included as variables.③

External Effects: This terminology is used to denote any variable that produces or tends to produce, a change in the system.

The above general classes of variables are intended as broad categories that should be helpful in identifying variables. It is likely, however, that there will be important variables that do not fit easily into one of the above categories and each problem needs to be carefully analyzed.

We wish to keep the number of variables to a minimum, it is important that all variables are independent.

In summary, the following points should be considered in the selection of variables:
1. Clearly define the problem. What is the main variable of interest (the dependent variable)?
2. Consider the basic laws that govern the phenomenon. Even a crude theory that describes the essential aspects of the system may be helpful.
3. Start the variable selection process by grouping the variables into three broad classes: geometry, material properties, and external effects.
4. Consider other variables that may not fall into one of the above categories. For example, time will be an important variable if any of the variables are time dependent.④
5. Be sure to include all quantities that enter the problem even though some of them may be held constant (e. g., the acceleration of gravity, g). For a dimensional analysis it is the dimensions of the quantities that are important--not specific values!
6. Make sure that all variables are independent. Look for relationships among subsets of the variables.

Notes

①把量纲分析应用到某个给定问题中时，最重要的步骤之一就是选择所涉及的变量。
②解决的办法要"精确"到什么程度取决于研究的目标。
③既然系统对外部的影响（如：力、压力和温度变化）的反应取决于系统材料的性质，与外部影响和反应相关的材料性质必须作为变量而被包括进去。
④考虑一下其他可能不属于上述任一范围的变量。例如，如果上述任何变量取决于时间的话，时间就是一个很重要的变量。

Reading Material B

Reynolds Number and Similarity

The nature of the flow pattern in a real fluid is profoundly affected by the relative magnitude of the forces arising from the inertia of the fluid and those due to its viscosity.① This relationship is expressed in terms of a dimensionless group, the Reynolds number:

$$(Re) = \frac{\rho v d}{\mu}$$

When the Reynolds Number for flow past a cylinder exceeds a critical value of roughly 200,000 a change takes place in the flow pattern: separation, instead of taking place at the locations indicated in Fig. 9-2, is delayed, and the streamlines closely follow the surface of the cylinder until well past the transverse diameter. The wake, instead of having a width greater than that of the cylinder, is substantially narrower, and the drag coefficient is much reduced.

In general, for a given boundary geometry, flow patterns are similar for equal Reynolds Numbers, and this law of similarity is extensively used in the interpretation of tests on scale models. The form of Reynolds Number indicates that it is larger the higher the velocity or the greater the size, and this limits the extent to which it is possible to simulate full - scale performance by model tests.[2] Thus, for example, it is not possible to demonstrate flow past a

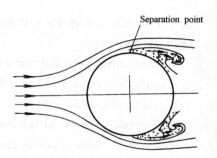

Fig. 9-2 Sketch of flow pattern in a prandtl channel

cylinder at Reynolds Numbers above the critical in a smoke tunnel of moderate size, since the required velocity is so great that there are practical difficulties in generating a satisfactory smoke trace. This limitation affects the observations that can be made on streamlined bodies such as aerofoils in the smoke tunnel.

The purpose of streamlining is to suppress flow separation and to ensure that, so far as possible, the streamlines follow the surface of the body, finally giving rise to a wake of the minimum possible width and a correspondingly small resistance to the flow. Experiment shows flow past an aerofoil in a smoke tunnel at (Re) ~150,000. It will be observed that, while the flow follows the lower surface smoothly, the streamlines diverge from the upper surface, though without the generation of the intensely turbulent wake associated with the cylinder. This aerofoil has a chord of 150 mm; a "real" aerofoil would be of much greater dimensions, the Reynolds Number would also be far greater, typically of the order of 10^7, and the streamlines would follow the upper surface along most of its length, giving rise to a narrow wake of width much less than that of the aerofoil.

Reynolds Number effects of this kind must always be taken into account in interpreting observations made on small-scale models, and the value of (Re) should always be calculated and recorded when reporting experiments involving fluid flow.[3]

It is a simple matter to construct models for use in a smoke tunnel, and topics that may readily be investigated include:

(a) Flow patterns for spheres, bluff and streamlined bodies and flat plates normal to the direction of flow, noting separation points and the size of wake generated. Correlation with measurements of resistance.

(b) Behaviour of aerofoils, including stall, effect of flaps and slots, and generation of wing-tip vortices.

(c) Flow through nozzles, orifices and diffusers.

(d) Flow round bends and corners; effect of guide vanes.

(e) Free jets.

(f) Flow patterns around buildings and for model aircraft and vehicles.

Notes

①实际流体流动模式的特征深受由流体惯性和粘滞性产生的力的相对值的影响。

②雷诺数的形式表明,速度越大或者尺寸越大,雷诺数就越大。这就限制了通过模型测试来模拟全尺寸性能的程度。

③在解释对按比例缩小的模型进行的观察时,这种雷诺数的影响必须予以考虑。在报告涉及流体流动试验时,Re 值应该始终计算并记录下来。

UNIT TEN

Text   Natural Convection

[1]　Heat transfer involving motion in a fluid caused by the difference in density and the action of gravity is called natural or free convection. Heat transfer coefficients for natural convection are generally much lower than for forced convection, and it is therefore important not to ignore radiation in calculating the total heat loss or gain. Radiant transfer may be of the same order of magnitude as natural convection, even at room temperatures, since wall temperatures in a room can affect human comfort.

[2]　Natural convection is important in a variety of heating and refrigeration equipment: (1) gravity coils used in high humidity cold storage rooms and in roof-mounted refrigerant condensers, (2) the evaporator and condenser of household refrigerators, (3) baseboard radiators and convectors for space heating and (4) cooling panels for air conditioning. Natural convection is also involved in heat loss or gain to equipment casings and interconnecting ducts and pipes.

[3]　Consider heat transfer by natural convection between a cold fluid and a hot surface. The fluid in immediate contact with the surface is heated by conduction, becomes lighter and rises because of the difference in density of the adjacent fluid. The motion is resisted by the viscosity of the fluid. The heat transfer is influenced by: (1) gravitational force due to thermal expansion, (2) viscous drag and (3) thermal diffusion. It may be expected to depend on the gravitational acceleration g, the coefficient of thermal expansion β, the kinematic viscosity v $(=\mu/\rho)$, and the thermal diffusivity $\alpha = (k/\rho c_p)$. These variables can be expressed in terms of dimensionless numbers: the Nusselt number, Nu, is a function of the product of the Prandtl number, Pr, and Grashof number, Gr, which, when combined, depend on the fluid properties, the temperature difference between the surface and the fluid, Δt, and the characteristic length of the surface, L. The constant c and exponent n depend on the physical configuration and nature of flow.

[4]　The entire process of natural convection cannot be represented by a single value of exponent n, but can be divided into three regions: (1) turbulent natural convection for which n equals 0.33, (2) laminar natural convection, for which n equals 0.25 and (3) a region that has (Gr · Pr) less than for laminar natural convection, for which the exponent n gradually diminishes from 0.25 to lower values.[①] Note that, for wires, the (Gr · Pr) is likely to be very small, so that the exponent n is 0.1.

[5]　To calculate the natural convection heat transfer coefficient, determine (Gr · Pr) to find whether the boundary layer is laminar or turbulent, then apply the appropriate equation. The correct characteristic length indicated must be used. Since the exponent n is 0.33 for a turbulent boundary layer, the characteristic length cancels out, and the heat transfer coeffi-

cient is independent of the characteristic length. Turbulence occurs when length or temperature difference is large. Since the length of a pipe is generally greater than its diameter, the heat transfer coefficient for vertical pipes is larger than for horizontal pipes.②

[6]   Convection from horizontal plates facing downward when heated (or upward when cooled) is a special case. Since the hot air is above the colder air, there is no theoretical reason for convection. Some convection is caused, however, by secondary influences such as temperature differences on the edges of the plate. As an approximation, a coefficient of somewhat less than half of the coefficient for a heated horizontal plate facing upward can be used.

[7]   Since air is often the heat transport fluid, simplified equations for air are given. Other information on natural convection is available in the general heat transfer references.

[8]   Observed differences in the comparisons of recent experimental and numerical results with existing correlations for natural convective heat transfer coefficients indicate that caution should be taken when applying coefficients for (isolated) vertical plates recommended by ASHRAE for situations with vertical surfaces in enclosed spaces (buildings).③ Improved correlations for calculating natural convective heat transfer from vertical surfaces in rooms under certain temperature boundary conditions have been developed.

[9]   Natural convection can affect the heat transfer coefficient in the presence of weak forced convection. As the forced convection effect, i.e., the Reynolds number, increases, the "mixed convection" (superimposed forced-on-free convection) gives way to the pure forced convection regime. Since the heat transfer coefficient in the mixed convection region is often larger than that calculated based on the natural or forced convection calculation alone, attention is called to references on combined free and forced convection heat transfer.④ The reference given before summarizes natural, mixed, and forced convection regimes for vertical and horizontal tubes. Local conditions influence the values of the convection coefficient in a mixed convection regime, but the references permit locating the pertinent regime and approximating the convection coefficient.

New Words and Expressions

humidity * [hju(ː)ˈmiditi]	n.	湿度
roof-mounted		屋顶安装的
baseboard	n.	踢脚板
casings [ˈkeisiŋz]	n.	壳
ducts [dʌkts]	n.	风管，管道
viscous [ˈviskəs]	a.	粘性的，粘滞的
diffusion [diˈfjuːʒən]	n.	扩散
diffusivity [difjuːˈsiviti]	n.	扩散性，扩散系数
Nusselt number		努谢尔特数
Prandtl number		普朗特数

Grashof number		格拉晓夫数
diminish [di'miniʃ]	vt.	减小，减少
turbulence ['tə:bjuləns]	n.	紊流，扰动
correlation * [ˌkɔri'leiʃəns]	n.	关系式
ASHRAE＝American Society of Heating Refrigerating and Air Conditioning Engineers		美国供热制冷和空调工程师协会
superimpose ['sju:pərim'pəuz]	vt.	加上，附加，叠加
forced-on-free convection		加上自然对流影响的受迫对流
regime * [rei'ʒi:m]	n.	区域，状态
pertinent * ['pə:tinənt]	a.	恰当的，相关的

Notes

①... less than for laminar natural convection：小于 laminar natural convection 的 Gr·Pr, ... for which the exponent n...：
which 代的是 the laminar natural convection。

②... larger than for horizontal pipes：
for 前面省略 the heat transfer coefficient。

③Observed differences... spaces（buildings）：
句中 observed differences 是主语; in the comparisons of... with... 介词短语作 differences 的定语, indicate 是谓语; that 引起的是宾语从句; coefficients for (isolated) vertical plates 是 applying 的宾语。

④... that...：
that 代的是 heat transfer coefficien, calculated... 过去分词作定语修饰 that。

Exercises

Reading Comprehension

I. Separate the following into three groups according to the text.
  A. gravity coils used in high humidity cold storage rooms and in roof mounted refrigerant condensers.
  B. gravitational force due to thermal expansion.
  C. the evaporator and condenser of household refrigerators.
  D. turbulent natural convection for which n equals 0.33.
  E. baseboard radiators and convectors for space heating.
  F. laminar natural convection, for which n equals 0.25.

G. cooling panels for air conditioning.
H. viscous drag.
I. a region that has (Gr·Pr) less than for laminar natural convection, for which the exponent n gradually diminishes from 0.25 to lower values.
J. thermal diffusion.

1. There is a variety of heating and refrigeration equipment in which natural convection is important.
   1) _____
   2) _____
   3) _____
   4) _____

2. The entire process of natural convection can be divided into three regions.
   1) _____
   2) _____
   3) _____

3. The heat transfer is influenced by.
   1) _____
   2) _____
   3) _____

Ⅱ. Match Column A with Column B according to the information given in the text.

A

Natural convection
① can affect
② is important in
③ can be defined as

The entire process of natural convection
④ can not be represented by
⑤ can be divided into

B

(a) a single value of exponent n.
(b) a variety of heating and refrigeration equipment.
(c) three regions.
(d) the heat transfer coefficient in the presence of weak forced convection.
(e) heat transfer involving motion in a fluid caused by the difference in density and the action of gravity.

Ⅲ. Say whether the following statements are True (T) or False (F) according to the text, making use of the given paragraph reference number.
1. Heat transfer coefficients for forced convection are generally much higher than for natural convection. (Para. 1)
2. Natural convection is not important in the evaporator and condenser of household refrigerators. (Para. 2)
3. Thermal diffusion can influence the heat transfer. (Para. 3)
4. Laminar natural convection, for which n equals 0.25 is not one of the regions of the entire process of natural convection. (Para. 4)
5. Since the colder air is above the hot air, there is no theoretical reason for convection. (Para. 6)

Vocabulary

Ⅰ. Find words in the text which mean almost the same as the following.
1. Para. (2) degree of moisture in the air (_____)
2. Para. (3) the quality or property of a fluid that causes it to resist flow. (_____)
3. Para. (4) make less; become less; (_____)
4. Para. (9) conditions or state; field; (_____)
5. Para. (9) relevant; applicable; (_____)

Now use the words you have found to complete the following sentences. Change the forms if necessary.
6. The exponent n gradually _____ from 0.25 to lower values.
7. Natural convection is important in the gravity coils which are used in high _____ cold storage rooms.
8. The motion is resisted by the _____ of the fluid.
9. Locating the _____ regime and approximating the convection coefficient are permitted in the reference books.
10. Local conditions influence the values of the convection coefficient in a mixed convection _____.

Ⅱ. Fill in the blanks with the words given below. Change the forms if necessary.

| viscous, turbulence, correlations, superimposed, roof-mounted |

1. The heat transfer is influenced by _____ drag and thermal diffusion.
2. Improved _____ for calculating natural convection heat transfer have been developed.
3. A map of Great Britain was _____ on a map of Texas to show comparative size.
4. _____ occurs when length or temperature difference is large.
5. Gravity coils can be used in _____ refrigerant condensers.

Reading Material A

Forced Convection

When heat transfer rates from natural convection are not sufficiently high, forced convection is used. As the name implies, in forced convection, the fluid is moved mechanically, generally by pumps, fans, blowers, or compressors. ① In most forced convection heat transfers, the flow is turbulent and will be so assumed here. However, when the fluid is quite viscous (for example, heavy oils, particularly at low temperatures), the flow may be laminar. In case of doubt, the Reynolds number should be calculated to make certain as to the type of flow taking place. ②

One of the most common types of forced convection heat transfer is that occurring inside pipes or ducts. In this section we are concerned largely with this type of heat transfer. However, the general principles developed here are applicable to other types of forced convection heat transfer problems.

The value of the film coefficient, h_c, for forced convection depends on the diameter of the passage D, the fluid velocity V, the mean stream density ρ, and the following properties of the mean film temperature: viscosity μ, specific heat c_p, and thermal conductivity k, Dimensional analysis may be used, in a manner similar to that used in considering free convection, to combine the variables into dimensionless groups, thus greatly reducing the experimental work required to determine the interrelationship of the various variables with h_c.

As a result of dimensional analysis, the following equation has been developed for turbulent flow,

$$\frac{h_c D}{k} = C \left(\frac{D\rho V}{\mu} \right)^e \left(\frac{c_p \mu}{k} \right)^f \tag{10.1}$$

Often, there is a variation in both the fluid density ρ and the velocity V as the fluid flows through its channel. However, for steady stable flow, the product ρV ($=G$) remains a constant, provided that the flow area is constant. The fluid density to be used in determining G must be the mean stream density at the point where V is determined.

The values of the constant C and of the exponents e and f in Eq. 10.1 are difficult to determine exactly but the most widely accepted values are: $C=0.023$, $e=0.8$ and $f=0.4$. Using these values, Eq. 10.1 becomes

$$\frac{h_c D}{k_f} = 0.023 \left(\frac{DV}{\mu_f} \right)^{0.8} \left(\frac{c_{p_f} \mu_f}{k_f} \right)^{0.4} \tag{10.2}$$

where the subscript f denotes that the properties to be used are those at the mean film conditions, It is to be noted that $h_c D/k$ is the Nusselt number Nu, DG/μ is the Reynolds number Re, and $c_p \mu/k$ is the Prandtl number Pr.

At this point it should be emphasized that experimental results obtained by careful investigators may differ from the results computed by applying Eq. 10. 2 by at least 25 percent. Some reasons for this difference are:

1. The assumption of a stagnant film is incorrect.

2. In many instances it is very difficult to evaluate the true mean film properties. This is particularly true when there are wide variations in temperature throughout the film.

3. It is very difficult to measure either the true temperature drop across the film or the rate of heat flow.

4. An oxide or other type of scale may form on the heat-transfer surface.③ Often the scale resistance cannot be readily determined separately and, hence, it is generally added to the resistance of the fluid film.

Inside film coefficients mat vary from less than unity to several thousand. Although Eq. 10. 2 does not always give the desired accuracy, in some cases it does narrow the expected range of values for the film coefficient, which may be satisfactory for engineering use if a small safety factor is included.④

Notes

①顾名思义。
②在有疑问的场合，应该计算雷诺数以确定发生的流动的形式。
③（氧化物或其它类）锈（氧化）皮。
④虽然方程10.2不总是得出期望的精确性，但在有些场合，它确实使得薄膜系数的期望范围变窄，如果加入一个小的安全因子，这或许在工程使用中是令人满意的。

Reading Material B

Convection

The term convection heat transfer refers to the heat exchanged between a surface and a fluid moving over the surface. The amount of heat thus transferred is dependent on the nature of the surface and its geometry and with the nature of the fluid and with its velocity over the surface as well as the temperature differences.① There are two types of convection heat transfers; namely, free (or natural) convection and forced convection.

Assume that the temperature of a fluid in contact with a surface is lower than that of the surface. The fluid will have a tendency to be heated by the surface. This heating causes the density of the fluid in direct contact with the lower density, this fluid will move upward carrying with it the energy that it absorbed. This fluid is replaced at the surface by other fluid which, in turn, is also heated and rises. This process continues, with a continuous fluid motion over the heated surface as long as the main body fluid temperature is less than that of the surface. A reverse of this process takes place when the surface temperature is lower than the main body fluid temperature.② Since this process is a natural one, it is termed natural or free convection.

As the name implies, forced convection occurs when the fluid is forced to flow over the heat transfer surface by external means, A fan, a blower, a compressor, or a pump may be the forcing agency.

The exact nature of convection heat transfer is very difficult to describe because of the large number of variables involved and because of the difficulty of measuring them accurately. For such conditions, the precise but very elaborate analysis of convection heat transfer cannot be justified.

The problem of convection heat transfer can be simplified by assuming that a stagnant film of the fluid is in immediate contact with the surface and that heat is transferred through this film by conduction.③ Even though this assumption does not describe the true situation, particularly for high fluid velocities over the surface, it gives approximate results that are satisfactory for many engineering purposes.

It may appear that the above mentioned equation can be used to determine the heat conducted through the assumed stagnant film. However, this equation calls for the thickness of the stagnant film. Since this film is an assumed one, its thickness cannot be measured. It is pointed out that the heat flow is proportional to the thermal conductance of the heat flow path, k/X. Designating this term as h_c and calling it the film coefficient, the equation becomes

$$Q = Ah_c(T_1 - T_2) \tag{10.3}$$

It is possible that a significant amount of heat may be transferred by radiation from a surface bounded by a fluid. In some situations, the fluid may be completely enclosed by the heating surface. The fluid may be a gas, such as air, which does not absorb a significant amount of radiant energy. In such a case the only heat transferred from the heated surface is by convection. When the fluid can absorb significant amounts of radiant heat energy and where the heated surface is exposed to other surfaces, the reader should refer to heat transfer texts, where this complicated method of heat transfer from a heated surface is explained.④

Notes

①这样传递的热量取决于表面的性质及其几何形状；取决于流体性质和表面上流体流速以及温差。
②当表面温度低于主流区温度时，产生相反的过程。
③通过假设有一层流体滞流膜与表面紧密接触并且热以导热方式传过该膜，对流热传递问题就可以简化。
④如果流体能吸收相当大量的辐射能而且如果受热表面暴露于其它表面，读者应该查阅热传递课文，在这些课文里解释了受热面热传递的复杂方法。

UNIT ELEVEN

Text   Drag of Three-Dimensional Bodies
(Incompressible Flow)

[1]   The total drag on a body is the sum of the friction drag and the pressure drag.
$$F_D = F_f + F_p$$
In the case of a well-streamlined body, such as an airplane wing or hull of a submarine, the friction drag is the major part of the total drag. Only rarely is it desired to compute the pressure drag separately from the friction drag.[①] Usually, when the wake resistance becomes significant, one is interested in the total drag only. Indeed, it is customary to employ a single equation which gives the total drag,
$$F_D = C_D \rho \frac{V^2}{2} A \qquad (11.1)$$

[2]   In the case of a body with sharp corners, separation always occurs at the same point. This results in a relatively constant value of C_D, as may be seen from the plot for the flat disk in Fig. 11-1. If the body has curved sides, however, the location of the separation point will be determined by whether the boundary layer is laminar or turbulent.[②] This location in turn determines the size of the wake and the amount of the pressure drag.

[3]   The foregoing principles are vividly illustrated in the case of the flow around a sphere. For very low Reynolds numbers ($DV/v<1$), the flow about the sphere is completely viscous and the friction drag is given by Stokes' law.
$$F_D = 3\pi\mu V D \qquad (11.2)$$
Equating this equation to Eq. (11.1) gives the result that $C_D = 24/\text{Re}$. The similarity between this case and the value of the friction factor for laminar flow in pipes is at once apparent. This regime of the flow about a sphere is shown as the straight line at the left of the log-log plot of C_D versus Re in Fig. 11-1.

[4]   As Re is increased beyond 1, the laminar boundary layer separates from the surface of the sphere, beginning first at the rear stagnation point. The curve of C_D in Fig. 11-1 begins to level off as the pressure drag becomes of increasing importance and the drag becomes more proportional to V^2. With further increase in Re, the point of separation moves forward on the sphere, until at Re$\approx$1,000 the point of separation becomes fairly stable at about 80° from the forward stagnation point.

[5]   For a considerable range of Reynolds numbers conditions remain fairly stable, the laminar boundary layer separating from the forward half of the sphere and C_D remaining fairly constant at about 0.45.[③] At a value of Re of about 250,000 for the smooth sphere, however, the drag coefficient is suddenly reduced by about 50 percent, as may be seen in Fig. 11-1. The reason for this lies in a change from a laminar to a turbulent boundary layer on the sphere. The

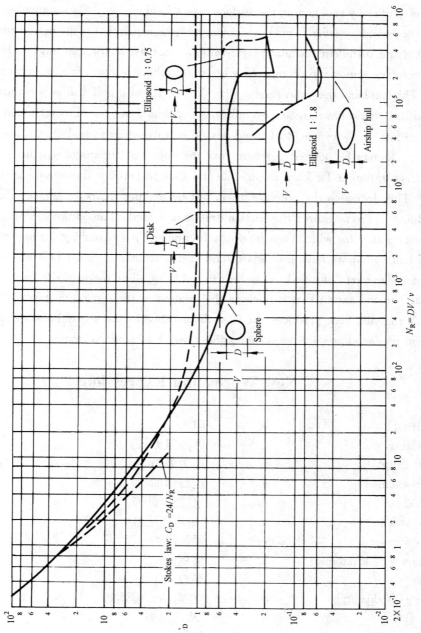

Fig.11-1 Drag coefficient for bodies of revolution

point of separation is moved back to something like 115°.

[6]   The transition from a laminar to a turbulent boundary layer may also be prematurely induced by artificially roughening the surface over a local region.④ By roughening the nose of the sphere the boundary layer is made turbulent and the separation point moved back. The added roughness and turbulent boundary layer cause an increase in friction drag, to be sure, but this is of secondary importance compared with the marked decrease in the size and effect of the wake. This explains the main reason why the surface of a golf ball is perforated. A smooth-surfaced ball would have greater overall drag and would not travel as far when driven.⑤

[7]   Plots of C_D versus Re for various other three-dimensional shapes are also shown in Fig. 11-1. It may be pointed out here that the object of streamlining a body is to move the point of separation as far back as possible and thus to produce the minimum size of turbulent wake.⑥ This decreases the pressure drag, but by making the body longer so as to promote a gradual increase in pressure, the friction drag is increased. The optimum amount of streamlining, then, is that for which the sum of the friction and pressure drag is a minimum. Quite evidently, from what we have learned, attention in streamlining must be given to the rear end, or downstream part, of a body as well as to the front. The shape of the forebody is important principally to the extent that it governs the location of the separation point (s) on the afterbody. A rounded nose produces the least disturbance in the streamlines and is therefore the best form for incompressible or compressible flow at subsonic velocities.

New Words and Expressions

drag [dræg]		n.	阻力
friction drag			摩擦阻力
pressure drag			压力阻力
well-streamlined		a.	流线型的
hull [hʌl]		n.	船壳,外壳
wake [weik]		n.	尾流,尾波
wake resistance			尾流阻力
customary *	['kʌstəməri]	a.	惯例的
flat disk			平盘
foregoing	[fɔː'gəuiŋ]	a.	在前的,前述的
sphere	[sfiə]	n.	球,范围
equate	[i'kweit]	vt.	使相等
versus *	['vəːsəs]	prep.	对
transition *	[træn'siʒən]	n.	过渡,变迁
prematurely *	[ˌpremə'tjuəli]	ad.	过早地
induce *	[in'djuːs]	vt.	引起,感应
roughen	['rʌfən]	vt.	使变粗糙

effectiveness [i'fektivnis]	n.	有效度，有效性
golf [gɔlf]	n.	高尔夫球
perforate ['pə:fəreit]	vt.	穿孔于，打眼于
smooth-surfaced	a.	表面平滑的
optimum * ['ɔptiməm]	a.	最适的，最佳的
forebody ['fɔ:ˌbɔdi]	n.	（机船）前部
afterbody ['ɑ:ftəˌbɔdi]	n.	（机船）后部

Notes

①Only rarely is it… from the friction drag.
only：置于句首，句子部分倒置；only rarely：只是偶尔。

②If the body… or turbulent：
句中 whether 引导的句子作介词 by 的宾语从句。

③For a considerable range… at about 0.45：
句子的主语是 conditions；谓语是 remain；句中的 the laminar boundary layer separating from… 和 and to remaining… 是分词独立结构作状语补充说明全句。

④The transition from a laminar to a turbulent boundary layer… over a local region：此句是一个被动结构的句子，主要结构是：The transition…may be…induced by…

⑤A smooth-surfaced ball would have greater…and would not travel as far when driven.
smooth-surfaced ball：表面平滑的球；overall drag：整体阻力；would not travel as far when driven：是个省略句，可还原为：would not travel as far as a rough-surfaced ball when it was driven.

⑥It may be pointed out… wake：
句中 to move… and thus to produce… 两个不定式短语并列作表语。

Exercises

Reading Comprehension

I. Match Column A with Column B according to the text.

A	B
1. the friction drag	a. a body with the shape that offers least resistance to the flow of air, water, etc.
2. the pressure drag	b. the forepart or front part
3. a streamlined body	c. the force coming from the friction
4. the wake resistance	d. the principles that is mentioned above

5. the foregoing principles
6. the rear stagnation
7. the point of separation
8. the forward stagnation point
9. forebody
10. subsonic velocities

e. the resistance coming from the wake
f. the force that comes from the pressure
g. the speed which is less than the speed of sound
h. the point from which the fluid and the body are separated
i. the point which is in the front of the body
j. the point which is at the back of the body

II. Complete the following sentences with the information given in the text.
1. The total drag on a body is the sum of the _____ drag and the pressure _____.
2. In the case of a body with sharp corners, separation always occurs at the _____.
3. It may be pointed out here that the object of streamlining a body is to move the point of _____ as far back as possible and thus to produce the minimum _____ of turbulent wake.
4. The optimum amount of streamlining, then is that for which the sum of the friction and pressure drag is a _____.
5. A smooth-surfaced ball would have greater overall drag and would not travel as when _____.

Vocabulary

I. Fill in the blanks with the words given below. Change the forms if necessary.

drag	optimum	customary	sphere	versus
transition	something like	prematurely	induce	effectiveness

1. How much do you earn for such a work? _____ $2000.
2. The _____ growth temperature for crops is from 10℃ to 25℃.
3. Now we are in the period of _____ and we should be ready for living a hard life.
4. It is _____ to employ a single equation which gives the total drag.
5. The _____ of the measures we've taken can be seen clearly and we should do something again before it's too late.
6. The treatment of fluid resistance in the foregoing sections has been the _____ of the boundary layer along a smooth flat plate located in an unconfined fluid.
7. This is a football match Shanghai _____ Sian and it must be very interesting and exciting.
8. The boy's parents died from traffic accident when the boy was only nine and he suffered a lot of the hardships of the world _____.
9. Our teacher had many illnesses _____ by overwork and he died while teaching on

the platform of the classroom.

10. I'm in charge of this block and beyond that street it is not the _____ of my influence.

II. Find words in the text which mean almost the same as the following.
   1. Para. 1: the force that slows down progress or make something move slowly (_____)
   2. Para. 1: in agreement with, according to, custom (_____)
   3. Para. 3: (in law and sport; often shortened to v. in print) against (_____)
   4. Para. 6: done, happening, doing something., before the right or usual time (_____)
   5. Para. 6: make a hole or holes in; make a row of tiny holes (in paper) so that part may be torn off easily (_____)

Reading Material A

Lift and Drag Concepts

When any body moves through a fluid an interaction between the body and the fluid occurs; this effect can be described in terms of the forces at the fluid-body interface.① This can be described in terms of the stresses—wall shear stresses, τ_w, due to viscous effects and normal stresses due to the pressure, p. Typical shear stress and pressure distributions are shown in Figs. 11-2. a and 11-2. b. Both τ_w and p vary in magnitude and direction along the surface.

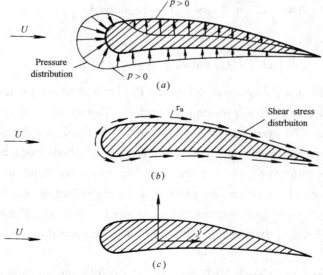

Fig. 11-2 Force from the surrounding fluid on a two-dimensional object:
(a) pressure force, (b) viscous force, (c) resultant force (lift and drag)

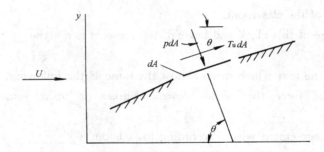

Fig. 11-3 Pressure and shear force on a small element of the surface of a body

It is often useful to know the detailed distribution of shear stress and pressure over the surface of the body. Many times, however, only the integrated or resultant effects of these distributions are needed. The resultant force in the direction of the upstream velocity is termed the drag, R, and the resultant force normal to the upstream velocity is termed the lift, L, as is indicated in Fig. 11.2.c.[2] For some three-dimensional bodies there may also be a side force that is perpendicular to the plane containing R and L.

The resultant of the shear stress and pressure distributions can be obtained by integrating the effect of these two quantities on the body surface as is indicated in Fig. 11-3. The x and y components of the fluid force on the small area element dA are

$$dF_x = (pdA)\cos\theta + (\tau_w dA)\sin\theta$$

and

$$dF_y = -(pdA)\sin\theta + (\tau_w dA)\cos\theta$$

Thus, the net x and y components of the force on the object are

$$R = \int dF_x = \int p\cos\theta dA + \int \tau_w \sin\theta dA \qquad (11.3)$$

and

$$L = \int dF_y = -\int p\sin\theta dA + \int \tau_w \cos\theta dA \qquad (11.4)$$

Of course, to carry out the integrations and determine the lift and drag, we must know the body shape and the distribution of τ_w and p along the surface. These distributions are often extremely difficult to obtain. The pressure distribution can be obtained experimentally without too much difficulty by use of a series of static pressure taps along the body surface. On the other hand, it is usually quite difficult to measure the wall shear stress distribution.

It is seen that both the shear stress and pressure force contribute to the lift and drag, since for an arbitrary body θ is neither zero nor 90° along the entire body. The exception is a flat plate aligned either parallel to the upstream flow ($\theta = 90°$) or normal to the upstream flow ($\theta = 0°$).

Although Eqs. 11.3 and 11.4 are valid for any body, the difficulty in their use lies in obtaining the appropriate shear stress and pressure distributions on the body surface.[3] Considerable effort has gone into determining these quantities, but because of the various complexities involved, such information is available only for certain simple situations.

Without detailed information concerning the shear stress and pressure distributions on a body, Eqs. 11.3 and 11.4 cannot be used. The widely used alternative is to define dimensionless lift and drag coefficients and determine their values by means of either a simplified analysis, some numerical technique, or an appropriate experiment. The lift coefficient, C_L, and drag coefficient, C_D, are defined as

$$C_L = \frac{R}{\frac{1}{2}\rho U^2 A}$$

and

$$C_D = \frac{L}{\frac{1}{2}\rho U^2 A}$$

where A is a characteristic area of the object. Typically, A is taken to be frontal area—the projected area seen by a person looking toward the object from a direction parallel to the upstream velocity, U. It would be the area of the shadow on a screen normal to the upstream velocity as formed by a light shining along the upstream flow. In other situations A is taken to be the planform area—the projected area seen by an observer looking toward the object from a direction normal to the upstream velocity. Obviously, which characteristic area is used in the definition of the lift and drag coefficients must be clearly stated.

Notes

① 当一个物体在液体里面运动时，物体和液体之间产生相互作用，这种效果可用物体-液体界面力来描述。
② 由此产生的逆速度方向的合力被称为阻力。由此产生的与逆速度成垂直方向的力被称为升力。
③ 如果没有关于剪应力和物体上压力分布的详细信息，方程11.3和11.4就不能使用。广泛使用的选择方法就是限定无量纲的升力和阻力系数并且确定它们的值，确定这些值时可以通过简化的分析方法（某种数学技术）或是通过适当的试验。

Reading Material B

Boundary-layer Separation and Pressure Drag

The motion of a thin stratum of fluid lying wholly inside the boundary layer is determined by three forces:
1. The forward pull of the outer free-moving fluid.
2. The viscous retarding effect of the solid boundary which must hold the fluid stratum imme-

diately adjacent to it at rest.

3. The pressure gradient along the boundary. The stratum is accelerated by a pressure gradient whose pressure decreases in the direction of flow and is retarded by an adverse gradient.

The treatment of fluid resistance in the foregoing sections has been restricted the drag of the boundary layer along a smooth flat plate located in an unconfined fluid. In the presence of a favorable pressure gradient the boundary layer is "held" in place. This is what occurs in the accelerated flow around the forebody. If a particle enters the boundary layer near the forward stagnation point with a low velocity and high pressure, its velocity will increase as it flows into the lower pressure region along the side of the body. But there will be some retardation from wall friction so that its total useful energy will be reduced by a corresponding conversion into thermal energy.①

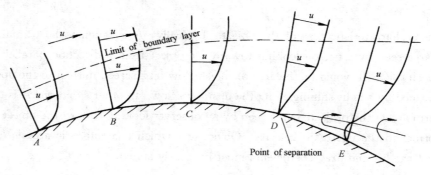

Fig. 11-4 Growth and separation of boundary layer owing to increasing pressure gradient. Note that U has its maximum value at B and then gets saller.

What happens next may best be explained by reference to Fig. 11-4. Let A represent a point in the region of accelerated flow, while B is the point where the velocity outside the boundary layer reaches a maximum. Then C, D, and E are points downstream where the velocity outside the boundary layer decreases. Thus the velocity of the layer close to the wall is reduced at C and finally brought to a stop at D. Now the increasing pressure calls for further retardation; but this is impossible, and so the boundary layer actually separates from the wall. At E there is a backflow next to the wall.

Downstream from the point of separation the flow is characterized by irregular turbulent eddies, formed as the separated boundary layer becomes rolled up in the reversed flow. This condition generally extends for some distance downstream until the eddies are worn away by viscous attrition. The whole disturbed region is called the turbulent wake of the body.

Because the eddies cannot convert their kinetic energy of rotation into an increased pressure, the pressure within the wake remains close to that at the separation point.② Since this is always less than the pressure at the forward stagnation point, there results a net pressure difference tending to move the body with the flow, and this force is the pressure drag.

Although the laminar and turbulent boundary layers behave in essentially the same manner at a point of separation. the location of the separation point on a given curved surface will be very different for the two cases. In the laminar layer the transfer of momentum from the rapidly moving outer strata through the viscous-shear process to the inner strata is slow and ineffective. Consequently, the laminar boundary layer is "weak" and cannot long stick to the wall against an adverse pressure gradient. The transition to a turbulent boundary layer, on the other hand, brings a violent mixing of the faster-moving outer strata into the slower-moving inner strata, and vice versa. The mean velocity close to the boundary is greatly increased. This added energy enables the boundary layer better to withstand the adverse pressure gradient, with the result that with a turbulent boundary layer the point of separation is moved downstream to a region of higher pressure.③

Notes

①但由于器壁摩擦而产生滞留，这样总的有用能量就会减少，减少的能量相应地转换成热能。
②因为涡流不能把它自身的旋转动力转化成增加了的压力，尾流里的压力和分离点的压力接近。
③这个增加了的能量可使得边界层能更好地经受逆向压力梯度。结果，紊流边界层里分离点向下游的高压区域移动。

UNIT TWELVE

Text   Actual Radiation

[1] Substances and surfaces diverge variously from the Stefan-Boltzmann and Planck Laws. W_b and $W_{b\lambda}$ are the maximum emissive powers at a surface temperature. Actual surfaces emit and absorb less readily and are called nonblack. The emissive power of a nonblack surface, at temperature T, radiating to the hemispherical region above it is written as[①]:

$$W = \varepsilon W_b = \varepsilon \sigma T^4 \qquad (12.1)$$

where ε is called the hemispherical emittance. The emittance is a function of the material, the condition of its surface and the temperature of the surface. Selected values and more extensive lists are given before.

The monochromatic emissive power of a nonblack surface is similarly written as:

$$W_\lambda = \varepsilon_\lambda W_{b\lambda} = \varepsilon_\lambda (C_1 \lambda^{-5}/e^{c_2/\lambda T} - 1) \qquad (12.2)$$

where ε_λ is the monochromatic hemispherical emittance. The relationship between ε and ε_λ is given by:

$$\varepsilon = (1/\sigma T^4) \int_0^\infty \varepsilon_\lambda W_{b\lambda} d\lambda \qquad (12.3)$$

[2] If ε_λ does not depend on λ, then, from Eq. 12.3, $\varepsilon = \varepsilon_\lambda$, surfaces with this characteristic are called gray. Gray-surface characteristics are often assumed in calculations. Several important classes of surfaces approximate this condition in some regions of the spectrum. The simplicity is desirable, but care must be exercised, especially if temperatures are high. Assumption of grayness is sometimes made, because of the absence of information relating ε_λ and λ.

[3] When radiant energy falls on a surface, it can be absorbed, reflected or transmitted through the material. Therefore, from the First Law of Thermodynamics:

$$\alpha + \tau + \rho = 1 \qquad (12.4)$$

where

α = fraction of incident radiation absorbed or absorptance

τ = fraction of incident radiation transmitted or transmittance

ρ = fraction of incident radiation reflected or reflectance

If the material is opaque, as most solids are in the infrared, $\tau = 0$ and $\alpha + \rho = 1$.[②]

[4] For a black surface, $\alpha = 1$, $\rho = 0$ and $\tau = 0$. Platinum black and gold black have absorptances or about 98% in the infrared which is as black as any actual surface is. Any desired degree of blackness can be simulated by a small hole in a large enclosure. Consider a ray of radiant energy entering the opening. It will undergo many internal reflections and be almost completely absorbed before it has a reasonable probability of passing back out the opening.

[5] Certain flat black paints also exhibit emittances of 98% over a wide range of conditions. They provide a much more durable surface than gold or platinum black and are frequently used

on radiation instruments and as standard reference in emittance or reflectance measurements.

[6] Kirchhoff's law, relating emittance and absorptance of any opaque surface from thermodynamic considerations, states that for any surface where the incident radiation is independent of angle or where the surface is diffuse, $\varepsilon_\lambda = \alpha_\lambda$.[3] If the surface is gray, or the incident radiation is from a black surface at the same temperature, then also $\varepsilon = \alpha$, but many surfaces are not gray. For most surfaces, absorptance for solar radiation is different than emittance for low temperature level radiation. This is because the wavelength distributions are different in the two cases, and ε_λ varies with wavelength.

[7] The foregoing discussion relates to total hemispherical radiation from surfaces. No discussion has been given to energy distribution over the hemispherical region above the surface, but this has an important effect on the rate of heat transfer in various geometric arrangements.

[8] Lambert's Law states that the emissive power of radiant energy over a hemispherical surface above the emitting surface varies as the cosine of the angle between the normal to the radiating surface and the line joining the radiating surface to the point of the hemispherical surface.[4] Such radiation is called diffuse radiation. This Lambert emissive power variation is equivalent to assuming that radiation from a surface in a direction other than normal occurs as if it came from an equivalent area with the same emissive power (per unit area) as the original surface.[5] The equivalent area is obtained by projecting the original area onto a plane normal to the direction of radiation. Black surfaces obey the Lambert Law exactly. It is approximate for many actual radiation and reflection processes, especially involving rough surfaces and nonmetallic materials. Most radiation analyses are based on the assumption of gray-diffuse radiation and reflection.

[9] In estimating heat transfer rates between surfaces of different geometries, radiation characteristics and orientations, it is usually assumed that: (1) all surfaces are gray or black, (2) radiation and reflection are diffuse, (3) properties are uniform over the surfaces, (4) absorptance equals emittance and is independent of the temperature of the source of incident radiation and (5) the material in the space between the radiating surfaces neither emits nor absorbs radiation.

[10] These assumptions are used because of the considerable simplification they provide, although results must be considered approximate.

New Words and Expressions

diverge [dai'və:dʒ]	vi.	偏离，离题
Stefan-Beltzmann Law		斯蒂芬-波尔兹曼定律
Planck Law		普朗克定律
emissive [i'misiv]	a.	辐（发）射的
nonblack		非黑体
hemispherical [hemi'sferikəl]	a.	半球的

emittance	[iˈmitəns]	n.	辐(发)射率
monochromatic	[mɔnəkrəˈmætik]	a.	单色的
spectrum *	[ˈspektrəm]	n.	光谱
incident	[ˈinsidənt]	a.	入射的
opaque	[əuˈpeik]	a.	不透明的
infrared	[ˈinfrəˈred]	n.	红外线区
platinum	[ˈplætinəm]	n.	白金
simulate *	[ˈsimjuleit]	vt.	模拟
enclosure *	[inˈkləuʒə]	n.	围绕物，围墙(栏)，箱
Kirchhoff Law			基尔霍夫定律
diffuse *	[diˈfju:s]	a.	漫射的
geometric	[dʒiəˈmetrik]	a.	几何的
Lambert Law			兰贝特定律
cosine	[ˈkəusain]	n.	(数)余弦
orientation *	[ˌɔːrienˈteiʃən]	n.	方位

Notes

①The emissive power of... is written as:
  句中 radiating... 为现在分词短语作定语修饰 the emissive power。

②If the material... and $\alpha+\rho=1$:
  句中 as 引导的是定语句从句，修饰说明 the material is opaque。

③Kirchhoff's Law,... $\varepsilon_\lambda = \alpha_\lambda$:
  句中 relating... 为现在分词短语作定语修饰 Kirchhoff's Law，句子的主语是 Kirchhoff's Law，谓语是 state，that 引导的是宾语从句($\varepsilon_\lambda = \alpha_\lambda$)，其中有两个 where 引导的定语从句修饰 any surface。

④Lambert's Law... surface:
  句子的主语是 Lambert's Law，谓语动词是 state，that 引出宾语从句，(主语是 the emissive power... the emitting surface, 谓语是 varied as); joining... surface 现在分词短语作定语修饰 the line。

⑤assuming that... 动名词短语作... to 的宾语; other than normal 修饰 direction。

Exercises

Reading Comprehension

Ⅰ. Answer the following questions by choosing the right choices or putting in the missing words.

1. How many kinds of laws are mentioned in the text?
   (a) Two
   (b) Four
2. What are they?
   (a) The First Law of Thermodynamics, Kirchhoff's Law, Stefan-Boltzmann, and Lambert's Law.
   (b) Kirchhoff's Law and Lambert's Law.
3. What do the following two laws state?
   (a) Kirchhoff's law states _____
   _____
   _____
   _____.

   (b) Lambert's law states _____
   _____
   _____
   _____.

II. Tell the kinds of radiations mentioned in the text by putting in the missing words according to the first letter given.

   1. i_____
   2. s_____
   3. l_____
   4. t_____ radiation (s)
   5. d_____
   6. a_____
   7. g_____

III. Put a tick before the correct ones according to the last two paragraphs.

   In estimating heat transfer rates between surfaces of different geometries, radiation characteristics and orientations, it is usually assumed that:

   1. all surfaces are gray or black.
   2. black surfaces obey the Lambent Law exactly.
   3. radiation and reflection are diffuse.
   4. properties are uniform over the surfaces.
   5. this has an important effect on the rate of heat transfer in various geometric arrangement.
   6. absorptance equals emittance and is independent of the temperature of the source of incident radiation.
   7. the incident radiation is from a black surface at the same temperature.
   8. the material in the space between the radiating surfaces neither emits nor absorbs radiation.

Vocabulary

I. Match the words in Column A with their corresponding definitions in Column B

A	B
1. spectrum	a. an enclosed space; something (as a fence) that encloses
2. simulate	b. imitate
3. enclosure	c. image of a band of colors (as seen in a rainbow) formed by a ray of light which has passed through a prism.
4. diffuse	d. placing or exactly determining the position of (sth.) with regard to the points of the compass.
5. orientation	e. poured or spread out; not concentrated; scattered;

Now use the words from (1-5) above to complete the following sentences. Change the forms if necessary.

6. Several important classes of surfaces approximate this condition in some regions of the _____.

7. These kinds of light are called _____ light.

8. Any desired degree of blackness can be simulated by a small hole in a large _____.

9. The _____ diagram is very important in these materials.

10. They say the space conditions can be _____ by scientists and specialists.

II. Fill in the blanks with the words given below. Change the forms if necessary

geometric	platinum,	emittance
monochromatic,	infrared,	

1. The _____ is a function of the material, the condition of its surface and the temperature of the surface.

2. These students of the Chinese Department can not fully understand _____ rays which belong to the special terms.

3. Certain flat black paints provide a much more durable surface than gold or _____ black and are frequently used on radiation instruments.

4. The discussion has an important effect on the rate of heat transfer in various _____ arrangements.

5. The _____ emissive power of a nonblack surface is similar to that kind of power.

Reading Material A

Radiation in Gases

Elementary gases such as oxygen, nitrogen, hydrogen and helium are essentially transparent to thermal radiation.[①] Their absorption and emission bands are confined mainly to the ultraviolet region of the spectrum. The gaseous vapors of most compounds, however, have absorption bands in the infrared region. Carbon monoxide, carbon dioxide, water vapor, sulfur dioxide, ammonia, acid vapors and organic vapors absorb and emit significant amounts of energy. Air containing water vapor and carbon dioxide is of primary concern to the heating and air-conditioning engineer.

Radiation exchange by opaque solids is considered a surface phenomenon. Radiant energy does, however, penetrate the surface of all materials. The rate of exponential attenuation of the energy is given by the absorption coefficient.[②] Metals have large absorption coefficients, and radiant energy penetrates only a few hundred angstroms at most. Absorption coefficients for nonmetals are lower. It is safe to consider radiation as a surface phenomenon unless the material is transparent. Gases, however, have small absorption coefficients, so the path length of radiation through gas becomes very significant.

Beer's Law states that the attenuation of radiant energy in a gas is a function of the product of the partial pressure of the gas times the path length ($p_g L$). The monochromatic absorptance of a body of gas of thickness L is then given by:

$$\alpha_{\lambda L} = 1 - e^{-\alpha \lambda L} \tag{12.5}$$

Since absorption occurs in discrete wavelengths, it is necessary to sum the absorptances over the spectral region corresponding to the temperature of the blackbody radiation passing through the gas. The monochromatic absorption coefficient, α_λ, is also a function of temperature and pressure of the gas. Therefore, detailed treatment of gas radiation is quite complex.

Table* Emittance of CO_2 and Water Vapor in Air at 75 F

Path Length	CO_2 (% by volume)			Relative Humidity, %		
ft	0.1	0.3	1.0	10	50	100
10	0.03	0.06	0.09	0.06	0.17	0.22
100	0.09	0.12	0.16	0.22	0.39	0.47
1000	0.16	0.19	0.23	0.47	0.64	0.70

Estimated emittance for carbon dioxide and water vapor in air at 297 K is a function of concentration and path length (Table*). The values are for a hemispherically shaped body of gas radiating to an element of area at the center of the hemisphere. Geometrical calculations are available. Generally, at low values of p_gL, the meat path length L or equivalent hemispherical radius for a gas body radiating to its surrounding surfaces, is four times the mean hydraulic radius of the enclosure. A room with a dimensional ratio of 1 : 1 : 4 has a mean path length of 0.89 times the shortest dimension when considering radiation to all walls.[3] For a room with a dimensional ratio of 1 : 2 : 6, the mean path length for the gas radiating to all surfaces is 1.2 times the shortest dimension. The mean path length for radiation to the 2×6 face is 1.18 times the shortest dimension. These values are for cases where the partial pressure of the gas times the mean path length approaches zero ($p_gL \approx 0$). The factor decreases with increasing values of p_gL. For an average room with approximately 2.44-m ceilings and relative humidity ranging from 10 to 75% at 297 K, the effective path length for carbon dioxide radiation is about 85% of the ceiling height, or 2.07 m. The effective path length for water vapor would be about 93% of the ceiling height, or 2.26 m. The effective emittance of the water vapor and carbon dioxide radiating to the walls, ceiling and floor of a room 4.88 m $\times$ 14.63 m with 2.44-m walls is in the following tabulation.

Relative Humidity, %	t_g
10	0.10
50	0.19
75	0.22

The radiation hear transfer from the gas to the walls is then:
$$q = \sigma A_w \varepsilon_g (T_g^4 - T_w^4) \tag{12.6}$$

This discussion of radiation in gases is somewhat superficial. The examples in Table* and the preceding text indicate the importance of gas radiation in environmental heat transfer problems. Gas radiation in large furnaces is the dominant mode of heat transfer, and many additional factors must be considered. Increased pressure broadens the spectral bands, and interaction of different radiating species prohibits simple summation of the emittance factors for the individual species. Departures from blackbody conditions necessitate separate calculations of the emittance and absorptance.[4] More complete treatments of gas radiation are available.

Notes

①热辐射实质上可以透过诸如氧、氮、氢和氦之类的单质气体。
②能量的指数衰减速率由吸收系数给出。
③在考虑到所有墙体的辐射时，尺寸比为1∶1∶4的房间中，平均辐射距离是最小长度的0.89倍。
④在非黑体的条件下就有必要分别计算发射率和吸收率。

Reading Material B

Radiation

Every free surface emits energy in the form of electromagnetic waves; the amount of energy is a function of the surface temperature. This emitted energy is known as radiant thermal energy. The nature of this radiant energy is not completely understood, but laws have been formulated that describe its behavior. It is recognized that, as with other forms of radiant energy, radiant heat energy is transmitted in the form of electromagnetic waves. The complete formulation of the laws governing radiant heat energy must consider that this energy is quantized, that is, the energy is transferred in quanta.[①] In contrast with other modes of heat transfer, no medium is required to transmit radiant energy. In fact some gases, for instance, carbon dioxide and water vapor, absorb some of the radiant energy passing through them.

For a fixed set of conditions, any free surface emits radiant energy of varying wavelengths. The frequency of vibration (ν) of radiant waves is dependent solely on the source of radiation and is independent of the medium through which they pass. The velocity of radiant waves (V) is a function solely of the medium through which they pass. Thus, the wavelength ($\lambda = V/\nu$) is a function of both the source and the medium.

All free surfaces receive radiant energy from all other surfaces that they can "see," that is, surfaces in direct line of sight. Most problems in radiation deal with the net radiant energy exchanged between a given surface and those that surround it. In common parlance, the term "heat exchanged by radiation" is used. It must be emphasized, however, that radiation is not heat. Heat is conducted to a surface. By virtue of the temperature of a surface, electromagnetic waves transmit energy from the surface. When these strike another surface, part of the energy will be absorbed, tending to increase the temperature of the surface struck by them, and part will be reflected. When the object is transparent, or partially so, to radiant waves, some or all of the radiant energy received by the surface will pass into the object. The transparency of an object to radiant energy is a function of the wavelength of the radiant waves. These statements relating to the radiant energy received by a surface may be put in equation form as follows:

$$\alpha + \rho + \tau = 1 \tag{12.7}$$

where α = absorptivity, or the portion of the radiant energy that is absorbed;
   ρ = reflectivity, or the portion of the radiant energy that is reflected;
   τ = transmissivity, or the portion of the radiant energy that is transmitted.

A black surface has an absorptivity close to unity. For this reason the term blackbody has been used to designate an imaginary object whose surface has an absorptivity of unity. Since no known surface completely absorbs radiant energy, the term blackbody refers to an ideal surface.② Kirchhoff conceived a method of completely absorbing radiant energy. Assume that a hollow sphere contains a very small opening, as is indicated in Fig. 12-1. Radiation entering this opening will be received by the back wall of the sphere. Here it will be partially absorbed and partially reflected to other parts of the walls of the sphere. The reflected waves are, in turn, partially reflected, so that each reflected portion is a progressively smaller portion of the energy entering the sphere until ultimately all of it is absorbed. Strictly speaking, some of the reflected radiant energy will pass out through the hole. However, the surface area of the sphere is πD^2. Hence, when the diameter of the sphere is chosen to be 50 times that of the opening, the inside surface area is 10,000 times that of the opening, and it may be assumed that the hollow sphere absorbs all of the radiant energy.③

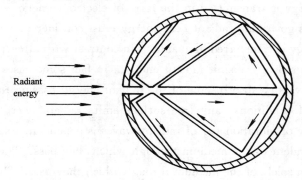

Fig. 12-1 Radiant energy absorbed in a hollow sphere.

The amount of radiant energy emitted by a surface is a function of the nature of the surface and its temperature. The term blackbody is also used to denote a surface that emits the maximum conceivable amount of radiant energy at any given temperature.④ There is no actual surface that is a perfect emitter, but the hollow-sphere concept may be used to establish a standard.⑤ The process of emission from the inner surface of the sphere is the reverse of that of absorption.

The total radiant energy emitted in a unit time by a unit area is known as the total emissive power and is designated by E. Since radiant energy is emitted over a range of wavelengths,

$$E = \int_{\lambda=0}^{\lambda=\infty} E_\lambda d\lambda \qquad (12.8)$$

where E_λ is the monochromatic emissive power. It is assumed that E_λ in E_q. 12.8 is a continuous function of λ.

Notes

①决定辐射热能定理的完整公式必须考虑这种能量是量子化的,即这种能量以量子的形式传递。

②由于现在还没有一种已知的表面完全吸收辐射能,术语"blackbody"指的是理想表面。

③因此，当该球体的直径选为该小孔直径的 50 倍时，内表面积是小孔面积的 10,000 倍，并且可以认为该空心球体吸收了所有的辐射能。
④术语"blackbody"也用来指一种表面，这个表面在任意指定温度下释放可以想象的最大辐射能。
⑤属于完善辐射体的实际表面是没有的，但空心球的概念可以用来建立一个标准。

UNIT THIRTEEN

Text   Categories of Compressible Flow

[1]　　The effects of compressibility become more significant as the Mach number increases. For example, the error associated with calculating the stagnation pressure of an ideal gas with $\rho V^2/2$ increases at larger Mach numbers.①

[2]　　To further illustrate some curious features of compressible flow, a simplified example is considered. Imagine the emission of weak pressure pulses from a point source. These pressure waves are spherical and expand radially outward from the point source at the speed of sound, c. For a stationary point source, the symmetrical wave pattern shown in Fig. 13-1a is involved.

[3]　　When the point source moves to the left with a constant velocity, V, the wave pattern is no longer symmetrical. In Figs. 13-1b, 13-1c, and 13-1(d) are illustrated the wave patterns at $t=3$ s for different values of V.

[4]　　From the pressure wave patterns of Fig. 13-1, we can draw some useful conclusions. Before doing this we should recognize that if instead of moving the point source to the left, we held the point source stationary and moved the fluid to the right with velocity, V, the resulting pressure wave patterns would be identical to those indicated in Fig. 13-1.②

[5]　　When the point source and the fluid are stationary, the pressure wave pattern is symmetrical (Fig. 13-1a) and an observer anywhere in the pressure field would hear the same sound frequency from the point source. When the velocity of the point source is very small in comparison with the speed of sound, the pressure wave pattern will still be nearly symmetrical. The speed of sound in an incompressible fluid is infinitely large. Thus, the stationary point source and stationary fluid situation are representative of incompressible flows. For truly incompressible flows, the communication of pressure information throughout the flow field is unrestricted and instantaneous ($c=\infty$).

[6]　　When the point source moves in fluid at rest the pressure wave patterns vary in asymmetry, with the extent of asymmetry depending on the ratio of the point source velocity and the speed of sound.③ When $V/c<1$, the wave pattern is similar to the one shown in Fig. 13-1b. This flow is considered subsonic and compressible. A stationary observer will hear a different sound frequency coming from the point source depending on where the observer is relative to the source because the wave pattern is asymmetrical.④ We call this phenomenon the Doppler effect.

[7]　　When $V/c=1$ pressure waves are not present ahead of the moving point source. The flow is sonic. For flow moving past a stationary point source at the speed of sound ($V/c=1$), the pressure waves are all tangent to a plane that is perpendicular to the flow and that passes through the point source.⑤ The concentration of pressure waves in this tangent plane suggests

the formation of a significant pressure variation across the plane. This plane is often called a Mach wave. Note that communication of pressure information is restricted to the region of flow downstream of the Mach wave. The region of flow upstream of the Mach wave is called the zone of silence and the region of flow downstream of the tangent plane is called the zone of action.

[8]　　When $V>c$, the flow is supersonic and the pressure wave pattern resembles the one depicted in Fig. 13-1d. A cone (Mach cone) that is tangent to the pressure waves can be constructed to represent the Mach wave that separates the zone of silence from the zone of action in this case. The communication of pressure information is restricted to the zone of action. From the sketch of Fig. 13-1d, we can see that the angle of this cone, α, is given by

$$\sin\alpha = \frac{c}{V} = \frac{1}{\text{Ma}} \tag{13.1}$$

Equation 13.1 is often used to relate the Mach cone angle, α, and the flow Mach number, Ma, When studying flows involving $V/c>1$. The concentration of pressure waves at the surface of the Mach cone suggests a significant pressure, and thus density, variation across the cone surface. An abrupt density change can be visualized in a flow field by using special optics.

[9]　　This discussion about pressure wave patterns suggests the following categories of fluid flow.

1. Incompressible flow: Ma$\leqslant$0.3. Unrestricted, nearly symmetrical and instantaneous pressure communication.
2. Compressible subsonic flow: 0.3$<$Ma$<$1.0. Unrestricted but asymmetrical pressure communication.
3. Compressible supersonic flow: Ma$\geqslant$1.0. Formation of Mach wave; pressure communication restricted to zone of action.

[10]　　In addition to the above-mentioned categories of flows, two other regimes are commonly referred to: namely. transonic flows (0.9$\leqslant$Ma$\leqslant$1.2) and hypersonic flows (Ma$>$5). Modern aircraft are mainly powered by gas turbine engines that involve transonic flows. When a space shuttle reenters the earth's atmosphere, the flow is hypersonic. Future aircraft may be expected to operate from subsonic to hypersonic flow conditions.

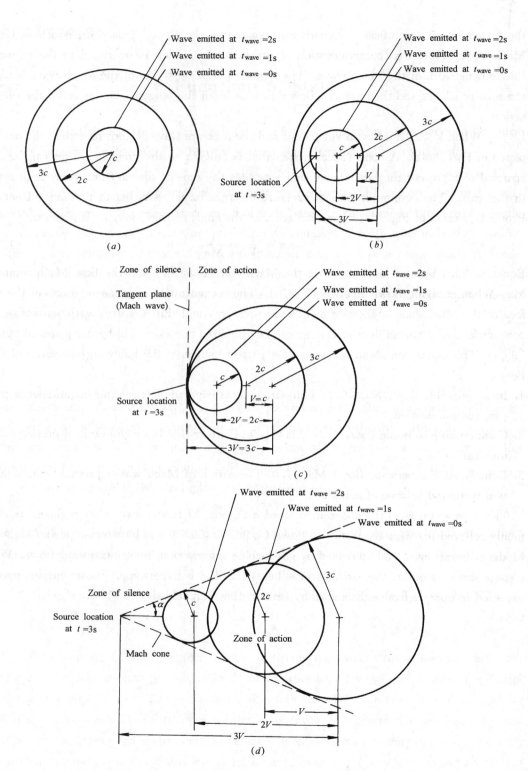

Fig. 13-1 (a) Pressure waves at $t=3$s; $V=0$ (b) Pressure waves at $t=3$s; $V<c$
(c) Pressure waves at $t=3$s; $V=c$ (d) Pressure waves at $t=3$s; $V>c$

New Words and Expressions

category * [ˈkætigəri]	n.	种类
the Mach number		马赫数
stagnation [stægˈneiʃən]	n.	停滞
emission [iˈmiʃən]	n.	散发
pressure wave		压力波
symmetrical [siˈmetrikəl]	a.	对称的，匀称的
stationary * [ˈsteiʃənəri]	a.	静止的
unrestricted [ˈʌnristriktid]	a.	不受限制的
instantaneous * [ˌinstənˈteinjəs]	a.	瞬间的，即刻的
asymmetry [æˈsimitri]	n.	不对称
subsonic [ˈsʌbˈsɔnik]	a.	亚音速的，亚声速的
asymmetrical [ˌæsiˈmetrikəl]	a.	不对称的
Doppler effect		多普勒效应
sonic [ˈsɔnik]	a.	音速的
tangent [ˈtændʒənt]	n.	正切，切线
perpendicular [ˈəːpəːpənˈdikjulə]	a.	垂直的，正交的
Mach wave		马赫波
downstream	ad.	在下游的
cone [kəun]	n.	锥形物，锥面
abrupt * [əˈbrʌpt]	a.	突然的
visualize * [ˈvizjuəlaiz]	vt.	使可见，见到
optic [ˈɔptik]	n.	光学
transonic [trænˈsɔnik]	a.	跨音速的
hypersonic [ˈhaipəˈsɔnik]	a.	特超音速的
shuttle [ˈʃʌtl]	n.	航天飞机

Notes

①For example,... Mach numbers:
句中 associated with... 为过去分词短语作定语修饰 the error，全句的主语是 the error associated with... at larger Mach numbers。

②Before doing this... in Fig13-1:
句中 that 引导的是宾语从句，这一宾语从句中有 if 引导的条件从句，条件句的主语是 we 谓语动词是 held 和 moved，主句的主语是 the resulting pressure wave patterns。

③When the point source... the speed of sound:

句中 with 引导的是分词独立结构作状语修饰全句。

④A stationary observer... is asymmetrical：

句中 coming... 为现在分词短语作定语修饰 frequency；depending on... 为现在分词短语作状语修饰全句。

⑤For flow moving... the point aource：

句中 moving... 为现在分词短语作状语修饰 flow；

that is... and that... 为定语从句修饰 a plane。

Exercises

Reading Comprehension

Ⅰ. Match Column A with Column B according to the text：

A	B
1. A point source	a. the waves which are symmetrical
2. a stationary point source	b. the speed which is constant
3. the symmetrical wave	c. the pressure wave patterns thus produced
4. a constant velocity	d. the pressure source is at a point wave pattern
5. the resulting pressure	e. rate of occurrence or number of repetitions in a given time for a sound
6. sound frequency	f. something which are not symmetrical
7. in asymmetry	g. the pressure source is at a stationary point
8. a moving point source	h. the pressure source is at a moving point
9. the zone of silence	i. the region which is free from action
10. the zone of action	j. the region in which the action occurs

Ⅱ. Complete the following sentences with the information given in the text：

1. The effects of compressibility become more significant as _____ increases.

2. When the point source and the fluid are stationary the pressure wave pattern is _____ and an observer anywhere in the pressure field would hear the _____ sound frequency from the point source.

3. when the point source moves in fluid _____ the pressure wave patterns vary in _____ with the extent of asymmetry depending on the ratio of the point source velocity and the speed of _____.

4. A stationary observer will hear a different sound frequency coming from the point source depending on where the observer is relative to the source because the wave pattern is asymmetrical. We call this phenomenon the _____.

5. The region of flow upstream of the Mach wave is called _____.

6. The region of flow downstream of the tangent plane is called _____.

7. Incompressible flow: Ma _____ 0.3. Unrestricted, nearly symmetrical and instantaneous pressure communication.
8. Compressible subsonic flow: 0.3 _____ Ma _____ 1.0. Unrestricted but asymmetrical pressure communication.
9. Compressible supersonic flow: Ma _____ 1.0. Formation of Mach wave; pressure communication restricted to zone of action.
10. In addition to the immediately above-mentioned categories of flows, two other regimes are the following: one is transonic flows _____ and the other is hypersonic flows _____.

Vocabulary

I. Fill in the blanks with the words given below. Change the forms if necessary.

category	hypersonic	emission	shuttle
stationary	transonic	instantaneous	perpendicular
abrupt	visualize		

1. When a space shuttle reenters the earth's atmosphere, the flow is _____, that is to say Ma>5.
2. The _____ of a volcano is smoke and ashes and generally it is very dangerous.
3. If we use the special optics an abrupt density change can be _____ in a flow field and it is easy to do this.
4. This kind of bombs is called _____ bomb which will explode in an instant.
5. Yesterday Mr. Zhang drove his new car in the street and collided with a _____ van and both engines were badly damaged.
6. We must be careful for the journey because the road is full of _____ turns.
7. There are many _____ of bikes and some of them are very expensive and some are much cheaper.
8. The _____ of "Challenge" of the United States exploded while traveling away from the atmosphere of the earth in 1986 and killed all the seven crew members.
9. Pressure waves are all tangent to a plane that is _____ to the flow and that passes through the point source.
10. A _____ plane is the one that fly faster than the speed of sound and when you hear the sound of it, the plane has already gone out of sight.

II. Match the words in Column A with their corresponding definitions in Column B.

A	B
1. category	a. sudden; unexpected
2. instantaneous	b. division or class in a complete system or grouping

3. abrupt c. happening, done, in an instant
4. subsonic d. (of speed) less than that of sound
5. transonic e. (of speed) faster than that of sound

Reading Material A

Effect of Flow Cross Section Area Variations

When fluid flows steadily through a conduit that has a flow cross section area that varies with axial distance, the conservation of mass (continuity) equation

$$\dot{m} = \rho A V = cons\tan t \qquad (13.2)$$

can be used to relate the flow rates at different sections.[①] For incompressible flow, the fluid density remains constant and the flow velocity from section to section varies inversely with cross section area. However, when the flow is compressible, density, cross section area, and flow velocity can all vary from section to section. We proceed to determine how fluid density and flow velocity change with axial location in a variable area duct when the fluid is an ideal gas and the flow through the duct is steady and isentropic.[②]

An appropriate equation in the streamwise direction for the steady, one dimensional, and isentropic (adiabatic and frictionless) flow is obtained as

$$\frac{dV}{V} = -\frac{dA}{A}\frac{1}{(1-\text{Ma}^2)} \qquad (13.3)$$

$$\frac{d\rho}{\rho} = \frac{dA}{A}\frac{\text{Ma}^2}{(1-\text{Ma}^2)} \qquad (13.4)$$

We can use Eq. 13.3 to conclude that when the flow is subsonic (Ma<1), velocity and section area changes are in opposite directions. In other words, the area increase associated with subsonic flow through a diverging duct like the one shown in Fig. 13-2a is accompanied by a velocity decrease.[③] Subsonic flow through a converging duct (see Fig. 13-2b) involves an increase of velocity. These trends are consistent with incompressible flow behavior.

Equation 13.3 also serves to show us that when the flow is supersonic (Ma>1), velocity and area changes are in the same direction. A diverging duct (Fig. 13-2a) will accelerate a supersonic flow. A converging duct (Fig. 13-2b) will decelerate a supersonic flows. These trend are the opposite of what happens for incompressible and subsonic compressible flows.

Using Eq. 13.4, we can conclude that for subsonic flows (Ma<1), density and area changes are in the same direction, whereas for supersonic flows (Ma>1), density and area changes are in opposite directions. Since ρAV must remain constant, when the duct diverges and the flow is subsonic, density and area both increase and thus flow velocity must decrease. However, for supersonic flow through a diverging duct, when the area increases, the density

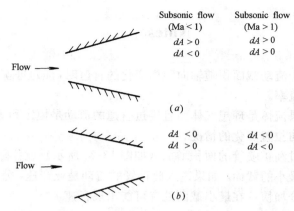

Fig. 13-2 (a) A diverging duct (b) A converging dct

decreases enough so that the flow velocity has to increase to keep ρAV constant.

By rearranging Eq. 13.3, we can obtain

$$\frac{dA}{dV} = -\frac{A}{V}(1 - \text{Ma}^2) \tag{13.5}$$

Equation 13.5 gives us some insight into what happens when Ma = 1. For Ma=1, Eq. 13.5 requires that $dA/dV = 0$. This result suggests that the area associated with Ma=1 is either a minimum on a maximum amount.

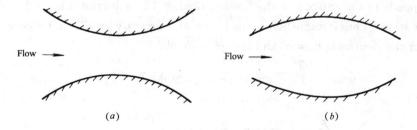

Fig. 13-3 (a) A converging-diverging duct; (b) A diverging-converging duct

A converging-diverging duct (Fig. 13-3a) involves a minimum area. If the flow entering such a duct were subsonic, Eq. 13.3 discloses that the fluid velocity would increase in the converging portion of the duct, and achievement of a sonic condition (Ma=1) at the minimum area location appears possible.[④] If the flow entering the converging-diverging duct is supersonic, Eq. 13.3 states that the fluid velocity would decrease in the converging portion of the duct and the sonic condition at the minimum area is possible.

A diverging-converging duct (Fig. 13-3b), on the other hand, would involve a maximum area. If the flow entering this duct were subsonic, the fluid velocity would decrease in the diverging portion of the duct and the sonic condition could not be attained at the maximum area location. For supersonic flow in the diverging portion of the duct, the fluid velocity would increase and thus Ma=1 at the maximum area is again impossible.

We conclude that the sonic condition (Ma=1) can be attained in a converging-diverging duct at the minimum area location.

Notes

①当流体稳定地流经一个流动截面积随轴向距离变化的管道时,质量守恒公式(13.2)可以用来说明不同位置的流率。

②我们接着来确定,如果流体是理想气体而且经过管道的流动是恒定和等熵时流体密度和流速随变面积风管轴向位置变化的情况。

③换句话说,亚音速穿过渐扩喷管的面积增加(如图13-2a所示)就伴随着速度的减少。

④渐缩渐扩喷管有一个最小的截面。如果进入此种管的流动是亚音速,公式13.3就显示了流速将在管的渐缩部分加快,在最小截面处有可能出现音速。

Reading Material B

Converging-diverging Duct Flow

It is convenient to use the stagnation state of the fluid as a reference state for compressible flow calculations. The stagnation state is associated with zero flow velocity and an entropy value that corresponds to the entropy of the flowing fluid.① The subscript 0 is used to designate the stagnation state. Thus, stagnation temperature and pressure are T_0 and P_0, we demonstrated that for the isentropic flow of an ideal gas, we obtain

$$\frac{T}{T_0} = \frac{1}{1 + [(k-1)/2]\text{Ma}^2} \tag{13.6}$$

$$\frac{p}{p_0} = \left\{ \frac{1}{1 + [(k-1)/2]\text{Ma}^2} \right\}^{k/(k-1)} \tag{13.7}$$

$$\frac{\rho}{\rho_0} = \left\{ \frac{1}{1 + [(k-1)/2]\text{Ma}^2} \right\}^{1/(k-1)} \tag{13.8}$$

A very useful means of keeping track of the states of an isentropic flow of an ideal gas involves a temperature-entropy (T-s) diagram as is shown in Fig. 13-4. Experience has shown, that lines of constant pressure are generally as are sketched in Fig. 13-4. An isentropic flow is confined to a vertical line on a T-s diagram.② The vertical line in Fig. 13-4 is representative of flow between the stagnation state and any state within the converging-diverging nozzle. Equation 13.6 shows that fluid temperature decreases with an increase in Mach number. Thus, the lower temperature levels on a T-s diagram correspond to higher Mach numbers. Equation 13.7 suggests that fluid pressure also decreases with an increase in Mach number. Thus, lower fluid temperatures and pressures are associated with higher Mach numbers in our isentropic converging-diverging duct example.

One way to produce flow through a converging-diverging duct like the one in Fig. 13-3a is to connect the downstream end of the duct to a vacuum pump. Neglecting friction and heat transfer and considering the air to act as an ideal gas. Eqs. 13. 6, 13. 7 and 13. 8 and a T-s diagram can be used to describe steady flow through the converging-diverging duct.

If the pressure in the duct is only slightly less than atmospheric pressure, we predict with Eq. 13. 7 that the Mach numbers levels in the duct will be low. Thus, with Eq. 13. 8 we conclude that the variation of fluid density in the duct is also small. The continuity equation leads us to state that there is a small amount of fluid flow acceleration in the converging portion of the duct followed by flow deceleration in the diverging portion of the duct.[3] We considered this type of flow when we discussed the Venturi meter, The T-s diagram for this flow is sketched in Fig. 13-5.

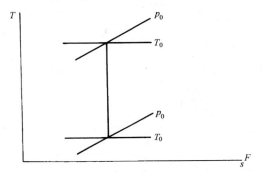

Fig. 13-4 The T-s diagram relating stagnation and static states

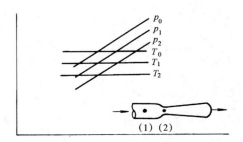

Fig. 13-5 The T-s diagram for Venturi meter flow

We next consider what happens when the back pressure is lowered further. Since the flow starts from rest upstream of the converging portion of the duct of Fig. 13-3a, Eqs. 13. 3 and 13. 5 reveal to us that flow up to the nozzle throat can be accelerated to a maximum allowable Mach number of 1 at the throat. Thus, when the duct back pressure is lowered sufficiently, the Mach number at the throat of the duct will be 1. Any further decrease of the back pressure will not affect the flow in the converging portion of the duct because information about pressure cannot move upstream when Ma=1. When Ma=1 at the throat of the converging-diverging duct, we have a condition called choked flow.

We have already used the stagnation state for which Ma=0 as a reference condition. It will prove helpful to us to use the state associated with Ma=1 and the same entropy level as the flowing fluid as another reference condition we shall call the critical state, denoted ( )*.

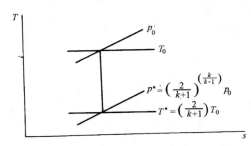

Fig. 13-6 The relationship between the stagnation and critical states

The stagnation and critical pressures and temperatures are shown on the T-s diagram of Fig. 13-6. For air (k=1.4),

$$(p^*/p_0)_{k=1.4} = 0.634 \quad (13.9)$$

and we see that when the converging-diverging duct flow is choked, the density of the air at the duct throat is 63.4% of density of the atmospheric air.

Notes

①滞止状态与零流速以及与流动流体相对应的熵值有关。
②an isentropic flow：等熵流动。
③连续方程式说明，在管道的渐缩部分有小量的流体流动加速度，随后在管道渐扩的部分又出现流动减速。

UNIT FOURTEEN

Text   Eddy Diffusivity and Application to Turbulent Flow

[1]　A characteristic phenomenon of turbulent flow is random velocity fluctuations superimposed on the time-average velocity.① These fluctuations result in bits or chunks of the fluid moving, at one instant, faster than the average velocity; at another instant, slower.② The fluctuations occur in the direction of flow and normal to it. Small mixing actions or eddy currents are established within the turbulent flow field. A small particle of fluid carried by an eddy current from a region of high velocity to one of low velocity gives up momentum to the slower fluid.③ The eddies cause an exchange of momentum between different layers of the moving fluid. If there is a temperature gradient, energy is exchanged by this mixing action in much the same way. If a mass concentration gradient exists, there is a similar mass exchange known as eddy diffusion. The difference between molecular and eddy diffusion lies in the microscopic or molecular mixing action vs. macroscopic or bit mixing action. As expected, eddy diffusion is relatively faster than molecular diffusion. The rate of eddy diffusion depends on the intensity of the velocity fluctuations, or turbulence. Since intensity of turbulence is determined by the Renolds number of the flow, the rate of eddy diffusion depends on the Reynolds number. The eddy diffusivity, ε_D, is defined by the same form of equation as that in molecular diffusion:

$$\dot{m}_B'' = \varepsilon_D (d\rho_B/dy) \tag{14.1}$$

where

    $\varepsilon_D =$ eddy diffusivity, m²/s

[2]　Because data on eddy diffusivities are rare and difficult to obtain, the mass transfer coefficient, analogous to the heat transfer coefficient in convective heat transfer, is usually defined and determined experimentally.④

[3]　Consider an airstream in steady turbulent flow over a wetted surface. It is assumed that the liquid-vapor interface is stationary at zero velocity. This results in a slow-moving layer of fluid next to the surface that is in laminar flow. Between this laminar sublayer and the main body of the turbulent stream there is a transition region, the buffer layer, in which the fluid may be alternately in laminar flow and in turbulent flow. Within the laminar sublayer, only molecular diffusion can occur; in the buffer layer, both molecular and eddy diffusion contribute to mass tranfer. In the turbulent region, eddy diffusion predominates and is so rapid that it almost equalizes the concentration gradient.

[4]　Because of the presence of the laminar sublayer, the rate of molecular mass diffusion from the wetted surface to the airstream, is:

$$J_B = -D_v(d\rho_B/dy)_i \tag{14.2}$$

where $(d\rho_B/dy)_i$ is the partial pressure gradient at the interface. Assuming that the gases are ideal and obey the Gibbs-Dalton Law, and that the total pressure is constant, then a partial pressure gradient must also exist in the air.[5] The wetted surface is impermeable to air, so a convective or bulk velocity must be established to counter the air diffusion rate. The total mass transfer from the wetted surface to the airstream must then be given by:

$$\dot{m}_B'' = -D_v(d\rho_B/dy)_i + \rho_{Bi}V_i \qquad (14.3)$$

where v_i is the convective velocity of the component B vapor at the interface, and the partial mass density of the water vapor at the interface is:

$$\rho_{Bi} = M_B p_{Bi}/R_g T_i \qquad (14.4)$$

[5] For the diffusion of one gas through a second stagnant gas, the simple molecular diffusion equation corrected by the factor P_{AM} accounts for the mass transfer contribution of the convective velocity.[6] For dilute mixtures, this contribution is small. The same correction factor can be used for this forced convection mass transfer process, at least at low mass transfer rates where v_i is small. The total mass transfer rate from the interface is:

$$\dot{m}_B'' = -D_v P_{AM}(d\rho_B/dy)_i \qquad (14.5)$$

[6] The concentration gradient $(d\rho_B/dy)_i$ must be evaluated experimentally. Rather than work with this gradient, it is common to define a mass transfer coefficient, h_m, It follows that:

$$\begin{aligned}\dot{m}_B'' &= (h_m M_B/R_g)(p_{Bi} - p_{B\infty}) \\ &= -(M_B D_v P_{AM}/R_g T_i)(dp_B/dy)_i\end{aligned} \qquad (14.6)$$

By mathematical rearrangement this becomes:

$$\begin{aligned}Sh_L &= h_m L/D \\ &= P_{AM}\left[d\left(\frac{p_B - p_{Bi}}{p_{B\infty} - p_{Bi}}\right)\bigg/d(y/L)\right]_i\end{aligned} \qquad (14.7)$$

where Sh_L is the dimensionless Sherwood number and L is some characteristic dimension of the mass transfer surface such as the length of a plate or diameter of a cylinder, Equation (14.7) gives a simple, but valuable, physical interpretation of the dimensionless mass transfer coefficient, i. e., the Sherwood number. It is seen as the dimensionless concentration gradient at the interface or mass transfer boundary.

[7] Mass transfer coefficients have been established experimentally for a number of flow geometries. Data on mass transfer is sparse compared with the wealth of data on heat transfer coefficients. Because of the analogy between these transfer processes, heat transfer data has been used to predict mass transfer coefficients. The reliability of such similarity relations has been well-established at low mass transfer rates for some flow geometries.

New Words and Expressions

eddy diffusion   对流扩散

random *	['rændəm]	a.	无规则的
fluctuation *	[ˌflʌktju'eiʃən]	n.	波动，起伏
chunk	[tʃʌŋk]	n.	（厚）块
momentum *	[məu'mentəm]	n.	动量
gradient	['greidjənt]	n.	（温度、气压等的）变化率梯度变化曲线
microscopic	[ˌmaikrəs'kɔpik]	a.	微小的，细微的
molecular	[məu'lekju'lə]	a.	分子的
analogous	['ənæləgəs]	a.	类似的，相似的
convective	[kən'vektiv]	a.	对流的
experimentally	[eksˌperi'mentli]	ad.	实验地
airstream		n.	气流
sublayer		n.	底层，下层
laminar sublayer			层流底层
buffer	['bʌfə]	n.	缓冲器
predominate	[pri'dɔmineit]	vi.	居支配地位
		vt.	支配，统治
equalize	['i:kwəlaiz]	vt.	使平等，使均等
the Gbbs-Dalton Law			道尔顿定律
impermeable	[im'pə:mjəbl]	a.	不渗透的，透不过的
stagnant	['stəgnənt]	a.	停滞的，不流动的
dilute *	[dai'lju:t]	a.	稀释的，淡的
Sherwood number			宜乌特准则
sparse	[spɑ:s]	a.	稀少的，稀疏的
analogy	[ə'nælədʒi]	n.	类似，相似

Notes

①A characteristic... velocity：
  句中 superiposed 过去分词短语作定语修饰 fluctuation。
②These fluctuations... slower：
  句中 moving faster than the average velocity 为现在分词短语作定语修饰 fluid；slower 后省略了 than 引出的比较部分，全部写出应为 moving slower than the average velocity。
③A small particle... to the slower fluid：
  句子的 A 主语是 A small partical of fluid carried... to one of low velocity，其中 carried... 为过去分词短语作定语修饰 fluid，谓语动词是 gives up。
④Because data on... experimentally：
  句中 analogous to... 为形容词短语作定语修饰 the mass transfer coefficient。
⑤Assuming that... is constant，...：为现在分词短语作状语；that... and that... 两个 that 都是 assuming 的并列宾语从句。

⑥ P_{AM} (the logarithmic mean density factor of the stagnant air): 静止空气的对数平均密度系数。

Exercises

Reading Comprehension

Ⅰ. Match Column A with Column B according to the first paragraph.

A	B
1. A characteristic phenomenon of turbulent flow	a. is relatively slower than eddy diffusion.
2. Eddy currents	b. is a similar mass exchange if a mass concentration gradient exists.
3. Eddy diffusion	c. is defined by the same form of equation as that in molecular diffusion.
4. The eddy diffusivity	d. are established within the turbulent flow field.
5. Molecular diffusion	e. is random velocity fluctuations superimposed on the time average velocity.

Ⅱ. Choose the best answer according to the text.

1. _____ is random velocity fluctuations superimposed on the time average velocity.
   A. A characteristic phenomenon of eddy diffusion
   B. A characteristic phenomenon of heat transfer coefficient
   C. A characteristic phenomenon of turbulent flow
   D. A characteristic phenomenon of convective velociy

2. An exchange of momentum between different layers of the moving fluid is caused by _____.
   A. turbulent flow.
   B. fluctuations
   C. the eddies
   D. the intensity

3. The rate of eddy diffusion depends on _____.
   A. the intensity of the velocity fluctuations or turbulence.
   B. the Reynolds number.
   C. a mass concentration gradient.
   D. A and B.

4. There is a similar mass exchange known as eddy diffusion if _____ exists.
   A. a mass concentration gradient
   B. a moving fluid

C. a slow-moving layer of fluid

   D. a transition region

5. The mass transfer coefficient is usually defined and determined experimentally because _____.

   A. the heat transfer coefficients in turbulent flow are rare and difficult to obtain.

   B. data on eddy diffusivities are rare and difficult to obtain.

   C. figures about laminar sublayer are rare and difficult to obtain.

   D. numbers concerning zero velocity are rare and difficult to obtain.

6. The fluid may be alternately in laminar flow and in turbulent flow _____.

   A. in the turbulent region, eddy diffusion.

   B. in a transition region, the buffer layer.

   C. in steady turbulent flow over a wetted surface.

   D. in a slow-moving layer of fluid.

7. All the following statements are true except _____.

   A. Only molecular diffusion can occur within the laminar sublayer.

   B. Both molecular and eddy diffusion contribute to mass transfer in the buffer layer.

   C. Eddy diffusion predominates in the turbulent region.

   D. Eddy diffusion is so rapid that it almost equalizes the mass transfer.

8. A convective or bulk velocity must be established to counter the air diffusion rate because _____.

   A. the gases are ideal and obey the Gibbs-Dalton Law.

   B. the total pressure is constant.

   C. a partial pressure gradient exists in the air.

   D. the wetted surface is impermeable to air.

9. Data on mass transfer is sparse compared with the wealth of data on _____.

   A. mass transfer coefficients.

   B. heat transfer coefficients.

   C. mass transfer rates.

   D. heat transfer rates.

10. Heat transfer data has been used to predict mass transfer coefficients because of _____.

    A. the analogy between these transfer processes.

    B. the data on mass transfer.

    C. the similarity relations.

    D. the low heat transfer rates.

Vocabulary

I . Find words in the text which mean almost the same as the following.

1. Para. (1) made or done aimlessly, without any plan.
2. Para. (1) moving up and down; fluctuating movement.
3. Para. (1) quantity of motion of a moving body (the product of its mass and velocity)
4. Para. (7) partial likeness or agreement
5. Para. (5) weakened by adding water or other liquid.

Now use the words you have found to complete the following sentences.

6. The teacher drew an _____ between the human heart and a pump.
7. If you need a _____ acid, you'd better ask him.
8. A characteristic phenomenon of turbulent flow is _____ velocity fluctuations superimposed on the time-average velocity.
9. Do falling objects gain _____.
10. We should pay much attention to the _____ in the exchange rates.

II. Fill in the blanks with the words given below. Change the forms if necessary.

| analogous | gradient | molecular | equalize | predominate |

1. Here is a forest in which oak-trees _____.
2. We should try our best to _____ incomes of the workers.
3. The mass transfer coefficient is _____ to the heat transfer coefficient in convective heat transfer.
4. In the buffer layer, both _____ and eddy diffusion contribute to mass transfer.
5. If there is a temperature _____, energy is exchanged by this mixing action in much the same way.

Reading Material A

Mean Temperature Differences for Parallel Flow and Counterflow Heat Exchangers

We assumed that either the temperatures of the two fluids were constant throughout or that their true mean temperatures were known. Under these conditions, the temperature difference to be used in calculating the heat flow can be obtained by simple subtraction. In engineering situations, the determination of the temperature difference is generally much more difficult.

Consider two fluids flowing in the same planes either in the same direction (parallel flow) or in opposite directions (counterflow).① When a fluid changes phase, there is no change in temperature provided the pressure is held constant. When this condition exists, it makes no difference as to which direction the fluid is flowing. On the other hand, when neither fluid changes phase, the direction of flow is very important. This condition will now be considered.

In the simple case, the fluids will be considered to flow in the same planes. If they also flow in the same direction, the flow is said to be parallel flow. When the two fluids flow in opposite directions, the flow is termed counterflow. Counterflow is illustrated in Fig. 14-1, and parallel flow is illustrated in Fig. 14-2.

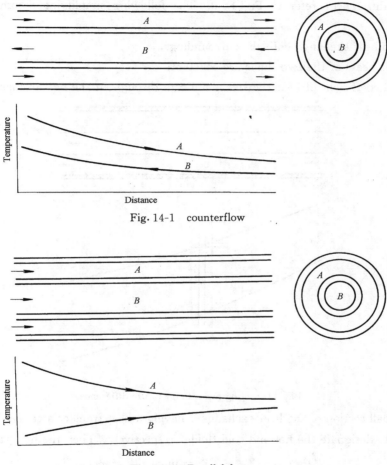

Fig. 14-1 counterflow

Fig. 14-2 Parallel fow

It should be noted for counterflow that as the flow passage is lengthened, the temperature difference between fluids A and B at any point in the flow passage becomes smaller and smaller. Thus, with a very long flow passage, the temperature of fluid B at its exit approaches that of fluid A at its entrance. Likewise the temperature of fluid A at its exit approaches that of fluid B as it enters. As the length of the flow passage increases without limit, the temperature difference between the two fluids in any point in the flow passage approaches zero and the heat transfer process approaches a reversible one. ②

On the other hand, for parallel flow as shown in Fig. 14-2, the temperature of the two fluids approaches each other at the exit. The longer the flow passage, the closer together the temperature of the two fluids will be at exit. However, the parallel flow heat transfer process cannot approach reversibility unless the temperature difference between the two fluids is small at entrance.[3]

It is apparent from examination of Fig. 14-1 and 14-2 that the true mean temperature difference of two fluids in a heat exchanger, where there is no change in phase, cannot be determined by simple subtraction of temperatures[4]. For a method of determining the true mean temperature difference, refer to Fig. 14-3. The following simplifying assumptions will be made:

1. There is no heat exchange with the surroundings.
2. The specific heats of the two fluids are constant.
3. The overall coefficient of heat transfer is uniform throughout the heat exchanger.

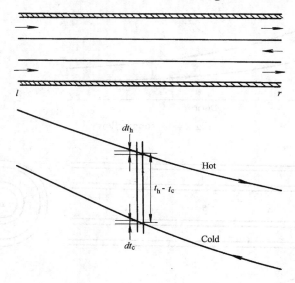

Fig. 14-3 Log mean temperature difference

Consider a small section of the heat exchanger, having a heat transfer area dA. Use the symbols h and c to designate the hot and cold fluids, respectively. Then the heat transfer is

$$d\dot{Q} = UdA(T_h - T_c) = \dot{m}_h c_{ph} dT_h = \dot{m}_c c_{ph} dT_c \tag{14.8}$$

also

$$\dot{Q} = UA\Delta T_m = \dot{m}_h c_{ph}(T_l - T_r)_h = \dot{m}_c c_{pc}(T_l - T_r)_c \tag{14.9}$$

where subscript l refers to the left side of the heat exchanger, and r refers to the right side. hence,

$$\Delta T_m = \frac{(T_h - T_c)_l - (T_h - T_c)_E}{\ln[(T_h - T_c)_l/(T_h - T_c)_E]} = \text{LMTD} \tag{14.10}$$

Since Eq. 14.10 contains the logarithm of a temperature ratio, the temperature difference ΔT_m computed by this equation is known as the log mean temperature difference (LMTD).

The mean temperature difference may also be approximated by assuming that the temperatures vary in straight lines throughout the heat exchanger. The temperature difference based on this assumption is known as the arithmetic mean temperature difference. Since this arithmetic mean is only an approximation, its use is not recommended, unless the temperature changes of both fluids are very small.

The expression for the log mean temperature was derived for counterflow. As may be shown, it holds true equally well for parallel flow and for a heat exchanger in which one of the fluids changes phase.⑤

Notes

①counter flow：逆（反，对）流。
②随着流道长度的无限增加，在流道中任一点处的两种流体间的温差接近于零，且传热过程接近于可逆过程。
③然而，顺流的热传递过程不能接近可逆过程，除非两种流体在进口处的温差就很小。
④通过对图 14-1 和 14-2 的观察，很明显热交换器中如果没有相位变化，两流体的真实平均温差不能用简单的减法来确定。
⑤对数平均温度的表达式由逆流导出。正如所示那样，它对顺流和其中的一种流体发生相变的热交换器来说也同样适合的。

Reading Material B

Finned-Tube Heat Transfer

The heat transfer coefficients for finned coils follow the basic equations of convection, condensation and evaporation. The arrangement of the fins used affects the values of constants and the exponential powers in the equations. It is generally necessary to refer to test data for the exact coefficients.

For natural convection-finned coils (gravity coils); approximate coefficients can be obtained by considering the coil to be made of tubular and vertical fin surfaces at different temperatures, and then applying the natural convection equations to each. This is difficult because the natural convection coefficient depends on the temperature difference, which varies at different points of the fin.

Fin efficiency should be high (80 to 90%) for optimum natural convection heat transfer. A low fin efficiency reduces the temperature near the tip. This reduces Δt near the tip, and also the coefficient, h, which in natural convection depends on Δt. The coefficient of heat transfer also decreases as the fin spacing decreases, because of interfering convection currents from adjacent fins and reduced free-flow passage; 6 to 12 mm spacing is common. Generally, high coefficients result from large temperature differences and small flow restriction.

Coefficients for a number of circular fin-on-tube arrangements, using fin spacing, δ, as the characteristic length, are correlated in the form $Nu=f(GrPr\delta/D_0)$ where D_0 is the fin diameter.[①] Data for free convection and radiation from wire and tube heat exchangers are given before.

Forced convection finned coils are used extensively in a wide variety of equipment. The fin efficiency for optimum performance is smaller than for gravity coils, since the forced-convection coefficient is almost independent of the temperature difference between the surface and the fluid. Very low fin efficiencies should be avoided, since inefficient surface gives a high (uneconomical) pressure drop. An efficiency of 70 to 90% is often used.

As fin spacing is decreased to obtain a large surface area for heat transfer, the coefficient generally increases because of higher air velocity between fins at the same face velocity and reduced equivalent diameter. The limit is reached when the boundary layer formed on one fin surface begins to interfere with the boundary layer formed on the adjacent fin surface, resulting in a decrease of the heat transfer coefficient, which may offset the advantage of larger surface area.[②]

Selection of the fin spacing for forced convection finned coils usually depends on economic and practical considerations, such as fouling, frost formation, condensate drainage, cost, weight and volume. Conventional coils generally are spaced 1.8 to 4 mm except where factors such as frost formation necessitate wider spacing.

Several means are used to obtain higher coefficients with a given air velocity and surface, usually by creating air turbulence, generally with a higher pressure drop: (1) staggered tubes instead of in-line tubes for multiple row coils, (2) artificial additional tubes, or collars or fingers made by suitably forming the fin materials, (3) corrugated fins instead of plane fins and (4) louvered or interrupted fins.

Heat transfer data are available for: one-row plate fin coils; straight fins; disc and spiral fins; circular fins.[③]

Data for one-row coils are shown. The thermal resistances plotted include the temperature drop through the fins, based on one square metre of total external surface area.

Notes

①对许多圆翅片管装置,用翅片间距 δ 作特征长度,传热系数列在 $Nu=f(GrPr\delta/D_0)$ 关系式中,式中 D_0 是翅片直径。
②一个肋片表面形成的边界层与相邻肋片表面形成的边界层开始相互干扰时就达到了极限,结果传热系数降低,这就可能抵消增大表面积带来的益处。
③可以得到单排肋片盘管、直肋、盘式和螺旋肋片、环形肋片等的传热数据。

UNIT FIFTEEN

Text   Centrifugal Pumps and Fans

[1]   Centrifugal pumps consist basically of an impeller rotating within a spiral casing.① The fluid enters the pump axially through the suction pipe via the eye. In single inlet pumps, the fluid enters on one side of the casing and impeller. In double inlet pumps, both sides are used for fluid entry and the impeller is usually of double width with a centre plate. It looks like two single entry impellers placed back to back.② This arrangement has the effect of doubling the flow rate at the same head.

[2]   The blades of a centrifugal impeller vary in shape depending upon the design requirements.③ The blade angle at inlet (β_1) is chosen so that the relative velocity meets the blade tangentially ('no shock' condition) and since under design conditions $v_{w1}=0$ it follows that β_1 depends upon u_1 and v_{f1} only.④ Thus, head considerations do not affect β_1. However β_2 (the blade angle at outlet) is very much affected by them.

[3]   The theoretical head developed by the centrifugal pump is given by Euler's equation

$$H_{th} = v_{w2}u_2/g$$

(provided $v_{w1}=0$) and, therefore, for given tip speed (u_2) depends entirely upon the outlet whirl component velocity v_{w2}.

[4]   Let us now examine the dependence of this component upon the blade angle at outlet β_2. Fig. 15-1 shows three different blade angles, often referred to as inclined backwards ($\beta_2<90°$), inclined forward ($\beta_2>90°$) or radial ($\beta_2=90°$). The figure also shows a combined velocity diagram for the three types of blades.

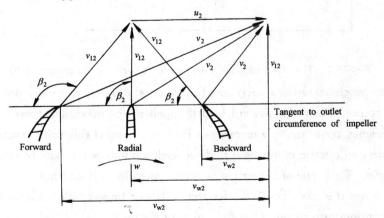

Fig. 15-1   Effect of blade outlet angle on the outlet velocity triangle

[5]   The diagrams are drawn for the same u_2 and v_{f2} for the three blade types. It is clear that as β_2 increases, the absolute velocity v_2 also increase. Therefore, the head developed depends upon β_2 and is larger for the forward inclined blades. However, it must be remembered that

the theoretical head given by Euler's equation is the total head developed by the impeller and, hence, embraces both the static and velocity head terms.⑤ Reference to Fig. 15-1 will show that the large head developed by the forward inclined impeller blades includes a large proportion of velocity head since v_2 is very large. This presents practical difficulties in converting some of this kinetic energy into pressure energy. The losses in a diffuser may be substantial, and are difficult to control.

[6]   The most common blade outlet angles for centrifugal pumps are from 15° to 90°, but, for fans, the range extends into forward inclined blades (well-known multi-vane fans) with β_2 as large as 140°.

[7]   The effect of outlet blade angle on the performance characteristics is shown in Fig. 15-2. It is seen that the forward-bladed impeller generates greater head at a given volume, but it must be remembered that a substantial part of this total head is in fact the velocity head.

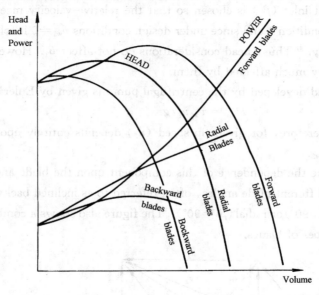

Fig. 15-2   The effect of blade outlet angle on performance characteristics

[8]   The power characteristics also show fundamental differences, which are of considerable practical importance. For the backward-bladed impeller, the maximum power occurs near the maximum efficiency point and any increase of flow rate beyond this point results in a decrease of power. Thus, an electric motor used to drive such a pump or fan may be safely rated at the maximum power. This type of power characteristic is called self-limiting.

[9]   This is not the case, however, for the radial- or forward-bladed impellers, for which the power is continuously rising. Choosing an appropriate motor, therefore, poses problems, because to have one rated for maximum power would mean over-rating and an unnecessary expenditure if the pump will operate only near the maximum efficiency point.⑥ On the other hand a smaller motor rated just for the operating point may be in danger of being overloaded should the pump be operated by mistake at a flow rate greater than the design value corre-

sponding to the maximum efficiency point.⑦

[10]   Centrifugal pumps and fans occupy the lower range of type numbers, up to approximately 1.8 as shown in Fig. 15-3. In general, the lower the type number of these machines the narrower is the impeller in relation to its diameter.⑧

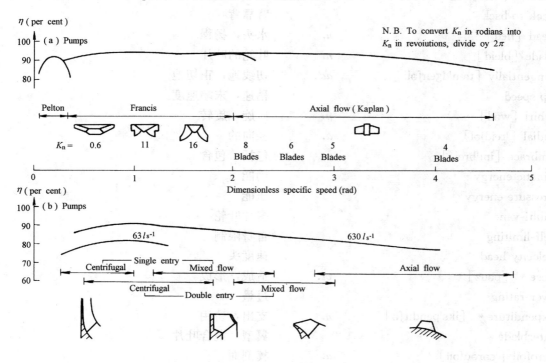

Fig. 15-3

[11]   The overall efficiencies of centrifugal pumps are high, of the order of 90 per cent in the range of type numbers between 0.8 and 1.6. They tend to fall off rapidly at lower type numbers, mainly because of the increased frictional losses in the long interblade passages of these narrow impellers.

[12]   Also, the efficiencies depend upon the size of the machine and, hence, the capacity handled.⑨ The larger the machine, the higher is the efficiency.

[13]   For centrigufal fans, the highest efficiencies are realized by the -aerofoilbladed- fans. They are basically of the backward-bladed type, but the blades have an aerofoil profile rather than being of the same thickness. Their range of type number is from 0.5 to 1.6 and maximum efficiencies are of the order of 90 per cent.

New Words and Expressions

centrifugal [sen'trifjugəl]   a.   离心的
fan [fæn]   n.   风机
impeller [im'pelə]   n.   转子，叶轮

spiral *	['spaiərəl]	a.	螺旋的
casing	['keisiŋ]	n.	机壳
axially	['æksiəli]	ad.	轴向地
suction	['sʌkʃən]	n.	吸入
back to back			背靠背
head	[hed]	n.	水头，扬程
blade	[bleid]	n.	叶轮的叶片
tangentially	[tæn'dʒenʃəli]	ad.	切线地，正切地
tip speed			稍速，末端速度
whirl	[wəːl]	n.	回旋，旋转
radial	['reidjəl]	a.	径向的
embrace	[im'breis]	vt.	包括，包含
kinetic energy			动能
pressure energy			压能
multi-vane			多片叶轮
self-limiting			自身限制
velocity head			速度头
pose *	[pəuz]	vt.	造成，形成
over-rating			过量
expenditure *	[iks'penditʃə]	n.	支出，费用
interblade			翼型，混合叶片
aerofoil	['ɛərəufɔil]	a.	翼剖面
profile	['prəufail]	n.	剖面

Notes

①Centrifugal pump... casing：

句中 rotating... 现在分词短语作定语修饰 an impeller。

②It looks like... back to back：

句中 placed back to back 过去分词短语作定语修饰 impellers。

③The blades of... the design requirements：

句中 depending upon 现在分词短语作状语补充说明全句。

④The blade... only：

句中 it follows that... 是句型，译为由此推断出；由此得出。

⑤However, it must be... velocity head terms：

句中 it must be remembered that... that 引导的是主语从句。

⑥Choosing... point：

句中 choosing an appropriate motor 动名词短语作主句的主语；to have one rated for maximum power 为动词不定式短语作 because 引导的原因状语从句的主语。

⑦On the other hand... the maximum efficiency point:

句中 being overloaded 动名词被动式作介词 of 的定语；should the pump be operated... 是与将来事实相反的虚拟条件句，if 省略，should 提前，引起倒装；... greater than... 形容词短语作定语修饰 a flow rate；... corresponding to... 现在分词短语作定语修饰 the design value。

⑧In general...：

句中 the lower... the narrower... 是"越……，越……"句型。

⑨Also,...：

句中 the size of the machine, the capacity handled 为 depend upon 的并列宾语。handled 为过去分词作定语修饰 capacity。

Exercises

Reading Comprehension

Ⅰ. Choose the best answer according to the text.
1. What kind of arrangement has the effect of doubling the flow rate at the same head?
    A. a double inlet pump with one impeller
    B. a single inlet pump with two impellers
    C. a double inlet pump with two impellers
    D. a single inlet pump with one impeller
2. All the following statements are true except _____.
    A. β_2 is very much affected by head considerations besides β_1.
    B. Centrifugal pumps consist of an impeller rotating within a spiral casing.
    C. The blades of a centrifugal impeller vary in shape depending upon the design requirements.
    D. The theoretical head developed by the centrifugal pump is given by Euler's equation.
3. What presents practical difficulties in converting some of the kinetic energy into pressure energy?
    A. The total head developed by the impeller embraces both the static and velocity head terms.
    B. The large head developed by the forward inclined impeller blades includes a large proportion of velocity head since v_2 is very large.
    C. The large head developed by the backward inclined impeller blades includes a small proportion of velocity head.
    D. The total head developed by the impeller embraces only the velocity head term.
4. All the following statements are not true except one.
    A. The maximum power of forward-bladed impellers occurs near the maximum efficiency point.

B. The maximum power of the backward-bladed impeller occurs with any increase of flow rate.

C. The maximum power of the backward-bladed impeller occurs mear the maximum efficiency point.

D. The maximum power of forward-bladed impellers occurs with any decrease of flow rate.

5. The overall efficiencies of centrifugal pumps are high, but tend to fall off rapidly _____.

   A. at lower type numbers
   B. with larger machines
   C. at higher type numbers
   D. with a lower flow rate

II. Complete the following sentences with the information given in the text.

1. Centrifugal pumps consist basically of an impeller rotating _____ a spiral casing and with the fluid entering the pump _____ through the suction pipe.
2. In _____ pumps, the fluid enters on one side of the casing and impeller.
3. In _____ pumps, both sides are used for fluid entry and the impeller is usually of _____ with a centre plate.
4. The blades of a centrifugal impeller vary _____ depending upon the design requirements.
5. It is clear that as β_2 increases, the absolute velocity v_2 also _____.
6. Give out the three different blade angles: _____, _____, _____.
7. It is seen that the forward-bladed impeller generates greater head at a given volume, but it must be remembered that a substantial part of this total head is in fact the _____.
8. In general, the lower the type number of these machines the narrower is the impeller in relation to its _____.
9. The efficiencies depend upon the size of the machine and, hence, the capacity handled. The _____ the machine, the _____ is the efficiency.
10. For centrifugal fans, the highest efficiencies are realized by the -aerofoil-bladed' fans. They are basically of the backward-bladed type, but the blades have an aerofoil profile _____ being of the same thickness.

Vocabulary

I. Fill in the blanks with the words given below. Change the forms if necessary.

impeller	fan	head	whirl
suction	radial	embrace	pose
expenditure	aerofoil		

1. The report _____ many important points and after the meeting we should discuss them and keep them in mind.
2. It's not worthwhile for you to spend a large _____ of money on such an unimportant matter.
3. An important factor in satisfactory operation of a pump is the avoidance of cavitation, both for the sake of good efficiency and for the prevention of _____ damage.
4. This water pump has a thirty meters _____ of water.
5. Now it is autumn and it is windy. The leaves _____ in the wind.
6. It is impossible for a helicopter to fly if it has no _____.
7. Since cavitation is determined by conditions at entrance to the impeller and not by those at discharge, an expression has been devised known as _____ specific speed, which is analogous to the usual specific speed except that the net head is replaced by the total _____ head above the vapor pressure head.
8. You ought to treat him well otherwise he might _____ a threat to you, and it is not good for you since you are a newcomer.
9. All the planes possess the same _____ for they apply the similar principles.
10. In the repair shop, there are several _____ drilling machines.

II. Match the words in Column A with their corresponding definitions in Column B.

A	B
1. impeller	a. the device used to drive, force or urge things moving forward
2. spiral	b. action of sucking; removal of air, liquid, etc. from a vessel or cavity so as to produce a partial vacuum and enable air-pressure from outside to force in liquid or dust
3. head	c. moving quickly round and round
4. whirl	d. body of water kept at a certain height (e.g. a water-mill or a hydro-electric power station); pressure or force (per unit of area) of a confined body of steam, etc.
5. suction	e. whirling movement

Reading Material A

Pump and the Pipe System

The relationship between the head loss h and the flow rate through the system is given by
$$h = KQ^2 \qquad (15.1)$$
as shown in Fig. 15-4, where B is above A. Clearly a pump P will be needed to supply the en-

ergy loss in the pipe system and, in addition, to provide energy equal to the difference in levels, because work must be done on the fluid in order to raise it from A to B against the gravitational force. [1] Thus, the total energy required for the flow from A to B to be maintained will be

$$E = \Delta Z + KQ^2 \qquad (15.2)$$

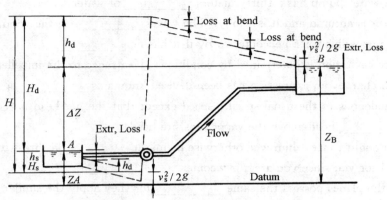

Fig. 15-4 Pump and pipe system

This equation is known as the system characteristic and the term ΔZ is called the static lift.

The example of Fig. 15-4, which also shows the total energy line and the hydraulic gradient line for the system, clearly demonstrates that the loss term KQ^2 incorporates the following losses.

(i) On the suction side of the pump:

$$h_s = K_1 \frac{v_s^2}{2g} + \frac{4fl_s}{d_c} \frac{v_s^2}{2g}$$

(ii) On the delivery side of the pump:

$$h_d = K_2 \frac{v_d^2}{2g} + \frac{4fl_d}{d_d} \frac{v_d^2}{2g} + \frac{v_d^2}{2g}$$

and
$$KQ^2 = h_s + h_d \qquad (15.3)$$

It will be seen from Fig. 15-4 that the total head rise in the pump H is, thus, equal to the sum of suction and delivery losses and the difference in levels between the reservoirs[2]:

$$H = h_s + h_d + \Delta Z$$

or
$$H = \Delta Z + KQ^2 \qquad (15.4)$$

which is the same as equation (15.2) because for the flow to be maintained the energy required by the system (E) must be equal to that supplied to it by the pump (H).

The system characteristic takes into account the difference in elevation, ΔZ, in addition to the head loss. A typical system characteristic is shown in Fig. 15-5. In a system handling air, the Z term is usually negligible because of the low value of air density.

For a rotodynamic pump, the head generated is not constant but is a function of discharge, the relationship between the two being the pump characteristic:

$$H = f(Q)$$

Clearly, then, if a rotodynamic pump operates in conjunction with a pipe system, the two must handle the same volume and, at the same time, the head generated by the pump must be equal to the system energy requirement at that flow rate.③ Therefore,

$$f(Q) = \Delta Z + KQ^2 \tag{15.5}$$

The solution of this equation is obtained graphically because, clearly, it is the intersection of the pump and system characteristics. This is shown in Fig. 15-6 and the point where the two characteristics cross is known as the operating point. This is the point on the pump characteristic at which it operates and, at the same time, it is also the point on the system characteristic at which the system operate. 'Pump matching' usually means the process of selecting a pump to operate in conjunction with a given system so that it delivers the required flow rate, operating at its best efficiency, which corresponds to the pump's design point.④

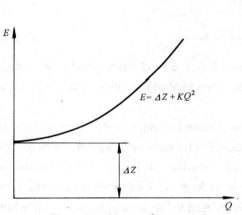

Fig. 15-5 System characteristic

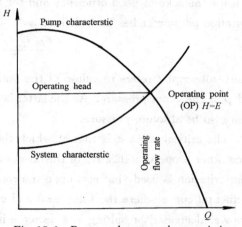

Fig. 15-6 Pump and system characteristics

The point on the system characteristic which corresponds to the required flow rate through the system is known as the duty required. Thus, for correct matching, the operating point should coincide with the duty required. This is not always easy to achieve because the accuracy with which the system resistance is estimated, in practice, is rather poor. We know that the effect on a fan application of the actual system resistance being different from that estimated. As a result, the flow rate delivered is greater than required and the fan operating efficiency is lower and, consequently, the power consumed would be unnecessarily in excess of that expected.⑤

Notes

①很清楚需要泵 P 来弥补管道系统中能量损失，并且还提供相当于水位差的能量，因此必须对流体作功从 A 提升到 B 以克服地心引力。

②从图 15-4 可以看出：泵的总扬程 H 等于吸水和输水水头损失及蓄水池之间高差之总和。

③于是很清楚，如果 rotodynamic pump 管道系统连机运行，两者必须处理相同的流量，与

此同时，泵所产生的水头必须满足该流量时系统的能量要求。

④"泵的选配"通常是指选择泵来和给定的系统一起工作，从而输送所需流量，并以对应于泵设计点的最佳效率运行。

⑤结果，输送流量超过所需流量，风机工作效率降低，因此，所耗电能就会毫无必要地超过预计值。

Reading Material B

Cavitation

An important factor in satisfactory operation of a pump is the avoidance of cavitation, both for the sake of good efficiency and for the prevention of impeller damage.[①] For pumps a cavitation parameter has been defined as

$$\sigma = \frac{(p_0)_{abs}/\gamma - p_v/\gamma - z_s - h_L}{h} \tag{15.6}$$

where subscript s refers to values at the pump intake, h is the head developed by the pump, and p_v is the vapor pressure. As the latter is normally given in absolute units, it follows that p_0 must also be absolute pressure.

The critical value σ_c is that at which there is an observed change in efficiency or head or some other property indicative of the onset of cavitation.[②] The value will depend not only upon what criterion is used, but also upon the conditions of operation. In Fig. 15-7 is shown an experimental curve where the total head and capacity were kept constant while the intake pressure was decreased, resulting in a decrease in σ. The critical value is fixed by the point where the efficiency was found to drop. A different value of σ_c would be found for a different capacity. For safe operation it is desirable to operate at values above the critical for the capacity involved. The critical value σ_c for any specified operating condition depends upon the design of the particular pump, and in any important installation it should be determined experimentally upon a model.

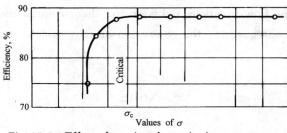

Fig. 15-7 Effect of varying the cavitation parameter

Since cavitation is determined by conditions at entrance to the impeller and not by those at discharge, an expression has been devised known as suction specific speed, which is analogous to the usual specific speed except that the net head is replaced by the total suction head above the vapor pressure head.[3] This is the numerator of Eq. (15.6) and is designated as NPSH, which stands for net positive suction head. The suction specific speed is then

$$S = \frac{n\sqrt{gpm}}{\text{NPSH}^{3/4}}$$

For a double-suction pump the total capacity should be divided by 2 for the determination of S.

Inasmuch as the critical value σ_c has been found to depend upon both the usual specific speed and the suction specific speed, there has been devised the relation.

$$\sigma_c = \frac{\text{NPSH}}{h} = \left(\frac{N_s}{S}\right)^{4/3} \qquad (15.7)$$

which is obtained by eliminating $n\sqrt{gpm}$ between the expressions for N_s and S. In order to obtain σ_c, it is necessary to use the critical value of NPSH in evaluating S.

Critical values of the cavitation parameter vary with the design of the pump, but typical approximate values for σ_c are 0.05 for a specific speed of $N_s=1,000$, 0.01 for $N_s=2,000$, and 0.30 for $N_s=4,000$. For values of N_s greater than 4,000 the Hydraulic Institute recommends that the value of S should be less than 8.140.

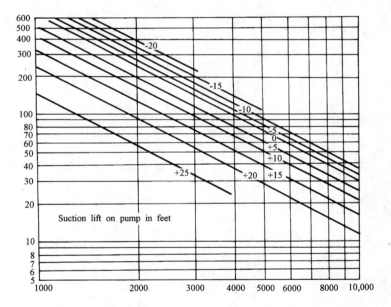

Fig. 15-8 Recommended limiting heads for single-stage, single-suction pumps as a function of specific speed and suction lift. At sea level with water temperature of 80 F

Introducing the critical value of σ into Eq. (15.6) we obtain

$$(z_s)_{\max} = \frac{(p_0)_{\text{abs}}}{\gamma} + \frac{p_v}{\gamma} - \sigma_c h - h_L \qquad (15.8)$$

which will give the maximum allowable elevation of the pump intake above the surface of the liquid. It is apparent from inspection of Eq. (15.8) that, to ensure freedom from cavitation, the pump should be set lower, particularly if (a) it is to be operated at a high elevation above sea level, (b) the total head developed is increased, (c) the specific speed for a given head is increased, or (d) the vapor pressure of the liquid is increased.

If the value of $(z_s)_{max}$ determined by this equation is negative, it indicates that the pump must be placed below the surface of the liquid. Recommended limiting heads for the prevention of cavitation for single-stage, single-suction pumps as a function of specific speed and suction lift (the elevation difference between the energy line at suction and the eye of the impeller) are given in Fig. 15-8.

Notes

①水泵满意运行的一个重要因素是避免气蚀现象，这样既是为了效率高，也是为了防止叶轮受损。
②临界值指的是，在效率或水头或某些其他性能方面出现了提示气蚀来临的可以观察到的变化。
③由于气蚀是由叶轮入口处的条件而不是出口的条件所决定，作为吸水比速的术语 由此产生，吸水比速相当于一般比速，只是净水头由高于水汽压头的总吸水头所代替。

UNIT SIXTEEN

Text   Manufactured Gases

[1]   Manufactured gas is defined herein as a combustible gas produced from coal, coke, oil, or by reforming of natural, liquefied petroleum gases or any mixtures thereof, and including any natural or liquefied petroleum gas if used for enriching.①

[2]   The manufactured gases may be divided into about 18 groups or classifications as follows:

[3]   1. Acetylene is primarily used for cutting and welding operations requiring high flame temperature and it has been used as an illuminant. It's made from calcium carbide and water.

[4]   2. Hydrogen as a fuel is limited to special industrial purposes. such as certain cutting and welding operation. It's made by electrolysis of water, by thermal cracking of natural gas and other hydrocarbons, and by the water gas reaction.②

[5]   3. Sewage gas is produced from sewage sludge in digesting equipment. Its heating value averages between 600 and 700 Btu per cu ft and consists of about two-thirds methane and one-third carbon dioxide.

[6]   4. Butane-air and propane-air gases consist of mixtures of butane or propane and air to provide fuel gases with any desired heating values from 450 to 2000 Btu. They are used as the gas supply for small communities and as peak load gas by many natural gas companies.③

[7]   5. Thermally cracked gas is made by decomposition of natural gas, liquefied petroleum gases, or gasoline. It's high in saturated and unsaturated hydrocarbons with some hydrogen.

[8]   6. Catalytically cracked gas is made by passing the gas or light hydrocarbon liquid to be cracked over nickel oxide catalyst maintained at a selected temperature by external heat.④ Regulated amounts of steam may be introduced. The gas is composed of CO and H_2 with appreciable amounts of N_2 and CO_2. Some of the uncracked gas or liquid vapor may be mixed with the cracked gas to increase the heating value.

[9]   7. Oil gases are made by thermal decomposition of oils which may vary from naphtha to heavy residuum high carbon oils. Their heating values vary from 300 to 400 Btu per cu ft and their primary use is for a peak load supplement by natural gas companies.

[10]   8. Refinery oil gas is produced in oil refineries from two chief sources, namely evolution of absorbed gases from crudes during the distillation process and as a by-product of refinery cracking operations. Depending upon the amount of hydrocarbons removed, the heating value may be from 1400 to 2000 Btu per cu ft.

[11]   9. Reformed gases are usually made by thermally cracking natural gas, propane, butane, or refinery oil gas in water gas generators or similar special equipment. The resultant gas varies appreciably in composition depending upon the equipment used and the percentage of the gas being cracked.⑤ Reformed gas contains hydrogen, carbon monoxide, and saturated and

unsaturated hydrocarbons.

[12]   10. Coal gas is made in retort by the distillation of the volatile matter from coal. It's high in hydrogen and methane with lesser amounts of carbon monoxide and illuminants.

[13]   11. Coke oven gas is made as by-product of coke ovens by the distillation of the volatile matter from the coal. Coke is the primary product. The gas produced is usually around 500⑤ Btu per cu ft with the combustible constituents consisting of hydrogen, methane, ethane, carbon monoxide, and illuminantes, At the end of a coking period the gas is primarily hydrogen, at the beginning it is high in methane. A low temperature coking process will produce a high-Btu gas, as there is little breakdown of the saturated hydrocarbons.

[14]   12. Produced gas is generated when air or oxygen is passed through a thick bed of hot coal or coke. The products of this process are CO, N_2 (from the use of air), and some CO_2. In actual practice, steam is added to the air to reduce clinker formation and the steam decomposition forms hydrogen in varying quantities.

[15]   13. Blast furnace gas is a by-product in the manufacture of pig iron in blast furnaces. For its heating value derived mainly from carbon monoxide is too low, it's usually used for heating purposes within the plant.

[16]   14. Blue gas, water gas, or blue water gas, is made by passing steam over hot coke, coal, or other carbonaceous material, and consists essentially of carbon monoxide and hydrogen with varying amounts of carbon dioxide and nitrogen.⑥ It burns with a blue flame.

[17]   15. Carbureted water gas consists of water gas as a base which has been carbureted or enriched with thermally cracked oil, natural gas, or liquefied petroleum gas. In addition to considerable percentages of CO and H_2, there are varying amounts of unsaturated hydrocarbons (illuminants) and saturated hydrocarbons. Nearly any desired heating value from 300 to 1200 Btu may be attained, depending upon the process employed.

[18]   16. Synthesis gas is made by various processes from coal, coke, naphtha or other hydrocarbons, and consists essentially of CO and H_2 in the ratio of 1 to 2. The crude gas also contains high percentages of CO_2.

[19]   17. Underground produced water gas made in underground coal seams by passing air, with or without supplemental oxygen or steam, through an ignited mass of coal, has been produced experimentally in several countries.⑦

[20]   18. Underground oil gases have been studied in the United States from the viewpoint of generating them via underground atomatic bomb explosions in oil shale formations to break up the shale rock and release the kerosene present.⑧ Then by retorting in place, petroleum fractions such as a fuel gas could be produced and brought to the surface.

New Words and Expressions

herein * [hiər'in]   ad.   此中，于此
combustible * [kəm'bʌstəbl]   a.   易燃的，可燃

coke *	[kəuk]	n.	焦炭，焦
liquify	['likwifai]	v.	（使）液化
thereof *	[ðɛə'ɔv]	ad.	因此，由此
enrich	[in'ritʃ]	vt.	使丰富
enriching			增热
acetylene	[ə'setili:n]	n.	乙炔
illumminant	[i'lju:minənt]	n.	照明剂
		a.	照明的
calcium *	['kælsiəm]	n.	钙
carbide *	['kɑ:baid]	n.	碳化物，碳化钙
electrolysis	[ilek'trɔlisis]	n.	电解作用
hydrocarbon *	[haidrəu'kɑ:bən]	n.	烃，碳氢化合物
sewage	['sju(:)idʒ]	n.	污水，污物
sludge	[slʌdʒ]	n.	软泥，煤泥
methane	['mi:θein]	n.	甲烷，沼气
dioxide *	[dai'ɔksaid]	n.	二氧化物
butane	['bju:tein]	n.	丁烷
propane	['prəupein]	n.	丙烷
decomposition *	[di:kɔmpəzi'ʃən]	n.	分解
saturate	['sætʃəreit]	vt.	使饱和
catalytically	[kætə'litikəli]	a.	催化的
nickel	['nikl]	n.	镍
naphtha	['næfθə]	n.	石脑油
residuum	[ri'zidjuəm]	n.	残留物，残渣油
refinery *	[ri'fainəri]	n.	精炼厂，提炼厂
monoxide *	[mɔ'nɔksaid]	n.	一氧化碳
retort	[ri'tɔ:t]	n.	蒸馏罐，碳化炉
volatile *	['vɔlətail]	n.	挥发物
constituent *	[kən'stitjuənt]	n.	成分，要素
breakdown *	['breikdaun]	n.	破裂，断裂
clinker	['kliŋkə]	n.	熔渣
pig	[pig]	n.	生铁
carburet	['kɑ:bjuret]	vt.	使…与碳化合
seam	[si:m]	n.	接缝
shale	[ʃeil]	n.	页岩
kerogen	['kerədʒən]	n.	油母岩

Notes

①Manufactured gas... for enriching：
   句中 produced from...；by... 过去分词短语做 a combustible gas 的定语；by 前省略了 produced；if used for enriching ＝ if it is usedd for enriching。

②It's made by..., by..., and by...：
   句中三个 by 短语并列修饰谓语动词 is made。

③They are used as..., and as...：
   两个 as 短语并列修饰谓语动词 are used。

④Catalytically cracked gas... by external heat：
   句中动词不定式 to be cracked... 作定语修饰 light hydrocarbon liquid；maintained... 过去分词短语作定语修饰 nickel oxide catalyst；by external heat 介词短语修饰 is made。

⑤The resultant gas... being cracked：
   句中现在分词短语 depending upon 作状语，补充说明修饰全句；being cracked 现在分词被动式作定语修饰 the gas。

⑥Blue gas,... and nitrogen：
   句中 is made by 和 cinsists essentially of 为全句的并列谓语。

⑦Underground produced water gas...：
   句子结构是主语（Underground produced water gas）＋被动结构（has been produced）＋地点状语（in several countries）；主语（Underground produced water gas）带有过去分词作的定语（made in underground coal seams by...）。

⑧Underground oil gases... the kerosenepresent：
   此句的结构是主语（underground oil gases）＋被动结构（have been studied）＋状语（in the United States 及 from the viewpoint of...）；from the viewpoint of：按照……的观点，根据……的观点。

Exercises

Reading Comprehension

Ⅰ. There are 18 kinds of the manufactured gases mentioned in the text. Now first put in the missing kinds of gases and then match Column A with Column B according to the text.

A	B
1. Acetylene	a. is usually used for heating purposes within the plant.
2. _____	b. is generated when air or oxygen is passed through a thick bed of hot coal or coke.

3. Sewage gas

4. _____

5. Thermally cracked gas

6. _____

7. Oil gases

8. _____

9. Reformed gases

10. _____

11. Coke oven gas

12. _____

13. Blast furnace gas

14. _____

15. Carbureted water gas

16. _____

17. Underground produced water gas

18. _____

c. is made as by—product of coke ovens by the distillation of the volatile matter from the coal.

d. is composed of CO and H_2 with appreciable amounts of N_2 and CO_2.

e. are mainly used for a peak load supplement by natural gas companies.

f. contains hydrogen, carbon monoxide, and saturated and unsaturated hydrocarbons.

g. is made in retort by the distillation of the volatile matter from coal.

h. is high in saturated and unsaturated hydrocarbons with some hydrogen.

i. is produced in oil refineries from two chief sources.

j. consists of water gas as a base which has been carbureted or enriched with thermally cracked oil, natural gas, or liquefied petroleum gas.

k. burns with a blue flame.

l. are used as the gas supply for small communities and as peak load gas by many natural gas companies.

m. is produced from sewage sludge in digesting equipment.

n. consists essentially of CO and H_2 in the ratio of 1 to 2.

o. is limited to special industrial purposes, such as certain cutting and welding operation.

p. is primarily used for cutting and welding operations requiring high flame temperature.

q. bave been studied in the United States

r. has been produced experimentally in several countries.

Ⅱ. Fill in the blanks with the information given in the text.
1. Acetylene is primarily used for cutting and welding operations requiring _____ and it has been used as an _____.
2. Sewage gas is produced from sewage sludge in _____.
3. _____ consist of mixtures of butane or propane and air to provide fuel gases with any desired heating values from 450 to 2000 Btu.
4. Thermally cracked gas is made by decomposition of _____, liquefied _____, or _____.

149

5. _____ are made by thermal decomposition of oils which may vary from naphtha to heavy residuum high carbon oils.
6. Refinery oil gas is produced in oil _____ from two chief sources, namely evolution of absorbed gases from crudes during the _____ process and as a by-product of refinery cracking operations.
7. _____ is made in retort by the distillation of the volatile matter from _____.
8. Coke oven gas is made as _____ of coke ovens by the distillation of the volatile.
9. Blast furnace gas is a by-product in the manufacture of _____ in blast furnaces.
10. Petroleum fractions such as a fuel gas could be produced and brought to the surface by _____.

Vocabulary

I. Fill in the blanks with the expressions given below. Change the forms if necessary.

| herein | combustible | liquify | thereof | enriching |
| sewage | residuum | refinery | clinker | constituent |

1. Manufactured gas is defined _____ as a combustible gas produced from coal, coke, oil, or by reforming natural, liquefied petroleum gases or any mixtures.
2. This gas is _____, and we must be careful to keep it far from fire.
3. The fishpond is getting shallower and shallower, and if you want to make it right to use, you have to pump up the water and then clean all the _____ on the floor.
4. What feul do you use for cooking? We mainly use the _____ petroleum gases.
5. Here is a problem and the solution _____.
6. _____ treatment is very important. Without it, we might have no clear water to drink.
7. This is a kind of combustible gas and the combustible _____ are hydrogen, methane, ethane, carbon monoxide, and illuminantes.
8. There is an oil _____ in this area and it is the largest in Asia.
9. In actual practice, steam is added to the air to reduce _____ formation and the steam decomposition forms hydrogen in varying quantities.
10. Any natural or liquefied petroleum gas can be called manufactured gas if used for _____.

II. Match the words in Column A with their corresponding definitions in Column B.

A	B
1. herein	a. in this
2. combustible	b. make or become liquid
3. liquify	c. of that; from that source

4. thereof
5. enriching

d. increasing heat
e. catching fire and burning easily

Reading Material A

Gaseous Fuels

Although various gaseous fuels have been used as energy sources in the past, heating and cooling applications are presently limited to natural and liquefied petroleum gases.

Types and Properties

Natural gas is a nearly odorless and colorless gas that accumulates in the upper parts of oil and gas wells. Raw natural gas is a mixture of methane (55 to 98%), higher hydrocarbons (primarily ethane) and noncombustible gases.① Some constituents, principally water vapor, hydrogen sulfide, helium, liquefied petroleum gases and gasoline are removed prior to distribution.

Typical compositions of natural gas distributed for use as fuel include: methane, CH_4 (70 to 96%), ethane, C_2H_6 (1 to 14%), propane, C_3H_8 (0 to 4%), butane, C_4H_{10} (0 to 2%), pentane, C_5H_{12} (0 to 0.5%), hexane, C_6H_{14} (0 to 2%), carbon dioxide, CO_2 (0 to 2%), oxygen, O_2 (0 to 1.2%), and nitrogen, N_2 (0.4 to 17%). Natural gases are sometimes divided into three types: high inert, high methane and high kJ, defined in Table 3.

Table 3 Group Classifications of Natural Gases

Group	Nitrogen, %	Density kg/m³	Methane, %	kJ/m³ Dry
I High inert type	6.3 to 16.20	0.795 to 0.852	71.9 to 83.2	35694 to 39160
II High methane type	0.1 to 2.39	0.710 to 0.739	87.6 to 95.7	37557 to 39904
III High kJ type	1.2 to 7.5	0.746 to 0.866	85.0 to 90.1	39904 to 41880

The composition of a natural gas depends on its geographical source. The composition of gas distributed in a given location can vary slightly since the gas is drawn from various sources, but a fairly constant heating value is usually maintained for control and safety purposes. The local gas utility is the best source of current gas composition data for a particular area.②

151

Heating values of natural gases vary from 33 500 to 44 700 kJ/m^3, but the usual range is 37 000 to 39 000 kJ/m^3. Unknown heating values for particular gases can be calculated from composition data.

Odorants (such as mercaptans) are added to natural gas to give it a characteristic odor for safety purposes.

Liquefied petroleum gases consist primarily of propane and butane, normally obtained as a byproduct of oil refinery operations or by stripping natural gas.③ Propane and butane are gaseous under usual atmospheric conditions, but can be liquefied by moderate pressures at normal temperatures.

Three liquefied petroleum gases are commercially available as fuels: butane. propane and a mixture of the two.

Commercial propane consists primarily of propane but generally contains about 5 to 10% propylene. It has a heating value of about 50150 kJ/kg or about 120 000 kJ/m^3 of gas. At atmospheric pressure, commercial propane has a boiling point of about -40℃. The low boiling point of propane makes it usable during winter in the northern United States and it is available in cylinders, bottles, tank trucks or tank cars.

Commercial butane consists primarily of butane but may contain up to 5% butylene. It has a heating value of about 49000 kJ/kg or about 120000 kJ/m^3 of gas. At atmospheric pressure, commercial butane has a relatively high boiling point of about 0℃. Therefore, butane cannot be used in cold weather unless gas temperature is maintained above 0℃ or butane partial pressure is decreased by dilution with lower boiling point gases. Butane is usually available in bottles, tank trucks or tank cars, but not in cylinders.

Commercial propane-butane mixtures with varying ratios of propane and butane are available, Their properties generally fall between those of the unmixed fuels.④

Propane-air and butane-air mixtures are used in place of natural gas in small communities and at peak loads by natural gas companies.

Manufactured gases are combustible gases produced from coal, coke, oil. liquefied petroleum gases or natural gas. These fuels are used primarily for industrial in-plant operations or as specialty fuels (e. g., acetylene for welding).

Notes

①methane 甲烷 (ethane 乙烷, propane 丙烷, butane 丁烷, pentane 戊烷, hexane 己烷)。
②当地煤气公司是某一个特定区域煤气成分资料的最佳来源。
③液化气主要由丙烷和丁烷组成,通常作为炼油厂的副产品或是分离天然气而得到。
④市场上有各种比例的商用丙、丁烷混合气,它们的特性一般介于上述两种燃料未混合时的特征之间。

Reading Material B

The future of plastic pipe at higher pressures

Participants in an AGA meeting panel on plastic pipe discussed the possibility of using polyethylene gas pipe at higher pressures.① Topics included the design equation, including work being done by ISO on an updated version, and the evaluation of rapid crack propagation in a PE pipe resin.② This is of critical importance because as pipe is used at higher pressures and in larger diameters, the possibility of RCP increases.③

Several years ago, AGA's Plastic Pipe Design Equation Task Group reviewed the design equation to determine if higher operating pressures could be used in plastic piping systems. Members felt the performance of our pipe resins was not truly reflected by the design equation. It was generally accepted that the long-term properties of modern resins far surpassed those of older resins. Major considerations were new equations being developed and selection of an appropriate design factor.

Improved pipe performance

Many utilities monitored the performance of plastic pipe resins. Here are some of the long-term tests used and the kinds of performance change they have shown for typical gas pipe resins.

Elevated temperature burst test

They used tests like the Elevated Temperature Burst Test, in which the long-term performance of the pipe is checked by measuring the time required for formation of brittle cracks in the pipe wall under high temperatures and pressures (often 80 degrees C and around 4-to 5-Mpa hoop stress).④ At Consumers Gas we expected early resins to last at least 170 hrs. at 80 degrees C and a hoop stress of 3 Mpa. Extrapolation showed that resins passing these limits should have a life expectancy of more than 50 yrs. Quality control testing on shipments of pipe made from these resins sometimes resulted in product rejection for failure to meet this criterion.⑤

At the same temperature, today's resins last thousands of hours at hoop stresses of 4.6 Mpa. Tests performed on pipe made from new resins have been terminated with no failure at times exceeding 5,700 hrs. These results were performed on samples that were squeezed off before testing.⑥ Such stresses were never applied in early testing. When extrapolated to operating conditions, this difference in test performance is equivalent to an increase in lifetime of hundreds (and in some cases even thousands) of years.

Environmental stress crack resistance test.

Some companies also used the Environmental Stress Crack Resistance test which measured brittle crack formation in pipes but which used stress cracking agents to shorten test times.

This test has also shown dramatic improvement in resistance to brittle failure. For example, at my company a test time of more than 20 hrs. at 50 degrees C was required on our early resins. Today's resins last well above 1,000 hrs. with no failures.

Notch tests

Notch tests, which are quickly run, measure brittle crack formation in notched pipe or molded coupon samples. This is important for the newer resins since some other tests to failure can take very long times. Notch test results show that while early resins lasted for test times ranging between 1,000 to 10,000 min., current resins usually last for longer than 200,000 min.

All of our tests demonstrated the same thing. Newer resins are much more resistant to the growth of brittle cracks than their predecessors. Since brittle failure is considered to be the ultimate failure mechanism in polyethylene pipes, we know that new materials will last much longer than the old. This is especially reassuring to the gas industry since many of these older resins have performed very well in the field for the past 25 yrs. with minimal detectable change in properties.

While the tests showed greatly improved performance, the equation used to establish the pressure rating of the pipe is still identical to the original except for a change in 1978 to a single design factor for all class locations.

To many it seemed that the methods used to pressure rate our pipe were now unduly conservative and that a new design equation was needed. At this time we became aware of a new equation being balloted at ISO. The methodology being used seemed to be a more technically correct method of analyzing the data and offered a number of advantages.

Notes

①AGA = American Gas Association 美国煤气协会。
②ISO = International Science Organization 国际科学组织；PE = poluethylene 聚乙烯。
③RCP = reinforced concrete pipe 钢筋混凝土管。
④他们使用象温升爆裂测试之类的测试。在这一测试中管系的长期性能通过测量高温和高压下管壁形成脆裂所需的时间来校核。
⑤装运时对这些树脂塑管质量检测有时会由于没有达到这一标准而对该产品拒绝使用。
⑥这些结果是在临测试前检出的（树脂）抽样得出的。

Appendix I Vocabulary

a least-square fit	最小二乘拟合	03
abrupt * a.	突然的	13
acceleration * n.	（物）加速，加速度	01
acetylene n.	乙炔	16
adiabatic a.	绝热的	02
adiabatically ad.	绝热地	04
adjacent * a.	邻近的，因此相连的	01
aerofoil a.	翼剖面	15
aeronautics n.	航空学	09
afterbody n.	（机船）后部	11
airstream n.	气流	14
algebraic a.	代数的	07
analogous a.	类似的，相似的	14
analogy n.	类似，相似	14
apparatus n.	装置	09
appreciable * a.	相当大的	08
appropriately ad.	适可地	05
approximately ad.	大体上	05
approximation n.	近似，近似值	03
arbitrarily ad.	随意地，任意地	05
arriveat	得出	05
ASHRAE(American Society of Heating Refrigerating and Air Conditioning Engineers) 美国供热制冷和空调工程师协会		10
asymmetrical a.	不对称的	13
asymmetry n.	不对称	13
atrest	静止	05
atmospheric a.	大气压的，空气的	06
axially ad.	轴向地	15
back to back	背靠背	15
baseboard n.	踢脚板	10
be referred to as…	指的是…	06
butane n.	丁烷	16
blade n.	叶轮的叶片	15
bodily a.	具体的，有形的	08
body force	质量力	05
breakdown * n.	破裂，断裂	16
buffer n.	缓冲器	14
calcium * n.	钙	16
capillarity n.	毛细作用现象	09
carbide * n.	碳化物，碳化钙	16
carburet vt.	使…与碳化合	16
carburetor n.	汽化器	09
casing n.	机壳	15
casings n.	壳	10
catalytically a.	催化的	16
category * n.	种类	13
categorize * v.	把…分类	01
centrifugal a.	离心的	04
chunk n.	（厚）块	14
clearance volume	余隙，容积	04
clinker n.	熔渣	16
coating n.	涂层	07
coefficient n.	系数	03
cohesive a.	内聚的	01
cohesive forces	内聚力	01
coke * n.	焦炭，焦	16
combustible * a.	易燃的，可燃	16
combustion n.	燃烧	01
compressibility n.	压缩（性）	03
compressible a.	可压缩	05
compression n.	压缩	04
compressor n.	压缩机，压气机	01
concentric a.	同轴心的	05
condenser n.	冷凝器	04
conductance n.	导热率	08
conductivity n.	导热系数	08

155

cone	n.	锥形物,锥面	13
configuration	* n.	构造,结构	01
constituent	* n.	成分,要素	16
contribution	n.	分配,分布	03
convection	n.	对流	08
convective	a.	对流的	14
correlating	* a.	相关的	03
correlation	* n.	关系式	10
correspondence	* n.	对应	03
cosine	n.	(数)余弦	12
credit(to)		把…归于,认为…	08
critical value		临界值	03
cross-section	n.	横断面,截面	07
cross-sectiona larea		横截面积	08
cryogenic	a.	低温(学)的	03
curvature	n.	弯曲	06
customary	* a.	惯例的	11
cyclic	a.	循环的	04
cylinder	* n.	气缸,圆筒	04
datum	n.	基准(点,面)	06
decomposition	* n.	分解	16
deflect	vt. & vi.	使偏离(斜),使转向	02
denote	* vt.	指示,表示	09
depict	* v.	描绘	05
desuperheated	a.	降温,降低蒸气过热度	04
determination	n.	测定	05
deviation	n.	偏离,偏向	06
differential	a.	微量(的)	02
diffuse	* a.	漫射的	12
diffuser	* n.	扩散器,喷雾器,扩压管	02
diffusion	n.	扩散	10
diffusivity	n.	扩散性,扩散系数	10
dilute	* a.	稀释的,淡的	14
dimensionless	a.	无量纲的	07
diminish	vt.	减小,减少	10
dioxide	* n.	二氧化物	16

displace	vt.	排(水)	01
disregard	vt.	忽视,不考虑	05
distorted	a.	失真了的	09
diverge	vi.	岔开,偏离,离题	06
Doppler effect		多普勒效应	13
downstream	ad.	在下游的	13
drag	n.	阻力	11
ducts	n.	风管,管道	10
dynamically	ad.	在动力学方面	09
eddy	n.	涡流	07
eddy diffusion		对流扩散	14
effectiveness	n.	有效度,有效性	11
elasticity	n.	弹力,弹性	09
electrolysis	n.	电解作用	16
elevation	* n.	高度	01
embrace	vt.	包括,包含	15
emission	n.	散发	13
emissive	a.	辐(发)射的	12
emittance	n.	辐(发)射率	12
empirical	* a.	以经验为根据的	07
empirically	* ad.	经验地,实验地	03
enclosure	* n.	围绕物,围墙(栏),箱	12
energy grade line		能量坡度线	06
energy head		能头	06
enrich	vt.	使丰富	16
enriching		增热	16
enthalpy	n.	焓	01
entropy	n.	熵(热力学函数)	01
equalize	vt.	使平等,使均等	14
equate	vt.	使相等	11
equilibrium	* n.	平衡,均衡	01
evaporator	n.	蒸发器	04
expander	n.	膨胀器,扩张器	02
expenditure	* n.	支出;费用	15
experimentally	ad.	实验地	14
experimentation	n.	试验,实验	07
expression	n.	式,符号	05
familiarity	n.	熟悉	06
fan	n.	风机	15

flat disk	平盘		11
fluctuation *	n. 波动,起伏		14
forced-on-free convection	加上自然对流影响的受迫对流		10
forebody	n. (机船)前部		11
foregoing	a. 在前的,前述的		11
format *	n. 形式		07
Fourier's Law	付立叶定律		08
friction drag	摩擦阻力		11
full-size	原尺寸		09
generalize *	vt. 归纳出		03
geometric	a. 几何的		12
geometric	n. 几何图形		09
golf	n. 高尔夫球		11
gradient	n. (温度,气压等)变化率 梯度变化曲线		14
graphical	a. 图的		07
Grashof number	格拉晓夫数		10
gravitational	a. 重力的		02
head	n. 水头,扬程		15
helical	a. 螺旋的,螺旋形的		04
hemispherical	a. 半球的		12
herein *	ad. 此中,于此		16
homogeneous *	a. 均匀的		01
hull	n. 船壳,外壳		11
humidity *	n. 湿度		10
hydraulic	a. 水力的,水压的		06
hydraulic grade line	水力坡度线		06
hydraulics	n. 水力学		09
hydrocarbon *	n. 烃,碳氢化合物		16
hydroelectric	a. 水力发电的		02
hypersonic	a. 特超音速的		13
illuminant	n. 照明剂 a. 照明的		16
impeller	n. 转子,叶轮		15
impermeable	a. 不可渗透的,透不过的		14
impractical	a. 不切合实际		09
in question	正被谈论的		05
in terms of	用…来表示		05
inasmuch(as)	因为,由于		06
incident	a. 入射的		12
incompressible	a. 不可压缩的		02
induce *	vt. 引起,感应		11
inertia *	n. 惯性,惰性,惯量		02
infinitesimal	a. 无穷小的,无限小的		02
infrared	n. 红外线区		12
inlet *	n. 进(入)口		02
insignificant	a. 不重要的,轻微的		09
insignificant	a. 小的,微不足道的		04
inspection	n. 检查		06
instantaneous *	a. 瞬间的,即刻的		13
insulating *	a. 绝热的		08
intake	n. 吸入,入口		06
integrate *	v. 积分		05
integration	n. 积分		08
interblade	翼型;混合叶片		15
intercept	vt. 拦截		06
interface	n. 结合面,分界面		09
interstage	a. 级间的,中间的		04
investigation	n. 调查		09
irreversibly	ad. 不可逆(转)地		04
isentropic	a. 等(定)熵的		04
isolation	n. 隔绝,隔离		07
isotherm	n. 等温线,恒温线		03
kerogen	n. 油母岩		16
kinematic	a. 运动(学)的		09
kinetic	a. 动力(学)的,动力的		01
kinetic energy	动能		15
Kirchhoff Law	基尔霍夫定律		12
Lambert Law	兰贝特定律		12
laminar	a. 流层的		07
laminar sublayer	层流底层		14
linear	a. 线性的		03
linearly *	ad. 线性地		08
liquify	v. (使)液化		16
log-logplot	双对数图		07

logarithmic *a.* 对数的		07
Mach wave 马赫波		13
magnitude * *n.* 量(级),数值		02
measurable *a.* 可测量的		07
mechanism * *n.* 机械装置,机械结构		01
methane *n.* 甲烷,沼气		16
microscopic *a.* 微小的,细微的		14
model *v.* 模拟(造)		02
modification *n.* 修改,改进		03
molecular *a.* 分子的		14
momentum * *n.* 动量		14
monochromatic *a.* 单色的		12
monoxide * *n.* 一氧化碳		16
Moody chart 莫迪图		07
multi-vane 多片叶轮		15
naphtha *n.* 石脑油		16
negligible * *a.* 可以忽略的		02
neutron *n.* 中子		01
nickel *n.* 镍		16
nonblack 非黑体		12
nozzle *n.* 喷管(嘴)		02
numerically * *ad.* 在数字上		04
Nusselt number 努谢尔特数		10
opaque *a.* 不透明的		12
optic *n.* 光学		13
optimum * *a.* 最适的,最佳的		11
orientation * *n.* 方位		12
over-rating 过量		15
parameter * *n.* 参数		03
particulate *n.* 微粒		03
partition function 分配函数		03
partition *n.* 分开,划分		03
penstock *n.* 进水管,压力水管,闸门		02
perforate *vt.* 穿孔于,打眼于		11
perpendicular *a.* 垂直的,正交的		13
pertinent * *a.* 恰当的,相关的		10
piezometer *n.* 测压计		06
piezometric *a.* 测压的		06
piezometric head 测压管水头		06
pig *n.* 生铁		16
pipeline *n.* 管线,管道		06
piston *n.* 活塞		02
pitot tube 毕托管		06
Planck Law 普朗克定律		12
platinum *n.* 白金		12
plot *vt.* 划分,标出		06
pose * *vt.* 造成,形成		15
Prandtl number 普朗特数		10
predominate *vi.* 居支配地位		14
vt. 支配,统治		
prematurely * *ad.* 过早地		11
pressure drag 压力阻力		11
pressure energy 压能		15
pressure wave 压力波		13
profile *n.* 剖面		06
progressive *a.* 进行的		08
projected area 投影面积		08
propagation * *n.* 传播		02
propane *n.* 丙烷		16
proportionality * *n.* 比例		08
proton *n.* 质子		01
prototype * *n.* 原形,足尺装置		09
purity *n.* 纯度		08
quantitatively * *ad.* 定量地		04
radial *a.* 径向的		15
random * *a.* 无规则的		14
Re axis Re 轴		07
Re curves Re 曲线		07
reciprocal *a.* 倒数的		03
reciprocating *a.* 往复的,来回的		02
reexpand *v.* 再膨胀		04
refinery * *n.* 精炼厂,提炼厂		16
refrigerant *n.* 致冷剂,冷冻剂,冷媒		04
refrigeration *n.* 制冷		04
regime * *n.* 区域,状态		10
regime * *n.* 格率,制度		07
residuum *n.* 残留物,残渣油		16
resultant * *a.* 作为结果而发生的		06

resulting	*a.* 由此产生的	06
retort	*n.* 蒸馏罐,碳化炉	16
reversible	*a.* 可逆的	04
reversibly	*ad.* 可逆(倒)地	04
Reynolds number	雷诺数	07
roof-mounted	屋顶安装的	10
roughen	*vt.* 使变粗糙	11
roughness	*n.* 粗糙度	07
saturate	*vt.* 使饱和	16
saturated	*a.* 饱和	01
saturation	*n.* 饱和(状态)	01
scale	*vt.* 换算	03
scale down	按比例缩减,降低	09
seam	*n.* 接缝	16
sediment	*n.* 沉淀,沉淀物	09
self-limiting	自身限制	15
sewage	*n.* 污水,污物	16
shaft *	*n.* 轴	01
shale	*n.* 页岩	16
Sherwood number	宣乌特准则	14
shuffle	*vt.* 搅乱,弄混	01
shuttle	*n.* 航天飞机	13
similarity	*n.* 类似,相似	09
similitude	*n.* 相同点,相似物	09
simulate *	*vt.* 看上去象,模仿	12
single-value	*n.* 单值	07
slab	*n.* 厚片	08
sludge	*n.* 软泥,煤泥	16
small-scale	*n.* 成比例缩小	09
smooth-surfaced	*a.* 表面平滑的	11
sonic	*a.* 音速的	13
spacing	*n.* 空隙	07
sparse	*a.* 稀少的,稀疏的	14
spatially *	*ad.* 在空间上	02
specific volume	比容	01
specific weight	容重	05
specifically	*ad.* 尤其	09
spectrum *	*n.* 光谱	12
sphere	*n.* 球,范围	11
spherical	*a.* 球形的	05
spiral *	*a.* 螺旋的	15
stagnant	*a.* 停滞的,不流动的	14
stagnation	*n.* 停滞	13
stationary *	*a.* 静止的	13
Stefan-Beltzmann Law	斯蒂芬-波尔兹曼定律	12
sub-layer	底层	07
sublayer	*n.* 底层,下层	14
subscript	*n.* 下符,下标	09
subsonic	*a.* 亚音速的,亚声速的	13
suction	*n.* 吸入	15
summation	*n.* 和,总数	05
summit	*n.* 顶点,决顶	06
superheated	*a.* 过热的	04
superimpose	*vt.* 加上,附加,叠加	10
surface force	表面力	05
symmetrical	*a.* 对称的,勿称的	13
tangent	*n.* 正切,切线	13
tangentially	*ad.* 切线地,正切地	15
the Gbbs-Dalton Law	道尔顿定律	14
the Mach number	马赫数	13
theoretician	*n.* 理论家	03
thereof *	*ad.* 因此,由此	16
thermal *	*a.* 热的	01
thermodynamics	*n.* 热力学	01
throttle	*n.* 节流阀	02
tip speed	稍速,末端速度	15
tortuous	*a.* 弯曲的	08
transient	*a.* (物)瞬变的	01
transition *	*n.* 过渡,变迁	11
transonic	*a.* 跨音速的	13
triple(point) *	*a.* 三相的(三相点)	03
truncated	*a.* 截短(断)的	03
turbo	*n.* 涡轮,透平	02
turbulence	*n.* 紊流,扰动	10
turbulent	*a.* 紊流,湍流	07
undesirable	*a.* 令人不快的,讨厌的	04
unicellular	*a.* 单细胞的,单孔的	08

unidirectional	*a.* 单向的		08
unrestricted	*a.* 不受限制的		13
upstream	*ad.* 逆流		06
validity *	*n.* 有效,效力		07
valve *	*n.* 阀门		04
velocityhead	速度头		15
versus *	*prep.* 对		11
vertically	*ad.* 终向地		05
vice versa	反过来(也是这样)		05
virial equation	维里方程		03
viscosity	*n.* 粘性		07
viscous	*a.* 粘性的,粘滞的		10
visualize *	*vt.* 使可见,见到		13
volatile *	*n.* 挥发物		16
volumetric	*a.* 容积的		04
wake	*n.* 尾流,尾波		11
wake resistance	尾流阻力		11
well-streamlined	*a.* 流线型的		11
whirl	*n.* 回旋,旋转		15

Appendix Ⅱ   Translation for Reference

第1单元

基本概念和定义

热力学的应用大部分都要求对系统及它的环境定义。热力系统定义为空间的某一区域或某一封闭面包围的物质质量，环境包括系统外面的一切物体，系统和环境由系统分界面分隔。这些分界面可以是运动的或固定不变的，可以是真实的也可以是假想的。

两个主要概念在任何热力系统中都适用，即能量和熵。熵计量某一给定系统分子的无序（程度），系统越混乱，它的熵就越大。相反，有序或不混乱的结构是一个低熵系统。

能量是产生某一效果的能力，并且可以分成储存能和瞬时能两类。储存型能量包括：热（内）能，u——由于分子运动和/或分子之间的作用力，系统所具有的能量。

势能，$P.E$——由于分子间存在的吸引力或系统的高度，系统所具有的能量：

$$P.E = mgz$$

式中　m——质量；

　　　g——当地重力加速度；

　　　z——相对于水平参考面的高度。

动能，$K.E$——由于分子速度，系统所具有的能量。

$$K.E = mv^2/2$$

式中　m——质量；

　　　v——穿过系统边界的流体速度。

化学能，E_c——由于组成分子的原子的排列，系统所具有的能量。

核（原子）能，E_a——由于使质子和中子构成原子核的内聚力作用，系统所具有的能量。

瞬时能包括：

热能，Q——系统由于温度不同，穿过边界传递的能量，总是朝着温度降低的方向。

功量——系统由于压力（或任何种类的力）不同，穿过边界传递的能量，它总是朝着压力降低的方向；如果该系统产生的总的效果能归纳成重物的升高，那么只有功量穿过边界。机械功或轴功，W，是由机械，如透平，空气压缩机或内燃机传递或吸收的能量。

流动功是进入或跨越系统边界的能量，这是由于在系统外某处的泵送过程发生流体进入该系统而引起的。它作为系统外边界面处的流体为迫使或推动相邻流体进入系统而作的功更容易理解。当流体离开系统时也会产生流动功。

$$\text{流动功（每单位质量）} = Pv$$

式中 P 是压力，v 是比容或单位质量排开的体积。

系统的参数是任何可观察到的系统特性。系统的状态通过列出它的参数来确定。最常见的热力学参数是：温度（T），压力（P）和比容（v）或密度（ρ）。另外，热力学参数还包括熵，储存能和焓。

热力学参数常常结合起来形成新的参数。焓（h）（参数结合得出的结果）定义为：
$$h = u + Pv$$
式中　u——内能；

　　　P——压力；

　　　v——比容。

给定状态的每一参数只有一个确定值，并且任一参数在给定状态下总保持同一值，不管物质是怎样到达这一状态的。

过程即状态的变化，定义为系统参数的任何变化。过程可以通过指定初、终平衡态，路径（如果是可辨认的）及过程中穿过系统边界发生的相互作用来描述。循环是一个过程，或更经常地是指一系列过程，在这些过程中系统的初、终态相同。因而，在循环结束时，所有参数都有与它们在初态时相同的数值。

纯物质具有均匀不变的化学成分。它能以多相存在，但所有的相中化学成分是相同的。

如果物质以饱和温度下的气态存在，则称为饱和蒸汽（有时用干饱和蒸汽这个术语来强调其干度为100％）。当蒸汽温度比其饱和温度高时，为过热蒸汽，过热蒸汽的压力和温度是独立参数，因为当压力保持不变时其温度可以增加。气体是高度过热的蒸汽。

第2单元

热力学原理在工程系统稳定流动组元中的应用

许多复杂的工程系统以稳定流动或周期流动运行，稳定或周期流动简化了热力学分析，这种系统由相互连接的稳定流动组元构成，这些组元根据其性能可分为四类：（1）轴功机械，（2）喷管和扩压管，（3）节流阀，和（4）热交换器。对这些组元变化特性的理解是了解下章讨论的热力装置的关键。

本章的目的是通过把热力学原理应用到含有该组元的控制体中来确定每类组元的热力变化。这种方法产生了该组元的"黑箱原则"特性，这种特性是为了评价整个系统性能所必须了解的。这并不意味着在决定该组元详细的内部过程中热力学原理不适用或无用。相反，在设计这样的组元时，对复杂的内部过程必须给予详细的考虑。但对这些内部过程的分析已超越我们现在任务的范围。

本章的分析是基于有一个进口和一个出口的控制体的稳定流动方程。此外，这在考虑流动方向上微元长度的控制体时是有用的。流体对应于微元的热传递速率和剪切功传递速率，在进出口间经历了微元的状态变化。这样我们就得出了微分关系：

$$\frac{\delta Q}{\dot{m}} + \frac{\delta W_{\text{shear}}}{\dot{m}} = dh + vdv - gdz$$

这种分析可以通过在不可压缩流体的流动、理想流体的流动，和在处于两相状态的纯物质的流动中应用来证明。这些例子阐明了四类稳定流动组元中每一类的基本特性。

第一类组元是由通过正或负轴功传递来改变流动状态的机械组成。有正轴功传递的机械通常指透平、往复式发动机、膨胀器、或液动电机，取决于使用场合和产生引起轴功传递的压力的方法。有负轴功传递的机械通常指压缩机、泵、或风机，取决于应用场合。

轴功机械的运行并不取决于在流动流体与设备内壁间达到热平衡，因此，轴功传递速率不受相对较慢的导热过程限制。更确切些，功量传递取决于设备内运动表面（透平或压缩机叶片或活塞端面）上的压力。这样，功量传递速率的极限值与流体中压力波（声音）传播的速度是有关的。这个速率通常很快，以致于对机械来说，功量的传递速度实际上受到该机械固体部件加速引起的力的限制（惯性应力极限）。

由于功量传递速度很快，轴功机械又很小，以致使流体留在机械里的时间周期相对于达到热平衡所需要的时间周期来说是短的。这样，设备基本是绝热的。注意有些热传递实际上在任何情况下都发生，但与轴功传递相比其量级是可以忽略的。这种情况对透平机械尤其正确，在透平机械中高功量传递速率是（经过叶片的）内部压力差的结果，该压差是由加速（偏斜）运动流体引起的。在往复式或容积式机械中，内力是作用在运动活塞端面或等同运动表面上（空间上均匀的）平衡压力的结果。

相对快的功量传递速率和由此而产生的小型机械的第二个结果是重力势能的变化通常可以忽略。甚至对水电站中使用的大型水轮机来说，只要控制体不包括进水管也是正确的。

前面的讨论表明，轴功机械可以合理地模拟为重力势能变化可略的绝热装置。而且，在许多实际情况下，总体流动的动能变化也是可略的。这样，热力学第一定律应用到代表这种类型机械的控制体上就得出：

$$-\dot{W}_{\text{shaft}} = \dot{m}(h_{\text{out}} - h_{\text{in}})$$

第 3 单元

状 态 方 程

纯物质的状态方程是当系统处于热力平衡状态时，压力，比容和温度之间的数学关系

$$f(P, v, T) = 0 \tag{3.1}$$

理论家使用统计力学的原理来（1）探索物质的基本参数，（2）预示基于微粒系统统计性质的状态方程或（3）提出有未知数的状态方程的函数形式。未知数可以通过测量物质的热力学参数来确定。以此为基础的基本方程是维里方程。

维里方程可表示为压力 P 的展开式或每单位质量体积 v 值倒数的展开式：

$$\frac{Pv}{RT} = 1 + B'P + C'P^2 + D'P^3 + \cdots \tag{3.2}$$

$$\frac{Pv}{RT} = 1 + (B/v) + (C/v^2) + (D/v^3) + \cdots \tag{3.3}$$

式中系数 B'，C'，D' 等，及 B，C，D 等称为维里系数。B' 和 B 是第二维里系数；C' 和 C 是第三维里系数。维里系数只是温度的函数，并且方程（3.2）和方程（3.3）中各系数值是相关的。例如，$B' = B/RT$ 及 $C' = (C-B^2)/(RT)^2$。

参数 R 是理想气体常数，定义为：

$$R = \lim_{p \to 0} (Pv)_T / T_{tp} \tag{3.4}$$

式中 $(Pv)_T$ 是沿等温线的压力和容积的乘积，T_{tp} 是规定的水三相点温度 = 273.16K。通用的最佳 R 值是 8.31434J/gmol·K。

Pv/RT 的数值也称为压缩因子，$Z = Pv/RT$，或

$$Z = 1 + (B/v) + (C/v^2) + (D/v^3) + \cdots \tag{3.5}$$

维里形式的一个优点是统计力学可用来预示低级系数，并给出维里系数的物理意义。例如，在方程（3.5）中，B/v 项是两个分子间相互作用的函数，C/v^2 是三个分子相互作用的函数等等。由于低级的相互作用是常见的，高级项的分配逐次减少。热力学使用分配函数或分布函数来决定维里系数。然而，一般来说是先选出第二第三系数的经验值。对高密度的流体，许多高级项是必要的，它们既不能从理论上得到满意的预示也不能由实验测量来确定。一般说来，一个四项的截断维里展开式对小于临界点值一半的密度是有效的。对较高的密度，可以使用附加项，该附加项按经验确定。

数字计算机使复杂得多的状态方程得以用来计算 P-v-T 值，甚至对高密度流体的计算。本尼迪特—韦布—鲁宾（Benedict-Webb-Rubin, B-W-R）状态方程和马丁—豪（Martin-Hou）方程已得到很大的应用，但一般应只限于对低于临界值的密度。斯特布里奇（Strobridge）提出了一个修改的本尼迪特—韦布—鲁宾（Benedict-Webb-Rubin, B-W-R）关系式，这在高密度时给出极好的结果，并可用于延展到液相的 P-v-T 函数。

斯特布里奇（Strobridge）提出了一个求氮气参数的状态方程，并且用于多数低温流体。该方程把 B-W-R 状态方程与由本尼迪特（Benedict）提出的适用于高密度氮气的方程相结合。这些方程已成功地应用于液相和气相，对液相扩展到三相点温度和凝固线，对气相从 10K 到 1000K，压力到 1000mPa。由斯特布里奇（Strobridge）提出的方程在测量的 P-v-T 数据不确定的范围内是准确的。最初由斯特布里奇（Strobridge）发表的该方程是

$$\begin{aligned} P = RT\rho &+ \left[Rn_1T + n_2 + \frac{n_3}{T} + \frac{n_4}{T^2} + \frac{n_5}{T^4} \right]\rho^2 \\ &+ (Rn_6T + n_7)\rho^3 + n_8T\rho^4 \\ &+ \rho^3 \left[\frac{n_9}{T^2} + \frac{n_{10}}{T^3} + \frac{n_{11}}{T^4} \right] e^{(-n_{16}\rho^2)} \\ &+ \rho^5 \left[\frac{n_{12}}{T^2} + \frac{n_{13}}{T^3} + \frac{n_{14}}{T^4} \right] e^{(-n_{16}\rho^2)} + n_{15}\rho^6 \end{aligned} \tag{3.6}$$

该方程线性项的15个系数通过对试验数据最小二乘拟合来决定。关于确定状态方程的方法和技术更进一步的资料，请查阅参考书。

在试验数据缺乏的情况下，范德瓦尔斯（Verder Waals））对比态定律可以预测流体参

数。正如凯曼林夫·奥尼斯（Kamerlingh Onnes）所提出的，对该定律的修改内容已用来改进低压时的对比。对比态定律提供了有用的近似法，并且许多对该定律的修改已在文献上发表。对预测参数值更复杂的处理是通过归纳得出的状态方程来进行。这些处理方法承认流体参数的相似性。这些方程一般允许通过引进参数来调整 $P\text{-}v\text{-}T$ 函数。有一个例子通过加入两个相关参数来考虑偏离对比态定律的情况。

第 4 单元

理想的基本蒸气压缩致冷循环

基本蒸气压缩循环的设备图如图 4-1 所示。这种循环的组成部分至少包括压缩机、冷凝器、膨胀阀和蒸发器。理想循环考虑的是由管道连接的无压力损失冷凝器和蒸发器，可逆绝热（定熵）压缩机和绝热膨胀阀之间的热传递，连接用的管道既没有压力损失也没有与周围环境的热传递。制冷剂以低压、低温的饱和蒸气形式在点 1 离开蒸发器进入压缩机，在压缩机中被可逆绝热（定熵）压缩。在点 2，制冷剂以高温高压的过热蒸气形式离开压缩机，进入冷凝器，在冷凝器中首先被降温，然后在定压下冷凝。在点 3，制冷剂以高压，中间温度的饱和液体形式离开冷凝器进入膨胀阀，在膨胀阀中发生不可逆绝热膨胀（焓不变）。在点 4，制冷剂以低压、低温、低干度蒸气形式离开膨胀阀，进入蒸发器，在蒸发器中可逆地定压蒸发到点 1 的饱和状态。对蒸发器和从冷凝器的热传递是在放热流体与吸热流体间不存在有限温差的情况下进行的。冷凝器降温过程中的情况除外。

从热力学第一定律可以得出能量平衡和某些性能参数。对基本蒸气压缩循环的每个组成部分应用第一定律的稳定流动（能量）方程，可导出下列关系式：

1-2　压缩　　　　　$_1\dot{W}_2 = -(h_2 - h_1)\dot{m}$　　　　　　　　　　(4.1)

2-3　冷凝　　　　　$_2\dot{Q}_3 = -(h_2 - h_3)\dot{m}$　　　　　　　　　　(4.2)

3-4　膨胀阀　　　　$h_3 = h_4$

4-1　蒸发器　　　　$_4\dot{Q}_1 = (h_1 - h_4)\dot{m}$　　　　　　　　　　(4.3)

在应用稳定流动方程中，略去动能和势能项，因为流速低以避免流体阻力和令人讨厌的压力损失，并且给定致冷系统内的高度变化通常很小，因此这些项在数值上是微不足道的。由于系统是循环的，在冷凝器中排出的热必须等于在蒸发器所吸收的热和压缩机功的总和。

性能系数（COP）被用来评价致冷系统的性能。COP＝制冷效果/输入的净功。

对基本蒸气压缩循环，从公式（4.1）和（4.3），COP 是：

$$COP = (h_1 - h_4)/(h_2 - h_1)$$

压缩机的性能特征以及在制冷循环中的应用在 1983 年设备卷第 12 章中分析。考虑的类型包括容积式压缩机（即，往复活塞式、回转式和螺杆式）和离心式压缩机。

在评价压缩机对热力系统的贡献时，有必要考虑压缩机进口和出口的制冷剂参数，这两点间的状态变化是（1）理想压缩机的可逆绝热（定熵）变化，（2）绝热但不可逆变化（流体流经压缩机时伴随熵的增加），理想压缩机的变化用绝热压缩机效率来描述。

对容积式压缩机来说，一个热力学的重要考虑是余隙容积的影响，即，留在压缩机内没有被运动部件排出的制冷剂体积。对活塞式压缩机来说，要考虑当活塞处于顶端、中心位置时活塞和气缸头间的余隙容积。在气缸排出压缩气体后，随着压力降到进口压力，余隙内的气体再次膨胀到较大体积。因此按进口压力和温度时的情况计量，压缩机排出的致冷剂质量比活塞扫过容积占有的质量要少，从数量上讲，这种结果可由容积效率 η_v 来表示。

$$\eta_v = m_a / m_t \tag{4.4}$$

式中　m_a——每冲程进入压缩机的新气的实际质量；

m_t——由排气体积代表的并在压缩机进口压力和温度时所确定的气体理想质量。

容积效率度量了在使致冷剂蒸气在循环中移动时，压缩机活塞排量（体积）的有效度。由于制冷剂的比容大不相同，致冷剂的选择会影响压缩机排气量传送的质量流量。

多级压缩机的设计参数之一是级间压力的选择，在级间压力处致冷剂温度由中间冷却器降低。在最佳级间压力时，总功最小。对理想气体（$Pv=RT$）的两级压缩来说，最佳级间压力是在吸气压力和排气压力的几何平均处，并导致两级功量相等。但是在制冷系统上使用多级压缩机不同于气体压缩机，因为级间压力处的冷却通常是由从循环某些其他部分转移来的致冷剂完成的。

第 5 单元

静止流体中压强的变化

考虑图 5-1 中静止流体微团。由于微团非常小，我们可假设其密度为常数。现假设微团中心点的压强为 p，而且假定微团的大小为 δx，δy，δz。作用在微团垂直方向上的力有质量力（微团内由于质量引起的重力作用）和表面力（来自周围液体而且垂直作用在微团顶部、底部以及四周）。由于流体是静止的，微团处于平衡状态，而且从各个方向作用在微团的力之和等于零。如果对水平方向的力求和，即 x 和 y 方向，那么仅仅起作用的力是在微团垂直面上的压力。为了满足 $\Sigma F_x=0$ and $\Sigma F_y=0$，作用在相对垂直面的压强必须相等，这样对于静止流体来说，就是，$\partial p/\partial x=\partial p/\partial y=0$。

对垂直方向力求和并设其为零，结果可以写为：

$$\frac{dp}{dz} = -\gamma \tag{5.1}$$

这是一般表达式，它表明了在铅垂方向压强的变化。负号表示当 z 变大（高程增加），压强变小。

为了计算静止流体中压强的变化，必须对方程 5.1 在适当的积分线之间积分。对于不可压缩流体（$\gamma = const$），方程5.1可以直接被积出来，它可以写成：
$$p - p_1 = -\gamma(z - z_1) \tag{5.2}$$
p是某一高程处的压强，这个表达式一般用于液体，因为它们的压缩性很小。仅在高程变化较大时，比如海洋，为了精确确定压强的变化，流体的压缩性才需考虑，当高程变化较小，用于气体时，方程5.2给出精确的结果。

对于静止流体，从自由液面垂直向下测定距离是方便的，如果h是自由液面以下的距离，而且液面上空气和蒸气的压强设定为零，方程5.2可以写成：
$$p = \gamma h \tag{5.3}$$

由于液面上总是有压强的，那么在某一深度h处的总压强可以由方程5.3的计算值加上液面压强给出。在很多情况下，这个液面压强可以忽略不计。

从方程5.3可以看出，在静止等密度连通的液体中，液面以下相同深度各点的压强是相等的。这表明，静止液体的等压面是水平面。严格地讲，是在任何地方都垂直于重力方向而且近似与地球同心的球面。从实用目的讲，这个曲面的有限部分可以被看作平面。

在图5-2中，设一个开口的容器，其表面没有压强。事实上任何液面上最小压强是它自己的蒸气压强。暂时略去这一点不计，根据方程5.3，任意深度h处的压强$p=\gamma h$。假设γ为常数，那么p和h之间有确定的关系。也就是，压强（单位面积上的力）等于表观密度为γ的流体的高度h。通常用流体柱的高度表示压强要比用单位面积上的压力表示更方便。

即使液面是在一定压强作用下，也只须将压强转换成该流体的等量柱高。把该柱高与图5-2所示的值相加，以得出总压。

前面的讨论已经用到液体中，而对某些有恒定表观密度γ的气体和蒸气也是适用的。这样通过关系式：
$$h = p/\gamma \tag{5.4}$$
压强p可以用任意流体的流体柱高度来表示。

方程5.2也可以写成如下形式：
$$z + \frac{p}{\gamma} = z_1 + \frac{p_1}{\gamma} = const \tag{5.5}$$

此式表明，对静止不可压缩流体，流体中任一点高度z与该点的压强水头p/γ之和等于任意其他点这两项之和，这样表达的意义是：在静止流体中，随高度增加，压强水头将减小，反之亦然，这个概念在图5-3中描述过。

第6单元

水力坡度线和能量线

$z+p/\gamma$这一项被称为测压管水头，因为它表示液体在测压管中上升的高度。水力坡度线是通过测压管液柱顶部的一条线。毕托管是一个小的开口管，它开口端指向上游。毕托管能截住流体的动能，所以能指示总水头，$z+p/\gamma+u^2/2g$。

熟悉能量线和水力坡度线的概念对不可压缩流体流动问题的解决是有用的。

如果沿管道安装一系列测压管，测压管中液体将上升到不同高度。通过这样一个想象系列液柱的顶端所画的线被称为水力坡度线。如果这种情况能存在而且保证相同的流动条件，可以观察到水力坡度线代表液体的自由表面。

水力坡度线表明沿管道的压强情况，因为假设剖面是按比例画的，那么在管道的任意一点，从管道到水力坡度线的垂直距离就是这一点的压强水头。在 C 点这个距离是零，所以它表示管道内部那点的绝对压强是大气压。在 D 点，管道是在水力坡度线的上方，表明那里的压强水头是 $-DN$。

如果管线剖面是按比例画的，通过在图上量取的方式，水力坡度线不仅能确定任意点的压强水头，而且仅仅通过观察就能了解沿整个管长压强的变化。只要是直管而且管径均匀，水力坡度线就是一直线。在长管线中经常出现微量弯曲的情况下，水力坡度线偏离直线的程度是小的。当然，除正常管道摩擦以外，如果有局部水头损失，水力坡度线会突然的下降。管径变化及由此而产生的速度变化，也会引起水力坡度线的突然变化。

正如图 6-1 所示，如果速度水头是常数，任意两点间水力坡度线的下降是这两点间的水头损失。因此在图 6-2 中，大管中的损失率比小管中的小得多。如果速度改变，正如图 6-2 和图 6-3 所表明的，在流动方向上水力坡度线实际上可能上升。

在图 6-1 中，从 A 点液面高度向下到水力坡度线的垂直距离代表从 A 点到任意点的 $V^2/2g+h_L$。所以坡度线的位置不取决管道的位置。因此，点绘水力坡度线不必计算各点的压强水头，相反，从 A 点到各点的 $V^2/2g+h_L$ 值是从通过 A 点的水平线向下量取的。这个过程通常更方便。如果管径是均匀的。只需确定几个点，通常仅需要两个点。

如果图 6-1 表示均匀管径按比例绘成的剖面，水力坡度线可以按如下方法绘制。在管道入口 A 点液面以下有一个跌落值，其值应等于 $V^2/2g$ 加上局部入口损失。在 E 点压强是 EF，在 F 点水力坡度线必须结束。如果管子在 E 点自由向大气排放，水力坡度线就必须通过 E 点。其他点的位置比如 B' 和 N 如果需要可以被计算出来。

如果 h_L 值是在通过 A 点的水平线下面量取，由此而产生的线如果是在水力坡度线以上 $V^2/2g$ 的距离范围内，那么这条线就表示了在任意基准面上方量取的总水头（H）的值。这条线是能量坡度线，表示能量减少速率。除非有来自水泵的能量输入，否则总能量坡度线在流动方向上总是沿程下降的。能量坡度线也不取决于管线的位置。

能量坡度线在图 6-1 到图 6-3 中显示。最后一个表明水头的主要损失是在岔开部分，正好超过最小管径段。

第7单元

圆形截面管道中不可压缩恒定均匀的紊流

封闭管道中紊流水头损失可以由达西（Darcy）公式给出：

$$h_\mathrm{f} = \frac{4fL}{d} \cdot \frac{\bar{v}^2}{2g}$$

从上式可以看出，除摩擦因子 f 以外，其他所有参数都是可测量的，在这个领域中广泛试验的结果确立了如下的比例关系：

(1) $h_\mathrm{f} \propto l$；
(2) $h_\mathrm{f} \propto \bar{v}^2$；
(3) $h_\mathrm{f} \propto l/d$；
(4) h_f 取决于管壁的表面摩擦；
(5) h_f 取决于流体的密度和粘滞性；
(6) h_f 不取决于压强。

为了保证由达西公式计算的 h_f 的准确性，f 值必须被选择，而且不是单值常数。f 值必须依赖上面所列的所有参数。用适合于量纲分析的式子表达，这包含：

$$f = \phi(\bar{v}, d, \rho, \mu, k, k', \alpha) \tag{7.1}$$

这里 k 是壁面粗糙度的度量，k' 是粗糙粒子间隔的度量，两者都具有长度的量纲，α 是形状因子（其值取决于粗糙粒子形状的无量纲参数）。在一般的粗糙管道中，量纲分析得出一个关系式：

$$f = \phi_2(\mathrm{Re}, k/d, k'/d, \alpha) \tag{7.2}$$

对于经验解，量纲分析只能指出各参数间的最佳组合；按上述所列变量表形式的摩擦因子的实际代数关系式必须通过试验确定。

1993 年，布拉修斯（Blasius）首先为紊流光滑管中的摩擦因子提出了准确的经验公式，即：

$$f = 0.079/\mathrm{Re}^{1/4} \tag{7.3}$$

这个公式在 Re<100,000 时，得出的光滑管水头损失误差在±5％范围内。

对于粗糙管，1933 年，尼古拉兹（Nikuradse）通过对一系列管道中水头损失的研究，证实了 f 对相对粗糙度 k/d 的依赖性，这些管道在内部粘贴一层砂粒，砂粒大小是可变的。这些试验没有研究粒子间隔 k'/d 或粒子形状因子 α 对摩擦因子的影响，但确表明对一类粗糙度来说是：

$$f = \phi_3(\mathrm{Re}, k/d) \tag{7.4}$$

完全有理由认为试验问题实际上不可能保持 k'/d 和 α 为常数，而由此来单独研究粗糙度 k/d 的影响。然而，通过依据雷诺数 Re 和相对粗糙度 k/d 得出 f 值时，所得结果的准确性确实表明同仅依赖相对粗糙度 k/d 而产生的结果比较，粒子间隔和形状的影响是可以忽略的。

所以，紊流管道流动水头损失计算是取决于使用经验性的结果而且最普通的参考源是莫迪图（Moody Chart）。此图是在一定的 k/d 范围内，以 f—Re 绘成对数坐标图，这种类型的数据图示一般被称为 Stanton 图。图 7-1 是典型的莫迪图,不同的分区可以被标出和说明。

(i) 标有'层流'(laminar flow)的直线段,代表 $f=16/Re$,是泊萧叶(Poiseuille)方程的图形表示。方程 $f=16/Re$ 在双对坐标图上被绘成斜率为 -1 的直线。而不依赖管道壁面的粗糙度。这一关系也表明,如果正确的 f 值被引用,达西公式适用于层流区。

(ii) 对于 $k/d < 0.001$,由于层流底层的存在,图 7-1 粗糙管曲线接近布拉修斯(Blasius)光滑管曲线,层流底层在紊流管壁附近形成,它的厚度随雷诺数(Re)的增大而减小。所以,对于表面粗糙度和雷诺数的某种组合来说,层流底层的厚度完全可以抵消壁面粗糙度的影响从而使流体就好象在管壁光滑的管道里流动似的。对于高雷诺数,大量的粗糙粒子伸出正在变薄的层流底层而使水头损失增加。

(iii) 在高雷诺数或管道具有高的 k/d 值时,所有粗糙粒子暴露在层流底层上面的流动中。在这种情况下,水头损失完全是由于造成管道粗糙度的每个粒子形成的涡团尾迹造成的。这种形式的水头损失被称为"形状阻力"。而与平均流速的平方成正比,也就是 $h_f \propto \bar{v}^2$。因此,根据达西公式 f 是常数,只取决于粗糙粒子的大小。这种情况通过部分 f—Re 曲线段表示在莫迪图上,这些曲线平行于 Re 轴而且在 Re 和 k/d 值较高的情况下出现。

第 8 单元

导 热

导热可以认为是通过物质分子间逐渐进行的能量交换而在物体(或物体联合体)内从高温区到低温区传递热量。在导热过程中,没有产生分子的具体的位移。然而,就金属来说,自由电子的运动大大有助于导热。

导热的基本定律归功于付立叶。该定律可表示如下。考虑稳态的单向热流通过一固体,如图 8-1 所示。取一横截面积为 A 的固体的厚片,该厚片垂直于热流路径。设厚片的厚度为 dx,厚片两端间的温差为 dt。从他的试验工作付立叶发展了如下关系:

$$\dot{Q} = -kA\frac{dT}{dx} \qquad (8.1)$$

式中　$\dot{Q}$——单位时间的热流量;

K——比例系数,称为导热系数;

dT/dx——热流方向上温度随距离的变化率。

在国际单位制中,导热系数表示为:

$$W/m^2 \div K/m = W/mK$$

大量的试验研究已得出了许多物质的导热系数值和温度对这些导热系数的影响。注意,任何金属的导热系数与任何气体的导热系数相比都是非常高的。已发表的金属导热系数值仅对指定纯度的金属才是正确的。尤其对那些具有最高导热系数值的金属,掺入少量其他金属就会引起导热系数明显的变化。

最佳的绝热固体应把它们的绝热性能归功于材料小孔内所含的空气或其他气体。这些小孔使热量经过长而弯曲的路径流经固体。另外，固体材料可得到的横截面积比投影面积小得多。实验证据表明，在使物质具有绝热值（性能）方面，许多单个小气孔要比有相同总体积的连接起来的一串气孔有效得多。任何给定的绝热材料，其导热系数都可能有很大的变化，因为导热系数取决于材料的密度、体积、小气孔的数量和吸湿量。

通过实验确定固体的导热系数，有几种可以接受的方法。只要适当注意，对成分已知的给定固体就可以得到相当准确的导热系数值。然而，要确定气体，蒸气，或液体的导热系数值却要困难得多，因为要从中取掉通过对流所传递的热量（与导热同时发生）几乎是不可能的，况且还没有包括准确测量其他因素的困难。因为这些原因，已发表的流体导热系数值都有大约10%～25%的误差。图8-2表示了在简单墙体中的热传导。假设墙体的宽度和高度要比墙体的厚度大得多，从而可以认为热流是单向的。墙体的一面维持均匀温度 t_1 另一面保持在温度 t_2。通过墙体的热量可以通过方程8.1积分得到。

考查附录中给出的各种物质的导热系数表明，对许多物质，其导热系数在相当大的温度范围内可以认为是恒定值。而且，对大多数物质，在信息可以得到的温度范围内，其导热系数是温度的线性函数。这样可以用导热系数的算术平均值 k_m 作为真实的导热系数。对简单墙体，方程8.1可积分如下：

$$\dot{Q} = \frac{k_m A}{X}(T_1 - T_2) \tag{8.2}$$

根据方程8.2，热流速率正比于热流面积，引起热流的温差，和 k_m/X 项。该项称为导热率。

当导热系数不随温度线性变化时，平均导热系数 k_m 就不容易确定。在这种情况下，就需要在方程8.1中把导热系数表示为温度的函数，然后进行积分。

第9单元

相似的定义

采用纯理论的方法确定给定流体流动的所有基本要素通常是不可能的，因此常常依赖于试验研究。通过基于量纲分析尤其是基于相似原理的系统程序，所作试验的数量可以大大地减小。相似原理允许使用某些关系式，通过这些关系式试验数据可以应用到其它场合。

这样，相似规律能使我们利用方便的流体做试验比如水、空气。还有，在水力学和空气动力学中，用对全尺寸装置按比例缩小的模型来做试验，可以以最小的费用而获得有价值的结果。相似原理使得用模型做试验获取原型的流动特征成为可能，原型就是全尺寸的装置。原型和模型中的流体不必是一样的，模型也不必比原型小。这样汽化器中的流动可以在很大的模型中研究；从入口到小型离心水泵转子的水流动可以通过入口到大转子模型来研究。

应该强调，模型尺寸不必与原型不同。事实上，它们可以是同一装置，这种情况下，变量是速度和流体的特性。

在模型试验中理想的特征之一是几何相似。重要的条件是流动模态几何相似，如果比例值使用 L_r 来表示，由此得出，面积随 L_r^2 而变化；体积随 L_r^3 变化。L_r 表示原型线性长度与模型对应长度的比值。圆满的几何相似并不总是容易得到的。例如，小模型的表面粗糙度不可能按比例减小，除非可以使它的表面比原型表面光滑得多。在沉淀物输送问题研究中，当材料精细到不切实际的情况下，按比例缩小底层材料是不可能的。细粉并不模拟砂子的特性。又如在河道研究中，水平比例受到可利用地面空间的限制，用于竖向的相同比例可能导致水流太浅以致毛细作用有显著的影响，而且坡度可能使流动成为层流。在这样的场合必须使用变态模型，这意味着竖向比例比水平比例大。如果水平比例用 L_r 表示，而竖向比例用 L_r' 表示，那么横截面积的比例为 $L_r L_r'$。

运动相似暗示几何相似而且另外它暗示在流场中所有相对应点的流速比值都是一样的。如果下标 p 和 m 分别表示原型和模型，速度比值 V_r 可以写为：

$$V_r = \frac{V_p}{V_m} \tag{9.1}$$

正如在下节中要解释的那样，L_r 的值将按照动力学的考虑来确定。

因为时间 T 具有 L/V 的量纲，时间比例就是：

$$T_r = \frac{L_r}{V_r} \tag{9.2}$$

以相似的方式，加速度比例是：

$$a_r = \frac{L_r}{T_r^2} = \frac{V_r^2}{L_r} \tag{9.3}$$

如果两个系统动力相似，相应的力必须在这两个系统中具有相同的比例。可能作用在流体微元上的力包括重力 F_G，压力 F_P，粘滞性 F_V 和弹性力 F_E。另外，如果流体微团处在液-气交界面上，就有表面张力 F_T，如果作用在流体微元上力的和不等于零，依据牛顿定律，微元将作加速运动。这样一个不平衡系统通过引入惯性力 F_I 可以转变成平衡系统。惯性力与作用力的合力大小相等方向相反，所以一般：

$$F_G + F_P + F_V + F_E + F_T + F_I = 0$$

在很多流动问题中，这些力中有些不存在或不显著。在图9-1中是两个几何相似流动系统的描述。假定它们也具有运动相似而且有作用力 F_G，F_P，F_V 和 F_I。那么动力相似就可达到，如果：

$$\frac{F_{G_p}}{F_{G_m}} = \frac{F_{P_p}}{F_{P_m}} = \frac{F_{V_p}}{F_{V_m}} = \frac{F_{I_p}}{F_{I_m}}$$

这里下标 p 和 m 象前述一样表示原型和模型。这些关系式也能表述成：

$$\left(\frac{F_I}{F_G}\right)_p = \left(\frac{F_I}{F_G}\right)_m \left(\frac{F_I}{F_P}\right)_p = \left(\frac{F_I}{F_P}\right)_m \left(\frac{F_I}{F_V}\right)_p = \left(\frac{F_I}{F_V}\right)_m$$

每一个方程是无量纲的。由于四个作用力，所以有三个独立表达式必须满足；对于三个作用力，有两个独立式必须满足，等等。

第 10 单元

自 然 对 流

由于密度差和重力作用引起流体运动而产生的热传递称为自然对流或自由对流。自然对流的传热系数一般远低于强迫对流，因此在计算总的得热量或失热量时，主要的一点就是不要忽略辐射热。辐射热传递与自然对流可以有相同的数量级，甚至在室温下也如此，因为室内墙体温度影响人体的舒适感。

在各种供热和致冷设备中自然对流是重要的：①在高湿度冷藏室内及室内安装的制冷剂冷凝器内使用的重力盘管，②家用冰箱的蒸发器和冷凝器，③空间采暖的踢脚板散热器和对流器，及④空调用辐射冷却板。设备外壳及其连接风道和管道的失热量和得热量中也包含自然对流。

现在来考虑冷流体和热表面间自然对流引起的热传递。与表面直接接触的流体由于导热而被加热，变轻，并且由于与相邻流体的密度差而上升。这种运动由于流体粘性而受到阻碍。热传递受下列因素影响：(1) 因热膨胀而引起的重力作用，(2) 粘性阻滞及 (3) 热扩散。这种热传递被认为取决于重力加速度 g、热膨胀系数 β、运动粘滞系数 $v(=\mu/\rho)$，及导热系数 $\alpha(=k/\rho c_p)$。这些变量可以用无因次数的形式给出：努谢尔特数，Nu，它是普朗特数 Pr 和格拉晓夫数 Gr 乘积的函数，Gr 与 Pr 的乘积，取决于流体特性、表面与流体间的温差 Δt，和表面特征长度 L。常数 c 和指数 n 取决于物体外形和流动性质。

自然对流的全部过程不能由单一的指数 n 表示，但可以分成三个区域：(1) 紊流自然对流，n 等于 0.33，(2) 层流自然对流，n 等于 0.25，(3) (Gr·Pr) 小于层流自然对流的区域，指数 n 从 0.25 逐渐减小到更低的值。注意，对金属线，(Gr·Pr) 可能会很小，所以 n 是 0.1。

为了计算自然对流传热系数，先算出 (Gr·Pr)，确定边界是层流还是紊流，然后应用合适的方程。必须使用已指出的正确的特征长度。由于紊流边界层的指数 n 是 0.33，特征长度消去，传热系数与特征长度无关。当长度或温差大时就产生紊流。由于管道的长度一般大于它的直径，竖管的传热系数大于横管的传热系数。

热面朝下（冷面朝上）的水平板对流是个特例。由于热空气在较冷空气之上，理论上不会产生对流。然而，一些次要影响，诸如平板边缘的温差，会引起一些对流。作为一种近似，可以使用这样一个（传热）系数，该系数比热面朝上的水平板的系数的一半稍低。

由于空气经常是传热流体，空气简化方程已经给出。其它有关自然对流的资料在一般传热参考书中可以得到。

将最近的实验和数据结果与现有的自然对流传热系数关系式相比较，观察到的差别表明，在封闭空间（建筑物）内的竖直表面使用 ASHRAE 推荐的（独立的）竖直平板传热系数时应该小心。计算房间内一定温度边界条件下竖直表面自然对流传热的改进关系式已发展起来。

在较弱的强迫对流情况下，自然对流会影响其传热系数。随着强迫对流效应，也就是雷诺数（Re）的增加，"混合对流"（加上自由对流的强迫对流）让位于纯强迫对流。由于混合对流的传热系数常常大于单纯自然对流或强迫对流的计算结果，故要参考自然对流与强迫对流综合作用的文献；前面给出的文献概述了垂直和水平管道的自然对流、混合对流、和强迫对流区。在混合对流中，局部条件影响对流系数值，但文献中允许选定适当的区域和近似取得对流系数。

第 11 单元

三维物体的阻力（不可压缩流体）

作用在物体上的总阻力是摩擦阻力和压差阻力之和：
$$F_D = F_f + F_p$$
对于流线型很好的物体来说，例如飞机的机翼或潜水艇的壳摩擦阻力是总阻力中的主要部分。一般不要求把摩擦阻力分离出来去计算压差阻力。通常在尾流阻力变得显著时，人们才对总的阻力感兴趣，事实上，习惯于使用一个方程来求出总的阻力

$$F_D = C_D \rho \frac{V^2}{2} A \tag{11.1}$$

对于具有尖角的物体，分离总是在同一点发生，这就产生了相对恒定值C_D。这种情况从图 11-1 平盘的曲线上可以看到。如果物体具有曲线型边界，分离点的位置将由边界层是层流还是紊流来确定。分离点的位置又确定尾流的宽度和压差阻力的大小。

上述原则在绕球体的流动中清清楚楚地得到了说明。在雷诺数（$DV/v<1$）很小的情况下，绕球体的流动完全处于粘性的作用下，而且摩擦阻力由 Stokes 公式给出。

$$F_D = 3\pi\mu VD \tag{11.2}$$

使这个方程与方程 11.1 相等，可以得出$C_D=24/\text{Re}$。这种情况与管道层流摩擦因子的相似性马上显示出来。绕球体流动的这个区域，在图 11.1 的C_D—Re 的双对数曲线图的左边被表示为一条直线。

当 Re 大于 1 时，层流边界层从球体表面分离，首先从后滞点开始。随着压差阻力占的比重增大，图 11-1 中的C_D曲线开始成水平状，而且阻力逐渐与V^2呈正比。随着 Re 的进一步增加，分离点在球面上向前移动，直到 Re=1,000，分离点大约在离前滞点 80°左右变得相当稳定为止。

在相当大的雷诺数范围内，条件保持相当稳定，层流边界层从球体的前半部分分离，而且C_D保持在 0.45 这一稳定值。然而对于光滑球体，当 Re 大约在 250,000 时，阻力系数突然减小大约 50%，这一现象可以在图 11-1 中看到，其原因是球体上边界层从层流向紊流的改变。边界层分离点向后移动到大约 115°。

从层流边界层向紊流边界系统的转变也可以通过人工地使某一局部区域的表面变粗糙来提前发生。通过使球体前端变粗糙，边界层变成紊流而且分离点向后移动。增加的粗糙度和紊流边界层必然导致摩擦阻力的增加,但可以肯定与尾流尺寸和影响的显著减小相比，

摩擦阻力的增加是次要的。这解释了为什么高尔夫球球面被穿孔的主要原因，表面光滑的球体将会有较大的整体阻力，因而在受力时不可能运动得象粗糙表面球体那样远。

其它各种形状三维体的 C_D—Re 图也在图 11-1 中显示。这里可以指出，使物体成流线形的目的是尽可能使分离点向后移，从而形成最小的紊流尾迹。这将减小压差阻力，但通过增加物体长度致使压强梯度逐渐增加，摩擦阻力也增加了。流线型的最佳程度是使摩擦阻力和压差阻力之和达到最小值。十分明显，从我们所学到东西来看，在流线形化的过程中，对物体的尾部或者下游部分必须同前部一样给予重视。原则上讲，物体前半部的形状是重要的，在某种程度上它控制分离点在后半部分的位置。圆形前缘对流线产生最小的扰动，所以对于亚音速不可压缩或可压缩流体是最佳的形式。

第 12 单元

实 际 辐 射

物质及表面对斯蒂芬－玻尔兹曼定律和普朗克定律有不同程度的偏离。W_b 和 $W_{b\lambda}$ 是在某一表面温度下的最大的辐射力。实际表面不太容易辐射和吸收，称为非黑（表面）。非黑表面的辐射力，在温度 T 时，辐射到非黑表面上方半球空间的辐射功率可写为：

$$W = \varepsilon W_b = \varepsilon \sigma T^4 \tag{12.1}$$

式中 ε 称为半球发射率。发射率是材料性质、表面状况和表面温度的函数。一些选择值以及更详尽的表格前面已给出。

非黑表面的单色辐射力类似地写为：

$$W_\lambda = \varepsilon_\lambda W_{b\lambda} = \varepsilon_\lambda (C_1 \lambda^{-5} / e^{c_2/\lambda T} - 1) \tag{12.2}$$

式中 ε_λ 为单色发射率。ε 和 ε_λ 之间的关系由下式给出：

$$\varepsilon = (1/\sigma T^4) \int_0^\infty \varepsilon_\lambda W_{b\lambda} d\lambda \tag{12.3}$$

如果 ε_λ 不取决于 λ，那么根据方程（12.3），$\varepsilon = \varepsilon_\lambda$。具有这种特性的表面称为灰表面。在计算中经常假设灰表面特性。表面的几种重要类型在光谱的某些区域近似符合这种假设，简单是理想的，但运用时必须小心，尤其是温度高的时候。由于缺乏 ε_λ 和 λ 之间关系的资料，有时会做灰体假设。

当辐射能投射到一个表面上，就会被吸收并反射或穿过物体透射。因而，由热力学第一定律：

$$\alpha + \tau + \rho = 1 \tag{12.4}$$

式中　α——投射辐射被吸收的份额即：吸收率；

τ——投射辐射被透射的份额即：透射率；

ρ——投射辐射被反射的份额即：反射率。

如果物体是不透明的，正如大多数固体在红外线区那样，$\tau = 0$，那么，$\alpha + \rho = 1$。

对黑体表面，$\alpha=1$，$\rho=0$ 及 $\tau=0$。白金黑体和纯金黑体在红外线区吸收率约为98%，与任何实际表面一样黑。任何理想的黑度都可以用在大空腔壁上的一个小孔来模拟。考虑进入孔口的一束辐射能，在它有可能从孔口返回之前，将经历多次内部反射，几乎被全部吸收。

某些纯黑色涂料在很广泛的条件下也显示98%的发射率。它们提供了比金或白金黑体耐用得多的表面，经常在辐射仪器上使用，并作为发射率或反射率测量中的参考标准。

基尔霍夫定律，是从热力学的观点考虑来说明任何不透明表面的发射率与吸收率之间的关系，阐明对投（入）射辐射与角度无关的任何表面或漫射表面来说 $\varepsilon_\lambda=\alpha_\lambda$。如果表面是灰表面，或投射辐射来自于同温度的黑体，那么还有 $\varepsilon=\alpha$，但许多表面不是灰表面。对大多数表面而言，对太阳辐射的吸收率与对低温辐射的发射率不同。这是由于在这两种情况下的波长分布不同，且 ε_λ 随波长变化的缘故。

前面讨论的是关于来自表面的总体半球辐射。没有讨论表面上方半球区域的能量分布，但这却对各种几何位置的传热速率有重要影响。

兰贝特定律，阐明发射表面上方半球面上辐射能的辐射力随某一角度的余弦（规律）变化，该角度是辐射表面的法线与辐射表面和半球面上点的联线之间的夹角。这样的辐射称为漫射。这种兰贝特辐射力变化相当于这样一种情况，假定来自某一表面非法线方向的辐射就好像是来自于与原表面具有相同辐射力（每单位面积）的等同面积所发生的辐射。这个等同面积可以通过将原表面投影到辐射方向的法向平面上来得到。黑表面完全遵循兰贝特定律。它近似于许多实际辐射和反射过程，在涉及粗糙表面和非金属表面时，尤其如此。大多数辐射分析是基于灰-漫辐射和反射这样的假定。

对不同几何形状、辐射特性和方向的表面，估计它们之间的传热速率时，常假定：①所有表面均是灰的或黑的，②辐射和反射是漫射，③整个表面参数均匀一致，④吸收率等于发射率并且与投射辐射源的温度无关，⑤两辐射表面间的物质既不发射也不吸收辐射。

这些假设由于它们提供的简化程度很大而被使用，虽然得出的结果只能认为是近似的。

第13单元

可压缩流体的分类

随着马赫数的增加，压缩性的影响也就更为重要。例如，在高马赫数的情况下，计算理想气体滞止压强的误差随 $\rho V^2/2$ 的增加而增加。

为了进一步说明可压缩流体的一些奇怪特征，考虑一个简单的例子。假想微弱的压强脉冲从点源传播出来，这些压力波呈球状，并以音速 c 辐射状从点源向外扩展。对于静止的点源，对称的波型模式表示在图 13-1a 中。

当点源以恒定速度 V 向左运动时，波型模式不再是对称的。图 13-1b，13-1c 和 13-1d 表示 $t=3$ 时 V 不同值时的波型模式。

从图 13-1 的压力波模式中,我们能得出一些有用的结论。做这一工作之前我们应该认识到,如果不是使点源向左运动,而是点源保持静止并让流体以速度 V 向右运动,由此而产生的压力波模式与图 13-1 所示相同。

当点源和流体均为静止时,压力波模式是对称的(图 13-1a),在压力场的任何地方,观察者能听到来自点源的相同声音频率。当点源速率与声音速率相比非常小时,压力波的模式基本上是对称的。在不可压缩流体中音速是无穷大的,所以,静止点源和静止流体情况是代表了不可压缩流体的。对于真实的不可压缩流体,压力信息在流场中的传播是自由的而且在瞬间完成。

当点源在静止流体移动时,压力波模式以非对称方式变化,非对称的程度依赖点源的速度与音速的比值关系。当 $V/c<1$,波型模式与图 13-1b 中表示的相似。这种流动被称为亚音速或可压缩的。因为波的模式是非对称的,静止观察者根据相对于点源的位置,会听到来自点源的不同音频的声音,我们称这种现象为多普勒(Doppler)效应。

当 $V/c=1$ 时,压力波不会出现在运动点源的前面,这时流动是音速的。当流体以音速($V/c=1$)流经静止点源时,压力波与通过点源且与流动方向正交的平面相切。压力波在这相切平面上聚集,这表明平面上有显著的压力变化形成,这个平面通常被称为马赫波。注意,压力信息的传播被限止在马赫波下游的流动区域里,马赫波上游的流动区域被称为静止区域,下游的流动区域被称活动区域。

当 $V>c$ 时,流动是超音速的,而且压力波模式同图 13-1d 中描绘的相似。与压力波相切的一个锥形(马赫锥)可被构造来表示马赫波,在这种情况下马赫波能把静止区域和活动区域分开。压力波信息传播被限制在活动区域内。从图 13-1d 我们能看到,这个锥的角度 $α$ 可以由公式得出:

$$\sin α = \frac{c}{V} = \frac{1}{\text{Ma}} \tag{13.1}$$

在研究 $V/c>1$ 的流动时,方程 13.1 通常用来表示马赫锥角 $α$ 和流动的马赫数的关系。压力波在马赫锥表面聚集,这表明通过锥面有显著的压强,从而是密度的变化。通过使用特殊的光学手段,可以看到在流场中密度的突然变化。

上述关于压力波模式的讨论表明下面流体流动的分类:
1. 不可压缩流动:$\text{Ma} \leqslant 0.3$,自由的,几乎对称的,瞬间完成的压力传播。
2. 可压缩亚音速流动:$0.3 < \text{Ma} < 1.0$,自由的,非对称压力传播。
3. 可压缩超音速流动:$\text{Ma} \geqslant 1.0$,马赫波形成,压力波传播被限定在活动区域。

除了上述提到的流动分类以外,另外两种情况通常提到。即,跨音速流($0.9 \leqslant \text{Ma} \leqslant 1.2$)和特超速速流($\text{Ma} > 5$)。现代航空器主要以空气涡轮发动机为动力,涡轮发动机涉及跨音速流。当航天飞机重新进入地球的大气层时,流动是特超音速的。可以预料未来的宇航器会在亚音速到特超音速之间的流动条件下飞行。

第 14 单元

涡流扩散系数及其在紊流中的应用

表示紊流特征的现象就是附加在时均速度上的随机速度波动。这些波动导致了少量或大量流体的运动，在某一时刻比平均速度快；在另一时刻，比平均速度慢。波动发生在流动方向和它的垂直方向上。小的混合作用即涡流在紊流区内形成。小的流体微粒由涡流携带着从高速区到低速区，向较慢的流体释放动量。涡流引起了运动流体不同层间的动量交换。如果有温度梯度存在，那么混合作用以几乎同样的方式传递能量。如果有质量浓度梯度存在，那么就有类似的质量交换，称为涡流扩散。分子扩散与涡流扩散的差别在于一个是微观的即分子的混合作用，另一个是宏观的即少量的混合作用。正如所预料的，涡流扩散比分子扩散相对较快。涡流扩散速率取决于速度波动即紊流的强度。由于紊流强度由流动的雷诺数决定，所以紊流扩散速率取决于雷诺数。紊流扩散系数，ε_D，由与分子扩散相同形式的方程表示：

$$\dot{m}_B'' = \varepsilon_D (d\rho_B/dy) \tag{14.1}$$

式中 ε_D ——涡流扩散系数，m^2/s

由于涡流扩散系数的数据很少且难以得到，质量传递系数类似于对流热传递的传热系数，常常靠试验来限定和确定。

考虑一下潮湿表面上方稳定紊流流动中的空气流，假设液一气接触面静止不动，速度为零。这就产生了贴近层流表面的缓慢运动的流体层。在层流底层和紊流主体间有一个过渡区即缓冲层，在缓冲层内流体会交替地以层流和紊流流动。在层流底层内，只能发生分子扩散；在缓冲层，分子扩散和对流扩散都有助于质传递。在紊流区，涡流扩散居支配地位，而且速度很快以致几乎使浓度梯度相等。

由于层流底层的存在，从湿表面到空气流的分子质扩散速度，是：

$$J_B = -D_v(d\rho_B/dy)_i \tag{14.2}$$

式中 $(d\rho_B/dy)_i$ 是接触面的分压力梯度。假设气体是理想气体，遵循道尔顿定律，并且总压力恒定，那么分压力梯度在空气中也肯定存在。湿表面是不透空气的，所以必须建立对流或主体速度以抵销空气扩散速度。从湿表面到空气流的总的质量传递必然有下式给出：

$$\dot{m}_B'' = -D_v(d\rho_B/dy)_i + \rho_{Bi}V_i \tag{14.3}$$

式中 v_i 是组分 B 蒸气在接触面处的对流速度；接触面处水蒸气的分质量密度是：

$$\rho_{Bi} = M_B p_{Bi}/R_g T_i \tag{14.4}$$

就一种气体经过另一种静止气体的扩散而言，由系数 P_{AM} 修正的简单分子扩散方程解释了对流速度对质量传递所起的作用。对稀释混合物，这种作用很小。对这种强制对流质量传递过程，可以使用相同的修正系数，至少在 v_i 很小的低质量传递速度时是这样。

接触面总的质量传递速度是：

$$\dot{m}_B'' = -D_v P_{AM}(d\rho_B/dy)_i \tag{14.5}$$

浓度梯度 $(d\rho_B/dy)_i$ 必须用试验来评价。通常的做法是不用这个梯度，而是限定质量传递系数 h_m。由此可见：

$$\dot{m}_B'' = (h_m M_B/R_g)(p_{Bi} - p_{B\infty})$$
$$= -(M_B D_v p_{AM}/R_g T_i)(d p_B/d y_i) \quad (14.6)$$

通过数学重新整理变为：
$$Sh_L = h_m L/D$$
$$= p_{AM}\left[d\left(\frac{p_B - p_{Bi}}{p_{B\infty} - p_{Bi}}\right)\middle/ d(y/L)\right] \quad (14.7)$$

式中 Sh_L 是无因次宣乌特数，L 是质传递表面的某些特征尺寸，诸如平板的长度或圆筒的直径。方程（14.7）给出了对无因次传递系数，即宣乌特数，简单但有价值的物理解释。它被看作是接触面处或质量传递边界层处的无因次浓度梯度。

许多流谱的质量传递系数已试验得出。质量传递数据与大量热传递系数数据相比是稀少的。由于这些传递过程之间的相似性，热传递系数已经用来预测质量传递系数。对某些流谱，低质量传递速率时这种相似性关系的可靠性已经得到证实。

第15单元

离心式泵与风机

离心式泵基本上由在蜗壳里旋转的叶轮组成。流体经吸管通过入口轴向进入泵。在单吸式泵中，流体从蜗壳和叶轮的一侧进入。在双吸式泵中，流体从两侧进入，通常叶轮有两倍宽并且中间有隔板，看起来就象两个单吸叶轮背靠背地排列。这样的排列在相同的水头下具有双倍流量的功效。

离心式叶轮的叶片形状按设计要求变化，吸入侧叶片角度 β_1 要经过选择能使流体的相对速度与叶片相切（无冲击条件），而且既然设计条件是 $v_{w1}=0$，由此得出 β_1 仅依靠 u_1 和 v_{f1}。所以水头条件不影响 β_1，但对叶片出口角度 β_2 的影响却很大。

离心式泵的理论水头由欧拉方程给出
$$H_{th} = v_{w2} u_2/g$$
（假定 $v_{w1}=0$），所以对于给定的末端速度 u_2 而言，理论水头完全取决于出口的旋转分速度 v_{w2}。

现在让我们验证这个分量对叶片出口角度 β_2 的依赖性。图 15-1 表明三种不同叶片角度，通常被称为后向式叶轮（$\beta_2<90°$）、前向叶轮（$\beta_2>90°$）、径向叶轮（$\beta_2=90°$）。这个图也表示出三种不同类型叶轮的合速度图。

这些图是针对三种类型叶片在 u_2 和 v_{f2} 相同的情况下画的。很清楚，随着 β_2 增加，绝对速度 v_2 也增加。所以，形成的水头取决于 β_2，并且在前向叶片情况下较大。然而必须记住，由欧拉方程给出的理论水头是叶轮提供的总水头，因此它既包含静压水头也包含速度水头。参照图 15-1 表明，前向叶轮叶片提供的大水头，由于 v_2 很大，包含大部分速度水头。在把一些从动能向压能的转变过程中，这种情况带来实用上的困难，散流器中的损失是相当大的，因而也难以控制。

离心式水泵多数常用的叶片出口角是15°到90°，但是对于风机来说，这个范围可以延伸到β_2达140°的前向叶轮（众所周知的多级风机）。

出口叶片角对运行特性的影响表示在图15-2中。可以看出，在给定流量情况下，前向叶片叶轮产生较大水头，但是必须记住，事实上总水头中相当大的部分是速度水头。

功率特性也显示出本质的差别，这在实践中很重要。对于后向叶片叶轮，最大功率发生在最大效率点附近，而且这个点以外的任何流量增加将导致功率减少。因此，带动这样水泵和风机的电动机可以额定在最大功率点而且运转安全。这类功率曲线被称为自限的。

但是对于径向叶片或后向叶片叶轮情况则不是这样。它们的功率是连续增加的。所以，选择恰当电机就产生了问题。因为按最大功率额定，就意味着超过额定功率，而如果水泵仅运行在最大效率附近就会造成不必要的开支，另一方面，只额定在操作点的较小电机。如果水泵错误地在比对应于最大效率点的设计值更大的流量下运行，则可能有过载的危险。

离心式泵或风机具有较低的类型数，其范围大致到1.8，图15-3有所显示。一般来讲，机器类型数越低，相对于直径来讲，叶片就越狭窄。

离心式泵的全效率是高的，类型数在0.8到1.6之间时，其效率大约为90%。在较低类型数时，效率迅速下降，主要是由于狭窄叶片间长流道里的摩擦损失增加而引起的。

此外，效率取决于泵和风机的尺寸和容量。尺寸越大效率越高。

对于离心式风机，最高效率是由"翼型"叶轮风机实现的。这种风机基本上是后向型叶轮，叶片是翼型剖面，厚度不相同。类型数的范围是从0.5到1.6，最大效率在90%数量级。

第16单元

人 工 煤 气

人工煤气在这里是指从煤，焦炭，油产生的或者通过改制天然气、液化石油气或其他混和物而产生的可燃气体，如果用于增热的话，还包括天然气或液化石油气。

人工煤气大致可分为如下18组或类：

1. 乙炔气主要用于需要高火焰温度的切割和焊接操作，并已用作照明剂，由碳化钙和水制成。

2. 氢气作为一种燃料，只限于特殊的工业用途，如某种切割和焊接操作，它是通过水电解，通过天然气和其它烃热裂、以及通过水煤气反应制得的。

3. 污水气是在蒸煮设备中，由污水煤泥制得的，其平均热值是600～700Btu每立方英尺，其组成大约是2/3甲烷和1/3一氧化碳。

4. 丙烷一空气和丁烷一空气燃气是由丙烷或丁烷与空气的混合物组成而产生的燃气，这是一种可以在450～2000Btu之间得到任何期望热值的燃气。许多天然气公司把这种气作为向小社区供气的气源和调峰气源。

5. 热裂解气是由天然气、液化石油气或汽油分解而制得，其饱和烃和不饱和烃含量很高，也含有一部分氢。

6. 催化裂解气是在外热作用下使燃气或轻质烃液体通过保持在一选定温度的镍氧化物催化剂后裂化而成，可以引入一定量的水蒸气，由一氧化碳和氢以及适量的氮和氧组成。为了增加其热值，也可将相当数量的未裂解燃气或液体蒸气掺混进裂解气中。

7. 油制气是由从石脑油到高含碳量的厚剩余油之间的油分解制成，热值在每立方英尺300~400Btu 之间变化，主要用途是天然气公司用作高峰负荷供气的补充气源。

8. 油厂制气在炼油厂制得，主要有两个来源，即在分馏过程中从原油的吸收气体提炼而来或者是炼油厂裂解过程中的副产品，热值大约在每立方英尺1400~2000Btu，取决于烃脱除的多少。

9. 改制气（重整气）通常是天然气、丙烷、丁烷或油厂制气在水煤气发生器或类似的专用装置中热裂解制得，组分上变化很大，取决于所用设备和裂解的燃气比例。改制气含有氢、一氧化碳、饱和烃和不饱和烃。

10. 煤制气是在碳化炉中干馏煤中挥发性物质制得，氢和甲烷含量高，还含有少量的一氧化碳和照明剂。

11. 焦炉煤气是干馏煤中挥发性物质而得到的焦炉副产品，焦炭是主要产品。产生的燃气通常情况下大约每立方英尺500Btu，可燃成分有氢、甲烷、乙烷、一氧化碳和照明剂。在结焦过程结束时，燃气主要成分是氢。结焦开始时甲烷含量高。低温结焦过程可产生高热值燃气，因为只有少量饱和烃裂解。

12. 发生炉煤气是空气或氧气通过厚的热煤层或焦炭层时产生的。这个过程的产物是一氧化碳、氮气（用空气的原因）和一些二氧化碳。实际中常将水蒸气加进空气中来减少熔渣的形成，而且水蒸气分解产生不定数量的氢。

13. 高炉煤气是高炉炼铁的一种副产品。因为其热值主要来源于一氧化碳而且太低，所以一般用于厂内供热。

14. 蓝焰煤气、水煤气或蓝焰水煤气是由热焦炭、煤或其它碳质物料通入水蒸气制得的，主要含有一氧化碳和氢以及不定数量的二氧化碳和氮气，燃烧时是蓝色火焰。

15. 增热水煤气是以水煤气作为基准气并通过热裂解油、天然气或液化石油气而碳化或增热。除了有相当高的一氧化碳和氢含量以外，还含有不定数量的不饱和烃（照明剂）与饱和烃，根据采用的工艺，几乎可以得到从每立方英尺300~1200Btu 之间的任何期望热值。

16. 合成气是煤、焦炭、石脑油或其它类烃通过不同的工艺制得，基本上一氧化碳和氢按1:2构成，粗煤气二氧化碳含量也很高。

17. 地下发生水煤气是在地下煤层中空气在有或者没有氧或水蒸气补充的情况下通过点燃的煤堆制得，已经有几个国家进行了试验性生产。

18. 地下油制气已在美国进行了研究。研究是出于这样的观点，即通过核爆炸来炸开页岩层，释放存在的煤油，然后就地分馏，这样就产生了象燃气这样的石油部分并送往地面。

Appendix III Key to Exercises

UNIT ONE
Reading Comprehension

I. 1. h 2. g 3. f 4. e 5. d 6. c 7. b 8. a

II. 1. The most common thermodynamic properties are:
   temperature (T), pressure (P) and specific volume (V) or density (Q)

2. Additional thermodynamic properties include: entropy, stored forms of energy and enthalpy.

III. 1. Stored forms   Transient forms
    1) thermal (internal) energy   1) heat
    2) potential energy   2) work
    3) kinetic energy   3) flow work
    4) chemical energy
    5) nuclear (atomic) energy

2.
1) Heat—the mechanism that transfers energy across the boundary of systems with differing temperatures, always in the direction of the lower temperature.
2) Work—the mechanism that transfers energy across the boundary of systems with differing pressures (or force of any kind), always in the direction of the lower pressure.
3) Mechanical or shaft work is the energy delivered or absorbed by a mechanism, such as a turbine, air compressor or internal combustion engine.
4) Flow work is energy carried into or transmitted across the system boundary.

3.
1) (a) ... that can be defined as any change in the properties of a system.
   (b) ... specifying the initial and final equilibrium states, the path (if identifiable) and the interactions that take place across system boundaries during the process.
2) (a) ... exists as vapor at the saturation temperature.
      ... saturated vapor.
   (b) ... at a temperature greater than the saturation temperature,
      ... superheated vapor,

Vocabulary

I. 1. shuffled   2. transient   3. kinetic   4. combustion   5. saturation

6. shuffled 7. combustion 8. saturation 9. Kinetic 10. transient
Ⅱ.1. elevation 2. acceleration 3. adjacent 4. categorize 5. homogeneous

UNIT TWO

Reading Comprehension

Ⅰ. 略

Ⅱ. 1. turbines reciprocating engines, expanders, fluid motors,
2. compressors, pumps, fans.

Ⅲ.

1. The rate of work transfer — is limited by (3)
— is not limited by (1)
— depends upon (2)

2. 1) d   2) c   3) b   4) e   5) a

Vocabulary

Ⅰ. 1. inlet   2. propagation   3. inertia   4. negligible   5. spatially
6. propagation   7. inertia   8. inlet   9. negligible   10. spatially

Ⅱ. 1. adiabatic   2. hydroelectric   3. deflected   4. reciprocating   5. differential

UNIT THREE

Reading Comprehension

Ⅰ. 1.✓ 3.✓ 5.✓

Ⅱ. 1. T   2. F   3. T   4. F   5. F

Ⅲ. 1. C   2. D   3. D   4. C   5. B

Vocabulary

Ⅰ. 1. B   2. A   3. A   4. C   5. B

Ⅱ. 1. b   2. c   3. d   4. a   5. e
6. coeffcient   7. truncated   8. particulate   9. isotherm   10. approximation

UNIT FOUR

Reading Comprehension

Ⅰ. 1. 略（参考课文第一段）
2. 1) e   2) d   3) a   4) b   5) c

Ⅱ. 1. compressor, condenser, expansion valve evaporator

183

  2. positive displacement compressors (e. g. reciprocating piston, rotary and helical rotary) and centrifugal compressors

Ⅲ. 1. (1) a reversible adiabatic compressor

  (2) positive displacement compressors

  (3) centrifugal compressors

  (4) the piston compressor

  (5) a multistage compressor

  (6) gas compressors

2. (a)

 (1) low pressure

 (2) high pressure

 (3) constant pressure

 (4) undesirable pressure

 (5) the inlet pressure

 (6) the interstage pressure

(b)

 (1) low temperature

 (2) high temperature

 (3) medium temperature

 (4) the refrigerant temperature

(c)

 (1) saturated vapor

 (2) superheated vapor

 (3) low quality vapor

 (4) the refrigerant vapor

Vocabulary

Ⅰ. 1. C   2. A   3. B   4. B   5. A

Ⅱ. 1. valves, valve, valve,   2. compression   3. cyclic   4. refrigerants

 5. quantitatively   6. centrifugal   7. Volumetric   8. numerically

 9. cylinder   10. refrigeration

UNIT FIVE

Reading Comprehension

Ⅰ. 1. B   2. C   3. B   4. C   5. A

Ⅱ. 1. acting on the fluid element, the body force,

 2. at rest, must be zero,

 3. must be equal,

 4. larger, smaller,

5. large changes, the compressibility of the fluid, arrive at,
6. downward, the free liquid surface,
7. the same pressure, the same depth,
8. a definite relation
9. in terms of a height of a column of fluid, pressure per unit area.
10. under some pressure, convert this pressure into.

Vocabulary

I. 1. summation   2. integrate   3. concentric   4. disregard   5. depict
II. 1. body force   2. depict   3. spherical   4. integrate   5. specific weight
   6. summation   7. arbitrarily   8. Disregarding   9. concentric
   10. compressibility

UNIT SIX

Reading Comprehension

I. 1. c   2. b   3. d   4. e   5. f   6. g   7. h   8. i   9. j   10. a
II. 1. piezometric head, the level to which liquid will rise in a piezometric tube.
   2. with its open tube end pointing upstream, the totel energy head
   3. zero, atmospheric
   4. the pipe is straight and of uniform diameter
   5. the hydraulic grade line

Vocabulary

I. 1. deviation   2. intercepted   3. summit   4. Familiarity   5. plot
   6. curvature   7. inspection   8. upstream   9. resultant   10. Inasmuch as
II. 1. c   2. d   3. b   4. e   5. a

UNIT SEVEN

Reading Comprehension

I. 1. a   2. e   3. c   4. d   5. b   6. f   7. g   8. h   9. j   10. i
II. 1. friction factor   2. roughness, density and viscosity, pressure
   3. α, parameter, shape of   4. percent   5. exposed

Vocabulary

I. 1. validity   2. coating   3. turbulent   4. measurable   5. format
   6. experimentation   7. empirical   8. isolation   9. eddies   10. laminar
II. 1. a   2. b   3. d   4. c   5. e

UNIT EIGHT

Reading Comprehension

Ⅰ. 1. e   2. c   3. d   4. b   5. a

Ⅱ. 1. 1) A   2) C   3) E   4) G   5) I
     2. 1) B   2) D   3) F   4) H

Ⅲ. 1. T   2. F   3. T   4. F   5. T   6. T   7. F   8. T   9. F   10. T

Vocabulary

Ⅰ. 1. bodily   2. proportionality   3. insulating   4. appreciable
     5. linearly   6. proportionality   7. insulating   8. bodily   9. appreciable
     10. linearly

Ⅱ. 1. tortuous   2. cross-sectional area   3. conductivities   4. unicellular
     5. convection

UNIT NINE

Reading Comprehension

Ⅰ. 1. d   2. c   3. a   4. b   5. e   6. j   7. i   8. h   9. g   10. f

Ⅱ. 1. ... a program that can greatly reduced the number of tests and it is based on dimensional analysis and specifically on the laws of similitude or similarity

     2. ... the laws which enable us to make experiments with a convenient fluid such as water or air, for example, and then apply the results to a fluid which is less convenient to work with, such as gas, steam, or oil

     3. ... that the model and its prototype are identical in shape but differ only in size

     4. ... that the ratio of the velocities at all corresponding points in the flow is the same

     5. ... that if the ratio of the velocities at all corresponding points in the flow is the same, then the force at all corresponding points in the flow is the same, too

Vocabulary

Ⅰ. 1. similitude   2. investigation, investigation   3. prototype   4. denotes
     5. sediment   6. distorted   7. impractical   8. resultant   9. elasticity
     10. subscripts

Ⅱ. 1. similitude   2. prototype   3. sediment   4. distort   5. interface

UNIT TEN

Reading Comprehension

Ⅰ. 1. 1) A   2) C   3) E   4) G
     2. 1) D   2) F   3) I
     3. 1) B   2) H   3) J

II. 1. d   2. b   3. e   4. a   5. c
III. 1. T   2. F   3. T   4. F   5. F

Vocabulary

I. 1. humidity   2. viscosity   3. diminish   4. regime   5. pertinent
   6. diminishes 7. humidity   8. viscosity   9. pertinent 10. regime
II. 1. viscous   2. correlations   3. superimposed   4. Turbulence
   5. roof—mounted

UNIT ELEVEN
Reading Comprehension

I. 1. c   2. f   3. a   4. e   5. d   6. j   7. h   8. i   9. b   10. g
II. 1. friction, drag   2. same point   3. separation, size   4. minimum
    5. far, driven

Vocabulary

I. 1. Something like   2. optimum   3. transition   4. customary
   5. effectiveness
   6. drag   7. versus   8. prematurely   9. induced   10. sphere
II. 1. drag   2. customary   3. versus   4. prematurely   5. perforate

UNIT TWELVE
Reading Comprehension

I. 1. b   2. a
   3. (a) Kirchhoff's law states that for any surface where the incident radiation is independent of angle or where the surface is diffuse $\varepsilon_\lambda = \alpha_\lambda$.
      (b) Lambert's Law states that the emissive power of radiant energy over a hemispherical surface above the emitting surface varies as the cosine of the angle between the normal to the radiating surface and the line joining the radiating surface to the point of the hemispherical surface.

II. 1. incident
    2. solar
    3. low temperature level   ⎤
    4. total hemispherical   ⎬ ——radiation (s)
    5. diffuse
    6. actual
    7. gray-diffuse   ⎦

III. 1. ✓   3. ✓   4. ✓   6. ✓   8. ✓

Vocabulary
    I. 1. c   2. b   3. a   4. e   5. d   6. spectrum   7. diffuse   8. enclosure
       9. orientation   10. simulated
    II. 1. emittance   2. infrared   3. platinum   4. geometric   5. monochromatic

UNIT THIRTEEN
Reading Comprehension
    I. 1. d   2. g   3. a   4. b   5. c   6. e   7. f   8. h   9. i   10. j
    II. 1. the Mach number   2. symmetrical, same   3. at rest, asymmetry, sound
       4. Doppler effect   5. the zone of silence   6. the zone of action   7. $\leqslant$
       8. $<$, $\leqslant$ 9. $\geqslant$ 10. $0.9 \leqslant Ma \leqslant 1.2$, $Ma > 5$

Vocabulary
    I. 1. hypersonic   2. emission   3. visualized   4. instantaneous   5. stationary
       6. abrut   7. categories   8. shuttle   9. perpemdicular   10. transonic
    II. 1. b   2. c   3. a   4. d   5. e

UNIT FOURTEEN
Reading Comprehension
    I. 1. E   2. D   3. B   4. C   5. A
    II. 1. C   2. C   3. D   4. A   5. B   6. B   7. D   8. D   9. B   10. A

Vocabulary
    I. 1. random   2. fluctuation   3. momentum   4. analogy   5. dilute
       6. analogy   7. dilute   8. random   9. momentum   10. fluctuation
    II. 1. predominate   2. equalize   3. analogous   4. molecular   5. gradient

UNIT FIFTEEN
Reading Comprehension
    I. 1. A   2. A   3. B   4. C   5. A
    II. 1. within, axially   2. single inlet   3. double inlet, double width
       4. in shape   5. increase
       6. inclined backwards, inclined forward, radial
               $\beta_2 < 90°$ $\beta_2 > 90°$ $\beta_2 = 90°$
       7. velocity head   8. diameter   9. larger, higher   10. rather than

Vocabulary

I. 1. embraces 2. expenditure 3. impeller 4. head 5. are whirling
   6. fans 7. suction, suction 8. pose 9. aerofoil 10. radial

II. 1. a 2. c 3. d 4. e 5. b

UNIT SIXTEEN

Reading Comprehension

I. 1. p 2. o 3. m 4. l 5. h 6. d 7. e 8. i 9. f 10. g
   11. c 12. b 13. a 14. k 15. j 16. n 17. r 18. q

II. 1. high flame temperature, illuminant
    2. digesting equipment
    3. Butane—air and propane—air gases
    4. natural gas, petroleum gases, gasoline
    5. Oil gases
    6. refineries, distillation
    7. Coal gas, coal
    8. by—product
    9. pig iron
    10. retorting in place

Vocabulary

I. 1. herein 2. combustible 3. residuum 4. liquefied 5. there of
   6. Sewage 7. constituents 8. refinery 9. clinker 10. enriching

II. 1. a 2. e 3. b 4. c 5. d

图书在版编目（CIP）数据

建筑类专业英语．暖通与燃气．第一册/赵三元，阎岫峰主编．—北京：中国建筑工业出版社，1997（2023.2重印）

高等学校试用教材
ISBN 978-7-112-03035-4

Ⅰ．建…　Ⅱ．①赵…②阎…　Ⅲ．①建筑学—英语—高等学校—教材②采暖—英语—高等学校—教材③通风—英语—高等学校—教材④燃料气—英语—高等学校—教材　Ⅳ．H31

中国版本图书馆 CIP 数据核字（2005）第 090441 号

本书按国家教委颁发的《大学英语专业阅读阶段的教学基本要求》规定组织编写的专业英语教材。本册内容包括工程热力学、流体力学、传热学、燃气概况等。全书安排 16 个单元，每单元除正课文外，还配有两篇阅读材料，均配有必要的注释。正课文还配有词汇表和练习，书后配有总词汇表、参考译文和练习答案。本书供本专业学生三年级上半学期使用，也可供有关专业人员自学英语参考。

高等学校试用教材
建筑类专业英语
暖通与燃气
第一册

赵三元　阎岫峰　主编
王　鸣　马立山
王建华　张素宁　　编
杨印芳　　　主审

*

中国建筑工业出版社出版、发行（北京海淀三里河路 9 号）
各地新华书店、建筑书店经销
廊坊市海涛印刷有限公司印刷

*

开本：787×1092 毫米　1/16　印张：12¼　字数：298 千字
1997 年 6 月第一版　2023 年 2 月第二十六次印刷
定价：39.00 元
ISBN 978-7-112-03035-4
（32394）

版权所有　翻印必究
如有印装质量问题，可寄本社退换
（邮政编码　100037）